Assessment: Social Practice and Social Product

Assessment has become one of the most significant areas of interest in educational policy development, as well as the focus of complex political, economic and cultural expectations for change.

In *Assessment: Social Practice and Social Product*, US and UK contributors look beyond the obvious functions of assessment and focus attention upon the roles it performs in the social structuring of society. They examine some of the myths and assumptions underpinning testing. At both macro and micro levels of analysis, attention is drawn to the social and cultural contexts of assessment and to the lived experiences and interpretations of individuals and groups most directly affected.

This timely and unique collection is the first devoted explicitly to socio-cultural studies of assessment, and the first to attempt to map the terrain of thirty years of study in the field. The chapters are organized thematically, with background text providing comparative perspectives, key issues and ideas for further reading. It provides a wide-ranging, structured and accessible approach to the study of the socio-cultural origins and impacts of assessment and the pressures for more democratic, learner-oriented forms of assessment. *Assessment: Social Practice and Social Product* makes an important contribution to understanding current contradictions and tensions within and across assessment practices and policies.

Contributors: Harold Berlak; Patricia Broadfoot; Barry Cooper; Máiréad Dunne; F. Allan Hanson; Cathy Horn; David James; Mark LaCelle-Peterson; George Madaus; Andrew Pollard; John Pryor; and Harry Torrance.

Ann Filer is a Research Fellow at the University of Bristol Graduate School of Education. Her research interests include the sociology of assessment, pedagogy and pupil perspectives. She is co-director (with Andrew Pollard) of the longitudinal Identity and Learning Programme, tracking pupil careers through primary and secondary schools.

Assessment: Social Practice and Social Product

Edited by Ann Filer

London and New York

First published 2000
by RoutledgeFalmer
11 New Fetter Lane, London EC4P 4EE

Simultaneously published in the USA and Canada
by RoutledgeFalmer
Routledge Inc, 29 West 35th Street, New York, NY 10001

RoutledgeFalmer is an imprint of the Taylor & Francis Group

Typeset in Times by Taylor & Francis Books Ltd
Printed and bound in Great Britain by TJ International Ltd, Padstow,
Cornwall

British Library Cataloguing in Publication Data
A catalogue record for this book is available from the British Library

Library of Congress Cataloging in Publication Data
Assessment : Social Practice and Social Product / edited by Ann Filer.
  Includes bibliographical references and index.
  1. Educational tests and measurements – Social aspects – United States.   2. Educational
tests and measurements – Social aspects – Great Britain.   3. Examinations – Social
aspects – United States.   4. Examinations – Social aspects – Great Britain.   5.
Educational equalization – United States.   6. Educational equalization – Great Britain.
I. Filer, Ann.
LB3051.E265   2000
371.26'0973–dc21   99-055450

ISBN 0–415–22782–8 (hbk)
ISBN 0–415–22783–6 (pbk)

Contents

Contents

Illustrations

Figures

Tables

Preface

Patricia Broadfoot

Culture, discourse, identity and power: these are the buzzwords of postmodernism. They relate to a view of the world which recognizes no ultimate reality except that of subjectivity, no ultimate good except that which is culturally determined, no common values except that of valuing differences. If postmodernism has done nothing else, it has served to remind us of the limitations of science and its quest for control of the natural world. It has revived our collective awareness of the social and the part it plays in initiating, evaluating, deploying, inhibiting or applying the results of such endeavours. It has reminded us that if there is any constant in the social world, it is power, the pursuit and exercise of which in its myriad different forms underpins the fabric of society and the stability of its institutions.

Not the least important among these institutions is the multi-million pound, international industry of educational assessment and testing. Like colonialism before it, the activities associated with educational assessment and testing have steadily advanced during the twentieth century to a point where, at the present time, there can be no country and no mainstream school that is not subject to its sway nor any pupils, teachers or families who do not accept its importance. It is a remarkable conquest. From its modest beginnings in the universities of the eighteenth century and the school systems of the nineteenth century, educational assessment has developed rapidly to become the unquestioned arbitrator of value, whether of pupils' achievements, institutional quality or national educational competitiveness.

Equally remarkable has been the lack of any serious challenge to this hegemony. Despite sustained and at times impassioned debates about either the technical limitations of testing or its harmful impact on the curriculum, such concerns have been but glancing blows. They have provided no serious opposition to the apparently inexorable advance of assessment into every aspect of educational activity. It is a unique story, and one for which an explicit explanation is more than overdue.

Of more urgent concern, however, is the absence to date of a sustained scholarly attempt to determine the significance of this dominance. What are the consequences – social, educational and economic – of the contemporary world dominance of educational assessment? What price has been paid to achieve apparent transparency and equity in the judgement of relative merit? We do not know, for we are only now beginning to count the social cost of assessment in terms of disillusioned and disheartened losers and calculating, narrowly focussed winners, for while there has been no shortage of scholarly activity relating to educational assessment, this has not been typically about its social effects or about its impact on the teaching and learning process as a whole. Instead, it has been largely conceived within the prevailing paradigm as part of the continuing quest to develop more accurate and economic ways of measuring quality and achievement. But now, as the accepted certainties of the modernist era fall victim to the reappraisals of a new millennium, there is room for different questions and concerns to take the place of those thrown up by the scientific revolution a couple of centuries ago. It is a time for new issues and new arguments. In place of the sustained debates concerning the reduction of measurement error or the niceties of domain sampling that have so long characterised the scholarly world of assessment, there are other pressing needs to be resolved. These are not concerns about accuracy, utility and economy, nor are they arguments about practicability and cost, though these, inevitably, refuse to go away from the hard surfaces of reality. They are rather issues which derive from contemporary challenges to the scientific project as a whole and the revival of more humanistic debates about cultural integrity, equity and diversity.

A fundamentally modernist creation, educational assessment can be seen as the archetypal representation of the desire to discipline an irrational social world in order that rationality and efficiency could prevail. The engine that drove its rapid development was the aspiration that merit and competence should define access to power and privilege; that investment in education could be tailored to identified potential; that value for money could be convincingly demonstrated. All these were worthy aspirations, and they remain the dominant agenda of examinations and test agencies around the world who even today continue what is often a heroic struggle to provide equitable and defensible accreditation and selection mechanisms, to hold back the tide of corruption and nepotism that threatens to engulf the whole enterprise.

But even in those countries where the struggle to hold the pass of merit and competence is hardest, questions are even now being raised about the appropriateness of this nineteenth-century technology for shaping the education systems of today and the citizens of tomorrow. The impetus for current debates is essentially a practical one. Can an education system dominated by the demands of academic, written examinations deliver individuals capable of contributing effectively in the workplaces of tomorrow when it will be their social and personal skills, their adaptability and their initiative which will be at a premium? How can creativity be encouraged in education systems in which the rewards currently go to the dogged and the dutiful, the convergent and the conforming?

Important as these questions currently are for policy makers, they are only the tip of the iceberg. If the challenge of change and technology, the knowledge economy and lifelong learning have prompted the beginnings of a movement to question the tried and tested technologies of assessment that are so deeply embedded in our society, the more generic currents of globalization and postmodernity represent an even more fundamental challenge – a challenge to the very belief in the power of science itself to lead to social progress. It is in this latter debate that we find the roots of this book. At last, the more generic concern to question the legacy of the Enlightenment, and the belief in the virtues of rationality and science that have informed the development of Western culture ever since, have prompted scholars to begin to question the instrumental claims made for educational assessment. The growing challenge to modernist perspectives has led to a growing recognition that educational assessment needs to be seen as a social, as much as a scientific, activity and hence one that is deeply embued with the bias and subjectivity inherent in any human interaction.

Assessment: Social Practice and Social Product is perhaps the first collection of papers in this field to take an explicitly socio-cultural perspective. In its bold attempt to map out the territory of what an explicitly socio-cultural approach to studying educational assessment might comprise, the book raises new and profoundly important questions about every level of education from the micro-interactions of the classroom to the macro level of policy and international comparison. It addresses all the many facets of educational assessment. A number of the contributors draw on leading contemporary social theorists – Foucault, Lyotard, Baudrillard and Bourdieu in particular – to explore the key role that assessment plays in the social structuring of modern societies. These analyses begin to offer some insights into the reasons behind the unprecedented growth in assessment activity of all kinds in recent years. They provide the foundation for exploring the implications of such developments as new mechanisms of power and control and as a new means of legitimating social inequalities.

This is an intellectual project of the most fundamental kind. As LaCelle-Peterson argues in Chapter 2, the challenge to the 'nomothetic assumptions that gave birth to the mental measurement movement' are a 'portent for the prospects of the democratic ideal itself'. Once we can see educational assessment as a device that is embedded in the complex histories, cultures and power relations of societies, we can begin the project of teasing out the reasons behind the advent of highly centralized mass testing systems and their consequences; we can begin to explore the likely consequences of the market of performance indicators that drives efforts to 'get the scores up' regardless of their validity in terms of more generic definitions of quality or of the many differences in understanding, engagement and empowerment that they obscure.

If nothing else is certain in this rapidly changing world, the importance of more and better learning is universally acknowledged. In future, there will be no place for a single highway to achievement or a royal road of qualifications from which all but the favoured few are progressively banned. There is no doubt, therefore, that we face a significant challenge. We need to find a way of continuing to provide for those assessment functions of quality control and quality assurance, of accreditation and selection that an increasingly fluid society renders more important than ever before. Yet also we need to find a way con-structively to cope with an explosive growth in the volume of assessment activity as society increasingly turns to it to regulate an unprecedented range of activities that are now beyond more traditional forms of control. It is indeed a sad irony that at the very time when the first green shoots of liberation are beginning to appear in relation to the assessment of individual achievement as the exigencies of lifelong learning begin to open up a vista of personalized learning trajectories and on-demand testing, more and more of the other parts of our collective life are increasingly in thrall to the discourse of 'performativity'. Monitoring, auditing, regulating, quality assurance, accountability, appraisal and inspection are the new assessment mantra, the visible articulation of a brave new world in which it is assumed that the quality of social activity and institutional performance can be dissected piece by piece like a specimen upon the table, its organs laid bare to scrutiny, judgement and comparison. Likewise, the new creeds of criteria and transparency are supposed to reassure a sceptical world that the huge assessment effort now required and the associated widespread sacrifice of autonomy is justified by the evident gains they lead to in relation to both efficiency and equity.

So, it is time to reveal that the emperor has no clothes. Before we become even more fatally infected with the contagion of 'performativity' and its symptoms of pervasive judgement and comparison, we need to recognize the limitations of educational assessment as a useful but nevertheless, imperfect tool. Indeed, we need urgently to engage with its role as a 'social process' that affects intimately and often forever, the quality of an individual's capacity to learn. We need too to recognize assessment as a social product, in which the values and traditions of particular cultures and the interests of specific groups within them combine to produce particular definitions of quality or merit. Last but not least, we need to recognize the potential for assessment to be a powerful positive force in supporting lifelong learning, provided its role as part of the process of teaching and learning is properly understood. The publication of *Assessment: Social Practice and Social Product* represents a significant step towards all three of these goals.

Patricia Broadfoot
University of Bristol
July 1999

Acknowledgements

I would like to thank the participants of the 'Studentship in Socio-Cultural Contexts: The Role of Assessment' symposium which I convened for the British Educational Research Association Annual Conference at the University of York, 1997. The papers of my co-contributors to that symposium, David James, Harold Berlak, Harry Torrance, John Pryor and Andrew Pollard, are not necessarily those that they have written for this collection. Rather, those earlier papers represented an important and coherent set of ideas around which I began to shape my ideas for this book. I therefore extend my thanks to these and to all the other authors here, from the USA and the UK, who recognized the need for this collection and contributed so enthusiastically to its realization.

I would also like to thank my colleagues at Bristol, Patricia Broadfoot and Andrew Pollard, for their continued interest and encouragement through the production of this book. I would particularly like to thank Patricia Broadfoot for contributing a preface to the collection.

Authors are grateful for permission to reproduce material previously published elsewhere. In Chapter 7, data is reproduced from 'Mary's Story' in *The Social World of Children's Learning* (Cassell). Also in Chapter 7, Figure 7.2 and data from 'Harriet's Story' and 'Robert's Story' first appeared in *The Social World of Pupil Career* (Cassell). In Chapter 5, Figures 5.1 and 5.3 are reproduced from *Schools Curriculum and Assessment Authority, Key Stage 2 Tests* (DfEE) and Figure 5.2 from *Schools Examination and Assessment Council, Pilot Standard Tests: Key Stage 2* (SEAC/University of Leeds).

Ann Filer
University of Bristol

Introduction

Ann Filer

Assessment has become one of the most significant areas of interest in educational policy dev-elopment worldwide. This is occurring in relation to emergent educational systems as well as in the context of government interventions in established systems. There is a growing awareness of the limited scope and the limiting effects on teaching, learning and motivation of some traditional forms of assessment. This awareness, together with international economic and employment trends, has in recent years heralded interest in new forms of assessment. The importance of assessment for influencing teaching and curricula has not been lost on governments. Politicians are increasingly aware that what is taught, and how, can be indirectly asserted through the control of 'high stakes' assessment programmes (Torrance 1995; Broadfoot 1996). In multi-cultural, post-industrial societies, the trend towards a centrally prescribed content of assessed know-ledge increasingly clashes with assertions of the cultural and social differences and diversity of experience and need among populations of students. Reacting to claims for more culturally diverse representations, architects of national testing in the United States and the United Kingdom now assert the existence of underlying shared values as a basis of national unity. They make plain their belief that an alternative vision, of an underlying cultural homogeneity, can be overtly constructed and promoted through a nationally assessed body of knowledge (Berlak, see Chapter 10).

Educational assessment has thus become a highly contested area as the focus of complex political, economic and cultural expectations for change. In the context of the growing *social* significance of assessment, however, policy, public debate and the development of practice predominantly focus around the *technical* means by which policy is delivered. The focus is on whether to test and when, and on the efficiency and appropriateness of different techniques and systems. That is to say, what predominates in assessment policy and practice are those functions concerned with the structuring of educational experience and outcomes. Notwithstanding the growing significance of assessment in the social structuring of societies, debate rarely addresses more fundamental issues concerning the *social* functions and outcomes of assessment; a debate, indeed, that can undermine the legitimizing influence of assessment procedures (Broadfoot 1996: 14).

Assessment as 'social practice' and as 'social product' is not widely addressed in sociological, educational or even assessment-related research, and neither, I feel, is it well understood. To remedy this, I believe it needs a more distinct profile as an area of study that draws on epistemological and methodological discourses other than the technicist paradigm that prevails in assessment and policy debate. I use the term 'discourse' here to denote 'genre' or a way of talking about a matter that frames what can be said about it. In relation to educational assessment, two broadly distinct discourses can be identified:

1   *A technical discourse of assessment.* A technical discourse of assessment is one in which required *ends* – for example, practices of grading, comparing and selecting individuals or schools on the basis of test scores – are not generally in dispute. It is, rather, a discourse concerning the *means* whereby given ends can be achieved as fairly and objectively as possible. Within such a discourse therefore, technicalities concerned with test validity and reliability, criterion and norm referencing and so on will prevail. Such a discourse is thus about maintaining and improving confidence in systems of assessment and results; thus, ultimately, legitimizing the uses to which they are put (Filer 1993, 1995).

2   *A sociological discourse of assessment.* The term 'sociological' here also includes social-psychological, anthropological and some 'postmodern' studies. This discourse presents insights into the fact that, as well as having educational purposes, assessment fulfils a range of political and social functions within modern societies. These wider functions are concerned with social differentiation and reproduction, social control and the legitimizing of particular forms of knowledge and culture of socially powerful groups. In this, the discourse has a critical role in examining some of the myths and assumptions embedded in the activity of educational testing. It critiques the 'science' of testing and offers insights into the fact that assessment, from the most formal to the most informal, takes place within social contexts. Assessment is conducted 'on, by and for inherently social actors' (Wiliam 1997: 396) and so the social and cultural values, perceptions, interpretations and power relations of assessors and assessed carry important implications for processes and outcomes. The discourse is therefore particularly concerned with the social impact of assessment and the perpetuation of educational and social disparity, and its cumulative affects in shaping ways in which individuals and groups in society come to be seen, and to see themselves (Filer 1993, 1995).

Of course, the impacts of assessment do not only derive from the formal testing, grading and classification of students. I use the term 'assessment' in the title of the book to denote the full range of formal and informal judgements made of students in educational settings. As well as formal tests and examinations, the term also covers ongoing, formative and diagnostic judgements, day-to-day marking and recording and numerous informal, often implicit, evaluations made of students work, progress and potential. It is also important to remember that many assessments explicitly or implicitly embody a number of social, emotional and physical characteristics of students. Thus an assortment of behavioural, attitudinal, socioeconomic, cultural and family characteristics often constitutes a 'social diagnosis' in accounting for students' failure to make satisfactory progress or fulfil their potential. The work of teachers, schools and educational districts are, in turn, also 'assessed' by governments and their agents, by parents and local communities, employers, the media and so on.

This wide range of forms, relationships and origins of educational assessment are addressed by the authors in this book, writing within the contexts of current assessment practice in the United States and the United Kingdom.[1] Over the years, each of the authors in this collection has made substantial contributions to this assessment discourse. Some indeed have done pioneering work in the field going back to the 1970s, their writing providing substantial and wide-ranging historical, theoretical and critical basis for a sociology of assessment. In particular, I would cite Patricia Broadfoot among the British writers here, and George Madaus among the North Americans. Sociological, social-psychological and postmodern discourses around assessment are beginning very effectively to illuminate, critique and posit forms of educational assessment from completely new perspectives. In the context of the increasing political interest and social significance of assessment, such developments are crucial. In bringing this collection together, therefore, it is my hope that a clearer profile and articulation of this distinctive discourse will encourage more research in the area and the progressive development of that which exists.

Figure I.1 summarizes the scope of the book, which I have organized in five parts to broadly reflect a range of themes within the discourse.

These themes can be construed (albeit crudely) in terms of the 'chronological stages' of assessment as it moves through the successive contexts of policy formation (Patricia Broadfoot and Andrew Pollard; Mark LaCelle-Peterson), the technologies of testing (George Madaus and Cathy Horn; F. Allan Hanson), classroom practice (Barry Cooper and Máiréad Dunne; John Pryor and Harry Torrance) and the wider social milieu surrounding assessment practice (Ann Filer and Andrew Pollard; David James). In addition to the pairs of chapters, an editor's introduction addresses each of these four broad themes. The final part of the book consists of an editor's introduction and two chapters which discuss some postmodern perspectives on educational testing and the implications for future practice (Harry Torrance; Harold Berlak). At the centre of the model I have summarized some of the diverse academic, socio-cultural and economic outcomes of policy and practice that are addressed throughout. Through the series of short introductions, I set out some background issues and research relating to each of the themes, as well as some suggestions for further reading. Given the usual limitations on space, I shaped the introductions with several considerations in mind. First, in organizing the book in this way I wished to connect and integrate the chapters into related fields of research and theoretical perspectives and to help structure the flow of ideas

Figure I.1   Themes within sociological discourses of assessment

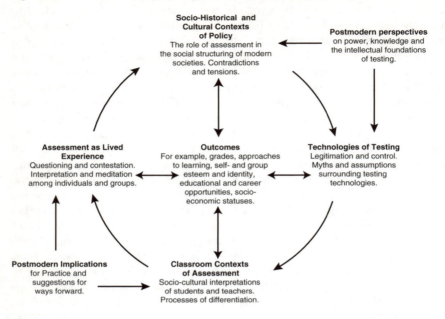

through the book. I also needed to maintain an overall balance across US and UK contexts and sources and highlight some important differences and comparisons. Also, as I describe above, I wished to present some key topics and readings as a stimulus and starting point for further study and research in areas of growing political and social significance.

Note

1   While the United States and the United Kingdom are the two sources of the chapters, in the latter contexts, readers will meet references to 'England' or 'England and Wales'. Education policy and systems of assessment have developed differently in England and Wales, Northern Ireland and Scotland. References to countries therefore generally reflect particular provision and contexts of research. The 'UK' is used more generally when referring to UK governments and to general policy directions.

References

Broadfoot, P. (1996) *Education, Assessment and Society*, Milton Keynes: Open University Press.

Filer, A. (1993) 'Classroom Contexts of Assessment in a Primary School', unpublished PhD, University of the West of England.

—— (1995) 'Teacher Assessment: Social Process and Social Product', *Assessment in Education* 2(1): 23–38.

Torrance, H. (ed.) (1995) *Evaluating Authentic Assessment*, Buckingham: Open University Press.

Wiliam, D. (1997) Review of Broadfoot (1996) in *British Educational Research Journal* 23(3): 396–7.

Part I

Socio-Historical and Cultural Contexts of Assessment Policy

Editor's Introduction

Ann Filer

Some Roles of Assessment in Modern Societies

Educational assessment fulfils a wider range of functions within modern societies than is generally recognized. Most political and public debate concerning assessment revolves around a limited number of purposes for assessment concerned with grading, selection and accountability. These purposes are generally associated with a nation's need to promote the knowledge and skills deemed necessary for current and anticipated economic, national–cultural and personal–social development. However, notwithstanding any shared perceptions at this general level that different nations might have regarding the purposes and desired outcomes of assessment, the particular systems for mass testing that they employ to meet such ends are often starkly different. A simple comparison of some key assessment traditions in the United States and England serves to make the point. The status of public examination systems has remained particularly entrenched in the English education system, as has trust in their powers to predict future occupational success (Broadfoot 1996). Historically, the emphasis in England has been on functions of certification and the progressive segregation and selection of students. This traditional emphasis remains in place alongside, although increasingly conflicting with, a more recent emphasis on schools' accountability for raising 'standards' for all, and on the concept of 'lifelong learning' (see Chapter 1). The history of mass education in the United States has seen much less overt emphasis on selecting educational elites than has been the case in England. Rather, its prime concerns have been with assessment for accountability and for monitoring and driving up 'standards' (see also Chapter 10). Underlying these historic concerns in the USA has been the expectation that schooling should function to socially integrate large immigrant populations into a common American identity. In that context, machine-scorable 'multiple choice' tests have prevailed, arising from the desire to collect 'objective' data for routinely monitoring and comparing large numbers of students, schools and educational districts cheaply and efficiently.

These examples, though brief and simplified, serve to illustrate some ways in which systems of assessment are more than a function of currently conceived educational and economic needs. Assessment processes and their educational and social outcomes are analysable as products of nations' histories, cultures and shifting political imperatives. To examine systems of assessment in this way, to perceive them as socio-historical and cultural processes and products as well as educational processes and products, serves as a starting point for a broader conception of the functions of assessment. That is to say, they take us beyond the more obvious functions of grading or certification, selection and accountability, and focus our attention upon the key role that assessment plays in the social structuring of modern societies.

Because systems of assessment are required to fulfil complex roles in modern societies, there is frequently a mismatch between policy intentions and outcomes. For example, contrasting with the intentions described above, many people argue that frequent mass testing in American schools has actually served to compound and perpetuate educational and social disparity, rather than alleviate it (see for example, US Congress, Office of Technology Assessment 1992; Darling-Hammond 1994). In Chapter 2 can be found an example of this concern. There, Mark LaCelle-Peterson reveals ways in which policy and test technologies embody hidden values such that they fail to represent the broad range of educational experience and needs of students. He reveals that the number and proportion of students whose first language is not English are increasing in US schools. It would be thought, he argues, that the needs of such students would figure largely within a system that is seeking to improve academic standards. Yet 'standards' are being pursued through the expansion of large-scale, undifferentiated assessment programmes, a policy which assumes that learners are a homogenous population. LaCelle-Peterson discusses ways in which tests, inappropriately structured for English-language learners, with culturally inappropriate knowledge content, serve to limit and distort rather than reveal the attainments of language minorities. They serve to obscure the educational needs of such pupils rather than support them. Readers will find further discussions of the relationship between inequitable assessment outcomes and factors relating to social class, gender and racial or cultural difference throughout this book.

Thus studies of the role of mass assessment in compounding and perpetuating educational and social disparities help to illuminate the relationship between assessment and processes of social reproduction. They explore ways in which assessment policy and technical practices derive from, and help perpetuate, forms of knowledge associated with the most powerful social, cultural and political groups in societies. That is, systems of national assessment can be seen as an expression of the cultural capital (Bourdieu and Passeron 1977) that underpins and *legitimizes* the reproduction of social and power elites in modern societies. This latter concern, relating to the role of assessment in legitimizing socially inequitable outcomes, is explored further in Part II.

Contradictions and Tensions in Current Assessment Policies

As I have described above, systems of mass assessment are required to fulfil complex and often contradictory roles in modern societies. In Chapter 1, Patricia Broadfoot and Andrew Pollard illustrate the tensions and contradictions arising from the incompatible requirements of current UK educational policy making. Their chapter also connects with important issues concerning the kinds of learning that societies wish to encourage and how that learning is assessed (see also Broadfoot 1998a, 1998b). Contrary to popular conceptions, assessment is not something that follows and is separable from learning. Rather, assessment shapes institutional learning. Different forms of assessment influence what is taught and how it is taught, what and how students learn. Throughout the twentieth century, many educationists have deplored the effects of public examinations on the quality of learning in English schools. Systems of assessment have been criticized for putting a premium on the reproduction of knowledge and passivity of mind at the expense of critical judgement and creative thinking (Broadfoot 1996: 175). Since the introduction of multiple-choice tests into American schools in the 1930s, they have been criticized for encouraging teachers to set tasks that promote de-contextualized rote learning and that narrow the curriculum to basic skills with low cognitive demands (Kellaghan and Madaus 1991; Darling-Hammond 1994; Herman et al. 1997). Recently, moreover, the learning needed for employment in post-industrial societies is being conceptualized in new ways. The proliferation of service industries and the changing character of work have created demands for transferable skills such as those of communication, information retrieval, problem solving, critical analysis, self-monitoring and self-assessment. As a result, we see a fast growing interest in the more formative, holistic, contextualized forms of assessment, often described under the umbrella terms of 'authentic' or 'performance' assessment. In vocational training, these are often referred to as 'competence-based' assessment. It remains the case, however, that traditional forms of assessment are not easily replaced, embedded as they are in complex histories, cultures and power relations of societies. Further, as Broadfoot (1988a: 473) argues, these traditional forms with their emphasis on scientific rationality (see Part II) are so pervasive in modern societies that they blind us to the potential for alternative forms of assessment.

Thus in the chapter from Broadfoot and Pollard, we see ways in which the UK government maintains policies aimed at 'raising standards' alongside developing those aimed at encouraging 'lifelong learning'. Both 'standards' and 'lifelong learning' are seen as key requirements for strengthening and maintaining a competitive UK economy. Yet as Broadfoot and Pollard show, there are very real contradictions between the forms of assessment needed to support these two different government policy initiatives. Hence, like governments worldwide, the UK government continues to struggle to meet increasingly diverse and complex requirements for assessment. At the same time, it fails to address the inevitable tensions, contradictions and unintended, inequitable outcomes which flow from the policies it promotes.

Suggestions for Further Reading

Patricia Broadfoot in *Education, Assessment and Society* provides an in-depth sociological and historical analysis of the role of assessment in modern educational systems and societies through a comparison of England and France.

For a comparison of testing in the United States and other industrialized nations, including England and Wales, see Chapter 5, 'How Other Countries Test', in *Testing in American Schools: Asking the Right Questions*. Chapter 7, 'Performance Assessment: Methods and Characteristics', provides a useful background to the development of new forms of testing and the implementation of change in the USA.

Assumptions that new forms of assessment will provide more equitable outcomes than traditional forms of testing in American schools are examined by US writers in the *Harvard Educational Review* (64(1)) symposium: 'Equity in Educational Assessment'.

A background to the development of authentic testing in England and Wales, together with some problems and possibilities in implementing new approaches, is explored in *Evaluating Authentic Assessment*, edited by Harry Torrance.

References

Bourdieu, P. and Passeron, J.C. (1977) *Reproduction*, London: Sage.

Broadfoot, P. (1996) *Education, Assessment and Society*, Milton Keynes: Open University Press.

—— (1998a) 'Records of Achievement and the Learning Society: a Tale of Two Discourses', *Assessment in Education* 5(3): 447–77.

—— (1998b) 'Quality Standards and Control in Higher Education: What Price Life-Long Learning', *International Studies in Sociology of Education* 8(2): 155–80.

Darling-Hammond, L. (1994) 'Performance-Based Assessment and Educational Equity', *Harvard Educational Review*, Symposium: Equity in Educational Assessment, 64(1): 5–29.

Herman, J.L., Klein, D.C.D. and Wakai, S.T. (1997) 'American Students' Perspectives on Alternative Assessment: Do They Know It's Different?', *Assessment in Education* 4(3): 339–52.

Kellaghan, T. and Madaus, G.F. (1991) 'National Testing: Lessons for America from Europe', *Educational Leadership* 49: 87–93.

Torrance, H. (ed.) (1995) *Evaluating Authentic Assessment*, Milton Keynes: Open University Press.

US Congress, Office of Technology Assessment (1992) *Testing in American Schools: Asking the Right Questions*, OTA-SET-519, Washington DC: US Government Printing Office, February.

1   The Changing Discourse of Assessment Policy

The Case of English Primary Education

Patricia Broadfoot and Andrew Pollard

Introduction

The changing focuses of English education policy in the 1990s can be seen as a reflection of the complexities arising from the postmodern challenge to the established thinking and practices of late modernity. This challenge, and reactivity to challenge, has given rise to new priorities, new forms of contestation and regulation and new forms of discourse across post-industrial nations worldwide in the closing decades of the century. In this chapter we explore the nature of contemporary educational discourse, taking English primary schooling as a case study of some of the underlying trends and tensions in society. In particular, we focus on the significance of the gradual establishment of a new hegemony of 'performance'[1] which, though first established by 'New Right' Conservatives, has survived a change in governing party. The first part of this chapter presents a brief overview of some of the key elements of the legislative reforms of the early 1990s and the particular concatenation of historical and political circumstances which gave rise to them. Moving beyond this, we then draw on Bernstein's work to highlight underlying consequences concerning school management, teacher professionalism and teaching and learning itself. Finally, in particular relation to the present New Labour government, we highlight the tension which exists between parallel discourses of 'performance' and 'lifelong learning'. Given the power differentials between teacher and taught embedded in these forms of discourse, we speculate on some outcomes at the level of social product and practice.

Primary education in England and Wales will never be the same again. The decade of unremitting change which followed the 1988 Education Reform Act – the most significant piece of educational legislation in half a century – has ensured that this is so. By the late 1990s, as the major wave of new policy initiatives began to ebb, it revealed a shoreline in which many of the principal features had been rearranged: the role of the headteacher and the way schools are managed; teachers' priorities and ways of working together; teaching methods and curriculum content. Perhaps to the casual observer, classroom practices and the activities of teachers and pupils appeared to have changed little. The constants of classrooms everywhere – talk, activity, display, a single teacher occupied with a large group of children – these are the defining characteristics of formal education today across the globe. Though it is possible that these too will begin to evolve as the technological developments of the information society become translated into institutional practice, for the present, schools and teachers, pupils and lessons are constants which we both recognize and understand, a familiar feature of our contemporary culture. It is all the more difficult, then, to appreciate the subtle yet profound redefining of the educational project that the last ten years has produced in English primary schools: the changes in relationships between headteacher and staff and between teachers themselves and between teachers and their pupils, and the product of these changes in terms of different attitudes, different goals, different concerns and different skills. This is an education system in which teachers' priorities in practice reflect a hard-won, and often still uneasy, compromise between new obligations and an enduring vision that has its roots in a different era.

The Primary Assessment, Curriculum and Experience (PACE) project was established in 1989 to monitor the impact of the momentous changes then being put in place following the passing of the 1988 Education Reform Act. Funded by ESRC in three stages (1989–92; 1992–4 and 1994–7), the PACE project was uniquely placed to document the unfolding story of change in primary schools and, in particular, to analyse the impact of the new National Curriculum and Assessment requirements on headteachers, teachers and pupils. In 1994 we described the PACE project as 'one of the many stepping stones in the quest to understand the nature of the educational enterprise and hence, how to provide for it most effectively' (Pollard et al. 1997: 4). Thus our research has been designed to help understand the origin and significance both of the policy initiatives imposed by Government and those which were the product of the attempts by teachers and headteachers to reconcile these requirements with their professional values and understandings. Why were these policy initiatives set in motion in the England of the late 1980s, and what, ultimately, is likely to be their significance for the nature and quality of pupils' learning? How can a case study of English primary education, and the way in which assessment is approached, illuminate more widespread changes in the power relations and modes of control of modern societies at the end of the century?

The Context for Change

Until the current National Curriculum was introduced, the only formal control of the content of education in English primary schools concerned the requirement to teach religious education, which was specified in the 1944 Education Act. Historically, England seems to have been unique in not having a national curriculum. Instead, it has traditionally relied on various kinds of assessment, particularly public examinations, to control the system. As in other countries, the existence of so called 'high-stakes' public examinations of 11-plus, 16-plus and 18-plus had provided a powerful focus for schools which were otherwise free to make their own decisions about content. However, there was a well recognized problem in providing coherence and continuity in the curriculum, with the result that children were sometimes exposed to the same curriculum content on several occasions. Entitlement and quality were also pressing issues (HMI 1978). Thus, one of the main stimuli for the introduction of a national curriculum was the desire to provide a broad, balanced and coherent curriculum for children aged between 5 and 16.

This concern had developed through the 1970s and 1980s from a sustained critique and sequence of moral panics concerning 'progressive' educational practices, an interpretation of the official recommendations of the Plowden Report (DES) of 1967. Despite research evidence of the continuing preponderance of conventional ways of working, progressivism was believed to dominate classroom practice in primary schools. There was considerable media attention over the period, including the occasional exposé, such as that in William Tyndale Primary School which caused a national scandal. Important political figures in both the Labour and Conservative parties became convinced that primary school education was too child-centred and unstructured. It was seen as being dominated by the professional ideologies of the teaching profession, and as failing to deliver sufficiently high standards in basic skills. Although it was a Labour prime minister, Jim Callaghan, who in 1976 initiated a 'great debate' on how to reform education, it was the Conservative administrations of Margaret Thatcher and John Major that moved forward with fundamental, system-wide legislation.

Other, more structural factors, were also significant in prompting such change. The 1970s and 1980s had seen a growth in international economic competition. This, together with growing financial pressures and an increased demand for state institutions to be accountable, underpinned a desire to curb the professional autonomy of teachers and to replace it with a much greater measure of central control. The underlying rationale here was provided by 'New Right' beliefs about the beneficial role of market forces and competition in driving up standards, and controlling 'producer interests' (Chubb and Moe 1992; Whitty et al. 1998). In such a model, assessment and measurement has a particular role in providing 'objective' information on which educational 'consumers' such as parents and governments can base their decisions. For this reason, there has been a significant development of a variety of forms of monitoring during recent years, including comprehensive information about standards, finance and many other aspects of educational provision.

It was also in the 1980s that a series of international surveys began to reveal how standards in England compared to those in other countries, and this has continued. The Third International Mathematics and Science Study (Keys et al. 1997) provides a recent illustration, showing as it did that English pupils apparently compare well with their peers in other countries on science achievement, but they are well down when it comes to mathematics. How far it is appropriate to trust such statistics is perhaps less important than recognizing the effect of such high profile studies on policy makers, who are keen to be seen to be responding to public unease about standards.

In addition to these general concerns, there were also a number of more specific developments. One of these was an unintended consequence of the almost total abandonment of 11-plus testing with the advent of comprehensive schools during the 1970s. This development left primary schools in particular free of almost any kind of formal curriculum or assessment control. It also meant that there was very little information about the standards being achieved in primary schools and in the lower years of secondary schools. Although the Assessment of Performance Unit had been set up in the 1970s to monitor national performance in particular subject areas, this was a spasmodic exercise and was not sufficient to reassure public disquiet.

The 1988 Education Reform Act

The expressed aim of an educational policy initiative almost unprecedented in its ambition and scope was, quite simply, to raise standards. This was to be achieved by raising expectations about pupil achievement, and by the imposition of a broad and balanced National Curriculum for all pupils to provide for continuity and coherence in their learning experience. A key element in the introduction of the National Curriculum was provision for a National Assessment system. This National Assessment system was designed not only to measure the performance of pupils at the end of four key stages (age 5–7, 7–11, 11–14 and 14–16), but also to make it possible for market forces to operate by providing the currency for the competition between schools to attract pupils that had also been built into the 1988 Act.

The design of the national assessment system drawn up by the Government's Task Group on Assessment and Testing (TGAT) envisaged an elaborate criterion-referenced structure of attainment targets, with pupils' achievement being recorded and reported at the end of key stages by means of a combination of teacher assessment and results from standard assessment tasks, externally provided assessment instruments. External assessment at the end of Key Stage 4 was to be in the form of the newly introduced GCSE (General Certificate of Secondary Education) examination. Significantly, such a comprehensive national assessment system could, and subsequently did, provide attainment data with which to compare not only individual students, but also the results of their schools, of Local Education Authorities and indeed of the nation as a whole in comparative league tables.

Although this evaluative purpose of National Assessment was not envisaged as being its only or even its prime rationale, this has nevertheless arguably proved to be the case. The original aim was that National Assessment should also provide formative and diagnostic information to guide teachers in the classroom as well as summative information for students, teachers and parents about the level of attainment of a given child at a given stage. However, the emphasis on using the resultant assessment information externally is reflected in the fact that the policy reforms following the 1988 Act made provision both for new reporting requirements to parents and for the formal publication of league tables of school results.

Change on the scale described is likely to cause turbulence in any education system, and the English reforms were no exception. The PACE study was not alone in documenting the anger and despair of teachers in the early years of this decade as they struggled to implement both the National Curriculum and National Assessment. Both were too demanding in terms of teachers' time and were perceived to be overprescriptive. By the middle of the 1990s, the National Curriculum had been 'reviewed' by Sir Ron Dearing. This review slimmed down the content of the National Curriculum and simplified the elaborate structure of criterion-referenced attainment benchmarks into a more simple system of level descriptors which would provide the basis for assessment and reporting achievement. National tests were then only to be imposed in the core subjects of English, maths and science and for Key Stages 2 and 3, and external markers were to be provided to lighten the load on classroom teachers. Furthermore, teacher assessment in both the 'core' and 'foundation' subjects was to have formally equal standing with the external standardized assessment test (SAT).

Arguably, it was the National Assessment requirements rather than the introduction of a National Curriculum *per se* which caused the major controversy in the education system over this period, particularly in primary schools. Our first PACE book, *Changing English Primary Schools?* (Pollard et al. 1994), reported the project's findings concerning teachers' experiences with, and attitudes to, both the National Curriculum and the assessment system during the early years of this decade. It made clear that teachers found the workload of implementing the new assessment requirements both an unacceptable burden in terms of the time required and equally unacceptable in terms of the prominence given to the explicit labelling and categorizing of pupils in terms of their level of achievement. Given that primary schools had little or no tradition of formal assessment since the demise of the 11-plus selection examination in most parts of the country, many teachers were ideologically opposed to conducting tests which they felt were neither meaningful or helpful. They also lacked professional experience in conducting such formal assessments and were thus faced with the need to develop new skills in this respect.

In 1993, many teachers refused to do the national tests on a formal basis, or else they carried them out as legally required but then declined to submit the results. This revolt was initiated by English teachers at Key Stage 3, who were objecting to the content of the tests and their inevitable washback effect on curriculum priorities. However, the fact that the non-compliance rapidly spread into primary schools as well provides a good illustration of the extent of the antipathy towards National Assessment that existed among primary teachers at that time.

As *Changing English Primary Schools?* makes clear, the causes of this antipathy were at a number of levels. The most obvious of these concerned issues of workload and time, and teachers' objections to a procedure that would take many days of effort for both teachers and pupils but would not, in their view, contribute to the facilitation of pupils' learning. However, beneath this were more fundamental concerns about the anticipated effect of such tests on the priorities and practices of English primary schooling. Perhaps it was already clear that the well-established English tradition of controlling schools by means of external assessment requirements was being redeployed in a new and powerful way to impose a particular set of curriculum priorities on schools.

In the years since 1988 and throughout the various stages of implementing the National Assessment system, there has been a clear tension between validity and reliability. The initial TGAT design had called for the creation of 'standard assessment tasks' which were as much like normal primary classroom activities as possible. However, the steadily growing emphasis year by year on the use of National Assessment results as an external indicator of school standards meant that the reliability of the information became increasingly important. In the context of 'league tables' of test results at school and LEA level being published in the national media, assessment procedures had to be rigorously controlled in order to ensure fairness in any comparison between different school's achievements. Given significant worries about the reliability of the more valid tasks of the early years of National Assessment, the consequence was a steady trend towards the use of formal, externally controlled paper and pencil tests at all levels.

Although externally set and marked tests provide for a greater level of comparability between classrooms, between schools and between LEAs, they inevitably suffer from the limitations of the technology used and cannot test the full range of curriculum goals. Furthermore, despite the fact that the teacher assessments were designed to complement external tests, there is nevertheless clear evidence that the growing importance of external tests at the end of primary school and halfway through secondary school is constraining the curriculum to focus on both the content and the procedures found in the tests (Pollard et al. 1997; Firestone et al. 1998)

Findings from the PACE study suggest that the attitudes and learning behaviour of children at the end of Key Stage 2 became more strongly evident as they experienced both a tightening of curriculum control and the impact of external and overt assessment. In summary, they tended to become increasingly 'performance-oriented', rather than 'learning-oriented'. They were very aware of the importance of 'good marks', getting things 'right'. However, in a climate of explicit and formal assessment, many of them avoided challenge and had a low tolerance of ambiguity (Pollard and Triggs, 2000).

Awareness of practising for tests is doubled in our Year 6 data compared with previous years. Thus, by Year 6, practice of particular skills and techniques had become a significant focus, while there was a fall in perceptions of learning for the acquisition of either information or skills. Providing opportunities for practice was clearly perceived as a learning intention, particularly in relation to writing and sums. Explicit reasons were given:

to get us ready for SATs
to get us ready for the sort of questions in SATs – to prepare us
to revise for SATs
practising for SATs – could be in the test
training for the tests in the summer

to practise letter writing
to practise for SATs
to get used to joining up letters for English – cos we'll lose marks

In the forthcoming volume *Policy, Practice and Pupil Experience*, Pollard and Triggs present further evidence to suggest that children's attitudes and learning behaviour have been significantly affected by the tightening of curriculum control that has taken place in response to the pressures of external and overt assessment. They describe how children are becoming 'performance-oriented', and the tension that this can create when compared with becoming 'learning-oriented'. They address the profound implications of this in influencing what is learned, when, for what purpose and in what way.

Back to Basics … Again?

After the Labour government came to power in May 1997, the performance-oriented trend continued. This was expressed most explicitly in the White Paper *Excellence in Schools* (DFEE 1997), which set out Labour's new drive to raise educational standards while also conveying its 'zero tolerance of failure'. Testing of pupils, league tables of school performance and school inspections were thus to continue and, in some respects, were extended. In parallel with these developments was an ever-increasing emphasis on the basics of literacy and numeracy coupled with pressure from influential policy makers for a return to more 'traditional' teaching methods, particularly whole class teaching. New targets were established for national levels of pupil attainment and, from September 1998, each individual school was required to set its own targets for the improvement of its pupils in nationally administered standard assessment tests. Local Education Authorities were also to be subject to requirements for target setting and inspection. Overall then, the extent of the control and monitoring of performance by central government and its agencies continues to increase.

In primary education, pupil performance at mathematics and English became even more significant indicators, and this emphasis was reinforced by a reshaping of National Curriculum priorities. Thus, in January 1988, the Secretary of State for Education, David Blunkett, announced that some of the requirements of the primary National Curriculum were being suspended for the next two years prior to completion of a further comprehensive curriculum review. Replacing the breadth of the ten-subject curriculum, only English, mathematics, science, information technology and religious education remained as required subjects. English schools were expected to continue teaching history, geography, design and technology, art, music and physical education – but to use their discretion over the time allocated and coverage attempted. The purpose of this reduction of National Curriculum requirements was expressed in terms of the government's determination to ensure that all children would leave primary school equipped with the necessary competence in the basics of literacy and numeracy.

Taken in the context of the various policy initiatives of the last ten years or so, the reduction of National Curriculum specification may be seen as an extremely significant development heralding the end of a particular policy chapter. On the one hand, it returned to teachers some of the flexibility that they enjoyed before the National Curriculum was introduced: to decide, for instance, how to respond to any particular curricular needs of the children in their school. On the other hand, it is likely to narrow the focus even more to 'the basics' of literacy and numeracy rather than, as in recent years, ensuring that all pupils have access to a broad and balanced curriculum.

This new phase of policy development clearly illustrates the themes which characterized changes in curriculum and assessment in England throughout the last decade: central control versus institutional and teacher autonomy; depth versus breadth in curriculum provision; standards and the desire to identify, measure and achieve clear targets in terms of pupil learning outcomes; the belief in the power of market forces fuelled by 'league tables'. These themes are the focus of the more theoretical analysis that follows.

Assessment, the 'Pedagogic Device' and Instrumentalism

From the outset of the PACE project, the work of Basil Bernstein (see Bernstein 1996) has proved particularly apposite as a framework for our theoretical inter-pretations. The capacity of Bernstein's conceptualization to embrace curriculum, pedagogy and assessment, and its concern with power, knowledge and consciousness as key variables, enabled us to successfully integrate the diverse perspectives of the PACE project. This integration has been achieved through the emergence of three core PACE themes, which we have identified as values, understanding and power. We have also used Bernstein's well-established concepts of the 'classification and framing of educational knowledge' to portray the interrelated trends that have taken place in primary schools over the period (Pollard et al. 1994)

The argument that schools, as well as teachers and pupils, are embedded in a dynamic network of personal identity, values and understandings (Pollard et al. 1994: 156) is central to the analysis of the PACE project. Personal identities, values and understandings 'are constantly developing in the light of internal and external interaction, pressure and constraints' (1994: 156) upon schools. Because of these dynamics, policy directives are translated into classroom prac-tice through a series of 'mediations'. That is, at each successive stage of the process of delivering education, actors are involved in a process of creative reinterpretation. In this too, Bernstein's analysis of the power of pedagogy to define and control the reconceptualization of the original message, provides a powerful theoretical model for examining the significance of the changes docu-mented in the PACE data.

The overall findings from the PACE study suggests that, through the 1990s, teachers have become more instrumental, moving from a 'covenant' to a 'contract'-based work ethic. However, at the same time they appear to be preserving a good measure of their traditional personal and moral account-ability. The findings also suggest that teachers have developed new curriculum expertise, while at the same time losing confidence in their ability to deliver. What then is the significance of these changes for primary pupils who are themselves also becoming more instrumental and 'performance'-oriented? These pupils are all too aware of the hurdles that lie before them and the skills they must acquire if they are to jump them. We believe that as different controlling groups within the education system seek to accommodate the new requirements on them, through a series of mediations, they are gradually changing the discourse through which the ideology and practice of primary education is expressed. This process of mediation, shaping a changing educational discourse, is conceptualized by Bernstein in terms of the 'pedagogic device' which he describes as 'the symbolic ruler for consciousness – the fundamental system for both creating and controlling the unthinkable' (1996: 50). It is possible to use this concept of the 'pedagogic device' (or mediating process) to analyse the significance of the changes that have taken place in policy and in pedagogy, curriculum and evaluation.

Bernstein locates that discourse of primary education which is now being progressively eroded, within a number of broad social science traditions of the 1960s. These had a common emphasis on 'competencies' and are characterized by a 'universal democracy of acquisition'. He cites, for example, the psychology of Piaget, the linguistics of Chomsky and the sociology of Garfinkel as instances of social scientific conceptualizations which in turn came to underpin the creation of educational approaches based on 'competencies'. These identified the subject as active and creative in the construction of a valid world of meaning and practice; and an educational approach which 'celebrated what we are rather than what we have become'. In such models, learning is conceptualized as accomplishments which are intrinsically creative and tacitly acquired, rather than instilled through formal instruction.

Radical as these educational ideas may seem, Bernstein argued that they found 'official' expression in the 1967 (DES) Report of the Plowden Committee, *Children and Their Primary Schools*, and in the next twenty years of primary school practice which the report's ideas profoundly shaped. He contrasts that 'competence'-based pedagogic model with one based on 'performance' which emphasizes a specific output from the acquirer, a particular text that the learner is required to construct and the acquisition of the specialized skills necessary to the creation of the required output. It is through the operation of explicit assessment procedures that learners will be made aware of the learning outcomes that will be valued. Their performance will in turn be a means of locating them in terms of a hierarchical judgement. In this power of assessment to control social and learning outcomes, we see the relevance of Bernstein's assertion that assessment is the 'purest form' of pedagogic control.

Tables 1.1 and 1.2 display, to contrastive effect, some important patterns related to 'liberal progressive' and 'performance' models. They are displayed in contrastive ways for analytic purposes, though of course the situation is more complex than this devise allows. This form of modelling derives from Bernstein (1996: 58), though he is in no way responsible for our adaptation and extension. The characteristics of Bernstein's 'performance' pedagogic model are readily recognizable in the developments currently taking place in primary schools as documented by the PACE project. As Tables 1.1 and 1.2 illustrate, the increasingly tight classification of the curriculum into clearly delineated subjects; the growing strength of the framing of both teachers and pupils' work so that they have less autonomy and choice; and the designation of times and spaces for particular purposes, are all clear indicators of the change towards a 'performance' pedagogic model.

The issues illustrated by the contrastive pedagogies in Tables 1.1 and 1.2 can be perceived to be embedded in two interrelated educational discourses. That is, they reflect a 'regulative discourse' (concerned with the creation of social order) and an 'instructional discourse' (Bernstein 1996). Changes in these 'regulative'

Table 1.1 *Some contrastive aspects of competence and performance models in relation to schools and teachers*

	A 'competence model' LIBERAL PROGRESSIVE EDUCATION	A 'performance model' PERFORMANCE EDUCATION
Schools and teachers	*'Invisible management' with relative professional autonomy*	*'Visible management' with relative professional regulation*
Organizational form	Professional, with flat management structure. Control through self-regulation, socialization and internalization of norms.	Mechanistic, with hierarchical structure and bureaucracy. Standardization for control and co-ordination.
Management style	Collegiate, with emphasis on proficiency, dialogue and consensus. Informality in relationships.	Managerial, with emphasis on efficiency and target setting for results. Greater formality in relationships.
Teacher roles	Teachers as facilitators, with affective dimensions seen as intrinsic to the teaching role.	Teachers as instructors and evaluators, with emphasis on cognitive and managerial skills.
Teacher professionalism	Professional covenant based on trust, and commitment to education as a form of personal development. Confidence and sense of fulfilment and spontaneity in teaching.	Professionalism is the fulfilment of a contract to deliver education, which is seen as a commodity for individuals and a national necessity for economic growth. Teacher confidence and fulfilment are less.
Teacher accountability	Personal and 'moral' accountability.	External and contractual accountability.
Whole school co-ordination	Relative autonomy and informal teacher collaboration.	Formal school planning with 'contrived' collegiality.
Economic costs	Expensive, because of sophisticated teacher education and time-consuming school practices.	Cheaper, because of more explicit teacher training and systematized school practices.

Table 1.2   Some contrastive aspects of competence and performance models in relation to classrooms and pupils

	A 'competence model' *LIBERAL PROGRESSIVE* *EDUCATION*	A 'performance model' *PERFORMANCE* *EDUCATION*
Classroom and pupils	*'Invisible pedagogies', with weak classification and frame*	*'Visible pedagogies', with strong classification and frame*
Autonomy	Considerable.	Limited.
Space	Flexible boundaries and use.	Explicit regulation.
Time	Flexible emphasis on present experiences.	Strong structuring, sequencing and pacing.
Activity	Emphasis on the realization of inherent learner capabilities through subject integrated and learner-controlled activities, such as projects.	Strong control over selection of knowledge and explicit promotion of specialized subjects and skills.
Evaluation	Emphasis on immediate, present qualities using implicit and diffuse criteria.	Emphasis on inadequacies of the product using explicit and specific performance criteria.
Control	Relatively 'invisible', with control inhering in interpersonal communications and relationships.	Explicit structuring and systems for classification and differentiation through instruction.
Pupil products	Pupil products are taken to indicate a stage of cognitive, affective or social development. Teachers 'read' and interpret learner products using specialized professional judgement and knowledge.	Pupil products are simply taken to indicate performance, as objectified by grades. Teachers instruct and assess using established procedures and criteria.
Pupil learning	Highlighting intrinsic motivation and encouraging mastery orientation. Potential for 'deep learning', but tendency to produce routinization and evasion.	Highlighting performance orientation. Tendency to produce instrumentalism and 'surface learning' or learned helplessness and withdrawal.

and 'instructional' discourses are perhaps most powerfully brought into being through changes in assessment practices. Thus recent profound changes to the language and practices associated with 'levels' and 'standards' in the evaluation of pupils, and with 'target setting', 'league tables' and 'value added' in the evaluation of schools, can be expected to create, through the 'regulative' discourse, profound changes in the social order, in social relations and social identities. Through the 'instructional' discourse, a change in such assessment language and practices can be expected to create changes in the ways in which particular knowledge and skills are inculcated.

The PACE data reflects just such a gradual but inexorable change in both the 'regulative' and 'instructional' discourses of English primary education. The concepts, vocabulary, perceptions, concerns and commitments of primary school teachers have been changing though the decade. While imposed assessment practices were once an affront to their values, professionalism and sense of self, they are increasingly seen as a taken for granted part of the job, with the achievement of 'targets' becoming a new vehicle for self-satisfaction and professional fulfilment.

Whither Lifelong Learning?

One interesting aspect of the performance discourse concerns whether it is consistent with the New Labour government's other educational aims and policies. This may be examined in terms of two broad issues.

First, it can be argued that there is a deep tension between the rhetoric of the much vaunted 'learning society' and the reality of the 'performance' culture which is being promoted by current policy making and by the accountability requirements which are being placed on schools.

The educational ideology of the learning society is one in which learners are empowered to want and be able to manage their own learning in an individualistic manner; where there will be more openness and opportunity and fewer prescribed spaces and times for learning, or defined outcomes or prescribed bodies of knowledge. One manifestation of this is a 1998 set of proposals from the Labour government on lifelong learning, *The Learning Age: A Renaissance for a New Britain* (DFEE 1998). However, we believe that the call for resilient and flexible learners, whose intrinsic motivation and mastery orientation will provide the foundation of future national economic and social development, is in tension with the systemic, performance-oriented changes which are being strengthened within the schools system. As was argued in a paper for the National Curriculum agency (Pollard 1997), the aims and structure of the National Curriculum for primary schools could helpfully be reconceptualized to enable teachers to achieve a new balance between basic skills, subject knowledge, learning dispositions and personal, social and moral development. Our analysis of the broad trends of change in primary education suggests that, if the performance orientation underpinned by high-stakes assessment continues to dominate, it may become increasingly difficult to encourage many pupils to adopt positive dispositions to learning. A narrow performance orientation, while satisfying short-term indicators, may thus have the unintended consequence of actually undermining longer term dispositions to learn through life, especially for those who are least successful in the current system. Ironically, it is just such school 'underperformers' that the lifelong learning initiatives are particularly designed to address.

Second, the trend that we have identified suggests the likelihood of growing tensions in the social fabric and towards the social exclusion of certain groups. This appears to be coming about as the instrumental 'performance'-oriented means to the end (of economic performance) becomes elevated into the end in itself. In such circumstances, society begins to lack any more fundamental basis for social solidarity than mutual competitiveness (Broadfoot 1996). We can already see some of these tensions manifest in contemporary debates about discipline in schools, crime and moral decline and in a climate in which schools increasingly feel the need to exclude certain pupils and compete with their neighbours for others. This climate of competitiveness and social polarization is reflected in PACE evidence that points to teachers' increasing concern about the performance and behaviour of children from particular social groups.

In short, both in its own terms of raising standards for the purposes of economic competitiveness and in relation to more profound issues of social solidarity, the current 'performance' emphasis, which is an increasingly defining feature of English schooling, may ultimately prove to be seriously counter-productive.

Conclusion

The PACE study as a whole has focused on a particular sector of English society, primary education, which is located within the broader sweep of history and social, cultural, economic and political change as we engage with new forms of modernity and postmodernity. Within the multi-faceted design of the PACE study, one particular focus echoes that of this book as a whole in being concerned with assessment as a social product. In this, it is seen as being moulded and fashioned by the ebb and flow of historical tradition, cultural assumptions and the changing social and economic and political contexts of English society at the end of the second millennium. In this chapter, our particular concern has been with assessment policy. We have explored some of the factors that have underpinned its recent evolution in the English context and the impact these policy changes have had on primary schools. The focus of our discussion has been the significance for pupils' learning of the new priorities now being required in primary schools. Of course, English primary schools were formerly famous for their embrace of a very different ideological tradition, but these have now been forced to come to terms with the imposition of assessment practices which embody fundamentally different assumptions about both the means and ends of education.

Above all, our analysis has focused on the significance of policy developments, not just for the immediate future of English primary schooling but in terms of the educational project as a whole, its role in society and its potential capacity to meet the challenges of a rapidly changing world. We have argued, in the words of Gray, that:

> the rhetoric about 'driving up standards' can be read as an attempt to realign education to the commodity values that increasingly define worthwhile or legitimate knowledge in post-industrial societies', i.e. 'the task of education is not the dissemination of a general model of life, not to transform students' minds but to supply the system with the merchandise it needs in the form of information and skills.

> (Gray 1990: 10)

We have progressed, almost imperceptibly, beyond the concerns articulated in the 'Great Debate' in England in the 1970s about standards and the need for more accountability within the education system. Indeed, the development of assessment as a policy device has also gone significantly beyond its role as a means of holding schools (and other institutions) accountable for educational standards. Nor is the concern fundamentally about raising standards, as central as this discourse apparently appears to be in current policy initiatives. Rather, we have entered an era in which the use of a particular application of assessment policy has led to a fundamental redefinition of the goals of education itself in terms of economic commodity values. As a result, it is becoming increasingly difficult for any of the players in the system even to articulate an alternative set of priorities, an alternative vision of desirable educational outcomes. As Elliott (1996: 76) suggests, contemporary assessment policies have played a central role in 'changing the rules which shape educational thought and practice. They are part of a language game which serves the interests of power and legitimates those interests in terms of the performativity criterion.' As a result, he suggests, 'the more marginalized and silenced are the voices who would articulate, given the social space to do so, a different vision of quality in education, of the pedagogical conditions which make it possible.'

To the extent that such voices are silenced, however, the likelihood of developing the type of educational institution that is needed to foster 'lifelong learning for all' is correspondingly reduced. In this chapter we have presented data that begin to suggest that the growing 'performance' orientation of English primary schools may lead to a substantial number of learners who are put off the business of learning at a relatively young age by the experience of failure. It is a pattern that is likely to be repeated at the level of secondary and higher education. Yet institutions find themselves increasingly powerless to remedy the situation, condemned as they are to pursue perpetually those elusive learning outcomes which form the basis of 'league tables' and other external quality assessments on which they will be judged.

This book as a whole explores the socio-cultural origins and implications of assessment practice. It does so through the successive contexts of policy formation, technological development, classroom practice and the lived experiences and perceptions of those who are assessed. The particular goal of this chapter has been to demonstrate that the current English obsession with a performance assessment policy is not, and cannot be, simply the application of a neutral technology: that tests are not 'valid irrespective of human expectation, ideas attitudes and wishes' (Feyerabend 1987: 5) but rather must be understood as a 'social technology' (Madaus 1994) rooted in contemporary power relations. Citing Hanson (1993), Madaus writes:

> They [tests and assessments] are not, and cannot be, measures or indicators of some purely objective, independently-existing state of affairs' writes Hanson, rather they 'act to transform, mould and even to create, what they supposedly measure.
>
> (Madaus 1994: 222; see also Chapters 3–4)

Thus as a policy device, the growing recourse to measures of 'performativity' (Lyotard 1979) has had, first, the effect of silencing alternative voices concerning the goals of education and how these goals may best be achieved. Second, when translated into practice, these policies mould individuals' views of themselves, both as learners and as people more generally in defining notions of success and failure and the reasons for it.

Thus, at the very moment when public education needs to break free of its familiar organizing principles and assumptions if it is to respond to the opportunities and challenges of the information revolution, it has become subjugated as never before to the educational assumptions of an earlier, modernist, industrial age. At the very time when the traditional role of educational assessment in providing for selection, legitimation and control needs to be replaced by an emphasis on assessment to support 'lifelong learning', there seems less chance than ever of such a change being realized. At present this contradiction lies largely buried beneath the rhetorical weight of the 'standards' agenda. Sooner or later, however, the tensions inherent in the profound changes in assessment discourse that have taken place in recent years will become apparent. The PACE study has revealed the beginning of the story; it is difficult to predict the end.

Note

1   It is important to note that the terms 'performance' and 'competence' as used by Bernstein (1996) and in this chapter have distinctly different meanings from those associated with 'performance' (authentic) and 'competence' testing as more generally understood in the field of assessment and as used elsewhere in this book.

References

Bernstein, B. (1975) *Class, Codes and Control*, Vol. III, London: Routledge.
—— (1990) *Class, Codes and Control*, Vol. IV, London: Routledge.
—— (1996) *Pedagogy, Symbolic Control and Identity*, London: Taylor & Francis.
Broadfoot, P. (1996) *Education, Assessment and Society*, Buckingham: Open University Press.
Chubb, J. and Moe, T. (1992) *Politics, Markets and America's Schools*, Washington, DC: Brookings Institution.
Croll, P. (ed.) (1996) *Teachers, Pupils and Primary Schooling*, London: Cassell.
Croll, P., Abbott, D., Broadfoot, P., Osborn, M. and Pollard, A. (1994) 'Teachers and Educational Policy: Roles and Models', *British Journal of Educational Studies* 42(2): 333–47.
Department of Education and Science (1967) *Children and Their Primary Schools*, Report of the Plowden Committee, London: HMSO.
DFEE (1997) *Excellence in Schools*, London: DFEE.
DFEE (1998) *The Learning Age: A Renaissance for a New Britain*, London: DFEE.
Elliott, J. (1996) 'Quality Assurance, the Educational Standards Debate, and the Commodification of Educational Research', *Curriculum Journal* 8(6): 63–83.
Feyerabend, P. (1987) *Farewell to Reason*, London: Verso.

Firestone, W., Winter, J. and Fitz, J. (1998) 'Different Policies, Common Practice: Mathematics Assessment and Teaching in the United States and England and Wales', AERA, San Diego.

Gray, J. (1990) 'The Quality of Schooling: Frameworks for Judgement', *British Journal of Educational Studies* 38(3): 204–23.

Hanson, F. Allan (1993) *Testing Testing: Social Consequences of the Examined Life*, Berkeley, CA: University of California Press

HMI (1978) *Primary Education in England*, London: HMSO.

Keys, W., Harris, S. and Fernandes, C. (1997) *Patterns of Mathematics and Science Teaching in Upper Primary Schools in England and Eight Other Countries*, The Third International Mathematics and Science Study 2nd National Report, Slough: NFER.

Lyotard, J.F. (1979) *The Post-Modern Condition: A Report on Knowledge*, Manchester: Manchester University Press, xxv, 31–7.

Madaus, G.F. (1994) 'Testing's Place in Society: An Essay Review of "Testing Testing: Social Consequences of the Examined Life", by F.A. Hanson', *American Journal of Education* 102: 222–34.

Pollard, A. (1997) 'Learning and a New Curriculum for Primary Schooling', paper presented to the SCAA conference on Developing the Primary School Curriculum: The Next Steps, June, London: SCAA.

Pollard, A., Broadfoot, P., Croll, P., Osborn, M. and Abbott, D. (1994) *Changing English Primary Schools? The Impact of the Education Reform Act at Key Stage One*, London: Cassell.

Pollard, A., Broadfoot, P., Osborn, M., McNess, E., Triggs, P. and Noble, J. (1997) 'Primary Assessment, Curriculum and Experience', symposium papers, British Educational Research Association, York.

Pollard, A. and Triggs, P., with Broadfoot, P., McNess, E. and Osborn, M. (2000) *Policy Practice and Pupil Experience: Changing English Primary Education*, London: Cassell.

Whitty, G., Power, S. and Halpin, D. (1998) *Devolution and Choice in Education: the School, the State and the Market*, Buckingham: Open University Press.

2 Choosing Not to Know

How Assessment Policies and Practices Obscure the Education of Language Minority Students

Mark LaCelle-Peterson

Introduction

Nearly one in four students in US primary and secondary schools comes from a home where a language other than English is dominant or influential, and both the number and proportion of such students is increasing (Anstrom 1996). Depending on one's definition of proficiency in English, as many as one in six students experience or are likely to experience 'obstacles to achievement' if their education is conducted exclusively in English.[1] What does this mean for an educational system that is seeking to reach new standards of academic excellence and which is 'betting' increasingly on large-scale assessment programmes to help accomplish this task? Since linguistic and cultural diversities are clearly 'megatrends' in US education, one might expect that consideration of the educational needs and characteristics of so-called limited English proficient (LEP) students would figure large in public discussion and policy deliberation. Not so. As in the early decades of the 1900s when immigration made language diversity a commonplace in expanding school systems across the US, demographic changes are widely acknowledged in commentary on social trends, but largely ignored in practice (Montero-Sieburth and LaCelle-Peterson 1991).

Unlike those earlier times, however, the stakes in educational attainment are higher for both individuals and society: the post-industrial economy affords no living-wage jobs for those whose school careers are cut short. In light of this, it bodes ill for us all that discussions of the education of students who are, in addition to tackling demanding academic studies, still learning English focus not on questions such as 'how does learning a second language impact a student's learning in other areas?' or 'how might educational programmes benefit from the languages and cultural experiences of English language learners (ELLs) and their family members?' or even 'what does the best research tell us about the average time it takes to learn well through a second language and about how individuals' time-to-proficiency varies around that average?' but focus rather on mandated time limits. Where one might hope to find vigorous discussion of educational options informed by rigorous research based on volumes of data, one finds instead partisan political rhetoric. In the most extreme example to date of simplistic (and xenophobic) political rhetoric trumping defensible educational practice, California voters in June of 1998 approved a draconian ballot referendum that largely restricts the educational options for students who are still learning English to a one-year immersion program (Crawford 1999). Opinion polls rather than research results are, unhappily, the surest barometer of trends in the education of ELLs.

The central premise of this chapter is that assessment policies and practices reflect and reinforce narrow and inadequate conceptualizations of the needs and characteristics of students in US schools for whom English is a second or other language; rather than informing public views and educational policies, assessment practices are captive to political imperatives that privilege language proficiency *per se* over cognitive development or academic achievement at the individual level, and that privilege assimilation and cultural erasure over political empowerment and maintenance of culture at the community level. Misconceptualizations of students' capabilities and needs persist despite ample research on language learning and academic achievement (see Thomas and Collier (1997) for a thorough review of the research and compelling original data and analysis), and despite clear recognition in the professional measurement standards that an individual's linguistic and cultural heritage and current level of proficiency in the language of the measurement instrument influences the meaning of obtained scores. As a result, US schools and school systems fail to use their own 'best practices' with ELLs, students who know a language other than English and whose proficiency in English is still developing.

Best evidence and technical standards notwithstanding, the assessment and education of ELLs in the USA is best understood as part of a larger social and political struggle. Through policy decisions at the state and local levels, US educators have too often chosen what is politically and socially expedient over what is known on the basis of solid research to promote academic achievement and multilingual accomplishment for ELLs. Through persistent selective inattention to available evidence in public debates, we as a society have chosen not to know, and the logic or meaning embedded in the structure of assessment policies, programmes and practices facilitates this choice more often than it challenges it.

Consideration of the role of assessment policies and practices in the education of students who are not monolingual English-speakers can elucidate both the political and educational dilemmas facing language minority communities in the USA and the failure of the mental measurement movement to deliver on its promise of ensuring that a rational, equitable and effective set of educational programmes and practices can be developed for all learners. Lest there be any misunderstanding, however, the interests of ELLs will not be served by doing away with standardized assessment; rather, we need assessment policies and practices that validate ELLs' learning and inform, rather than obscure, discussions of their education. Fair and accurate assessments are essential to any educational system as means of providing feedback to students (and their parents), feedback for teachers to guide instruction, and evidence for monitoring purposes. In fact, fairness and accuracy are inextricably interrelated in assessment: fairness in assessment must include (a) measuring the achievements of *all* students who are assessed with equal accuracy, and (b) ensuring that equally useful and adequate information is available on the educational status and progress of all students.

Three levels of assessment discourse will be examined to elucidate this larger struggle over language, meaning and identity in the education of ELLs in the US: the technical/academic professional discourse of testing and measurement standards; state and local testing policy discourse; and the muddled 'common-sense' discourse of building-level and district-level assessment practices. At each level, the education of ELLs is complicated and compromised by assessment policies and practices. Together, it will be argued, these discourse strands reflect a view of society and education that is rooted in the nomothetic assumptions of the positivist psychology that gave birth to the mental measurement movement and is characterized by assumptions of 'latent homogeneity'. A view that must be recognized and challenged by counter-discourses of 'manifest hetero-geneity'. Building on an analysis of the contradictions within and among these discourses, it will be argued that an equity-focused assessment framework based on a cultural view of identity and community connected to the emerging discourse of performance assessment is urgently needed. Consideration of actual cases where assessment policies have compromised the education or achievement of individuals and groups will be considered in the analysis.

First, however, a short discussion of terms is in order (definitions and names/labels are, after all, keys to creating and understanding the social construction of the world). In this chapter, students whose home language or mother tongue is a language other than English and who do not yet have equal or native-like proficiency in English will be referred to as English language learners (ELLs). This term is used for two positive reasons and despite an acknowledged weakness. First, the term ELL focuses on what students are mastering rather than on the fact that they have not yet done so (LaCelle-Peterson and Rivera 1994); in this it differs from the officially sanctioned term 'limited English proficient'. ELLs are in the process of learning English, and educators' standard way of describing students in the process of learning anything is to emphasize their anticipated accomplishment, whether we speak of the emergent literacy of young students (rather than their lifelong illiteracy up to that point) or refer hopefully to a university student as a chemistry major (rather than as 'laboratory-impaired'). We routinely refer to monolingual English-speaking students who are beginning the study of Spanish or Chinese as 'beginners' or 'level 1 students' rather than as 'limited-Spanish (or Chinese)-proficient'. The focus of assessment policy and practice would, I think, be different if we started with this term rather than with one that unduly privileges 'limitations'.

The second reason for preferring the term ELL is to emphasize the ongoing, open-ended process of second language acquisition. Where the term LEP encourages a focus on current level of proficiency rather than on progress, and on 'getting out of' the category rather than embracing the accomplishment, ELL is meant to emphasize process over either momentary measures of profi-ciency and reductionist categorization of learners. The term LEP encourages educators to view language learning as temporary, as if once the magic cut-off score (which varies among US states) defined as denoting 'proficiency' is reached, the second language acquisition process is no longer an important consideration in a child's education. In fact, of course, the whole number of students for whom second language learning is a part of educational reality and must be taken into consideration in instruction and assessment is much larger than the number identified as LEP. Though the stakes are highest for students whose levels of proficiency in English preclude equal learning opportunities in English-only classrooms, the influence of language and culture is continuous and multi-faceted rather than discrete and unidimensional. Language-related issues in learning and assessment do not disappear when a student's English proficiency score exceeds an arbitrarily set legal cut-off score.

Finally, despite the positive reasons for using ELL over LEP, one distinct problem remains: the term calls attention to only one aspect of student learning (developing English proficiency) and does not adequately reflect that fact that ELLs are also learning maths, sciences, literature, writing, music and so on. Indeed, our aspirations for ELLs must be broader, not narrower, than those we hold for monolingual English speakers. ELLs must meet the common academic standards in all subject areas, often through a second (or third) language. It must also be borne in mind that in seeking to meet all the demands placed on them, ELLs will exhibit all the individual differences in terms of learning styles, preferences for subject areas, and special aptitudes and learning needs that any other group of students exhibits. The story of ELLs education is never only about language, but at the same time it is always about language. Having tried unsuccessfully to come up with a more adequate term, I am resigned to bearing the inadequacy of 'ELLs' in mind while waiting for a more clever writer to propose a more fully accurate term.

Assessment Standards and ELLs: What We (Sometimes) Admit

The story of how assessment policies and practices keep us from understanding and/or promoting the educational well-being (and ultimately, employment opportunities, life chances and life experiences) of ELLs begins with the discourse of standardized assessment. It bears noting that the field of educational assessment has been in a relatively dynamic phase for the past ten to fifteen years. The heyday of selected-response testing as the dominant and highest mode of measuring any and every variable of interest is past, and varied modes of assessment that focus on process, performance and outcomes have gained in prominence. At the same time, large-scale assessment programmes have expanded and diversified, and are called upon to play a critical role in the ongoing standards-based reform movement. Indeed, assessment has played a pivotal role in the rhetoric of educational reform throughout the past two decades. Calls for accountability have relied on large-scale assessments to gauge the relative success of schools and districts and, in some states, to trigger intervention in or closer scrutiny of low-performing districts or buildings. In addition, large-scale assessments, often in the form of minimum competency tests, are increasingly used as 'high stakes' prerequisites for high school graduation and as policy prods to increased achievement (Garcia and Pearson 1994; Thurlow et al. 1997).

Still more recently, large-scale assessments have been proposed as a policy tool to increase student achievement by shaping classroom instruction and raising academic expectations (Garcia and Pearson 1994; Mitchell 1992; Stiggins 1997; Wiggins 1993). Reform-minded educators have proposed using new types of large-scale assessments as one element of systemic efforts to achieve higher educational standards, and work has begun on developing large-scale assessments that more closely parallel good instruction by requiring students to accomplish larger integrated tasks. Proponents see large-scale performance assessment as a potential policy 'fulcrum' with which to leverage improved instruction by posing tasks that are worth being 'taught to' (Mitchell 1992). Assessment policy has been, at various times and for various purposes, designed to provide information for accountability purposes, incentives for higher achievement and inducements to changes in instructional practices and academic standards.

Given that the 'arithmetic' of assessment follows the same patterns as that of curriculum – it is always easier to add than to subtract – it is no surprise that surveys of state assessment policies reveal a great deal of testing being done for a variety of purposes (North Central Regional Educational Laboratory 1996). States currently require or encourage the assessment of more students with more measures than ever before. While assessment has become a prominent element of reform efforts, the demographic changes noted earlier have brought increased ethnic, cultural and linguistic diversity among students, and for the purposes of this discussion, among test takers. Research has shown that gathering equally accurate information from diverse groups of test takers is no easy task; characteristics of tests, aspects of test development procedures and content of test items have all been shown to have differential impacts on different groups of learners (see Garcia and Pearson (1994) for a thorough review of the research base). But while meeting the twin goals of gathering accurate information on all students in a target population and treating each student and all groups of students fairly in the process has been recognized as challenging (for example, Garcia and Pearson 1994; LaCelle-Peterson and Rivera 1994; Liu et al. 1996, 1997; Mercado and Romero 1993; Zehler et al. 1994), the logic of testing contains an inherent reluctance to recognize this challenge.

Standardized assessment is, after all, based on the doctrine that identical treatment of what are assumed to be practically homogeneous learners will yield equally accurate and comparable data. All learners are assumed to be, indeed, *must be assumed to be* essentially interchangeable on all but the characteristic to be measured, and thus test administration handbooks call for all students to be treated the same in the interest of treating all students fairly and gaining equally accurate information on all test takers. Given the centrality of this tenet to the logic of standardized assessment, assertions that testing all students identically may constitute unequal treatment creates considerable dissonance. Indeed, the logic of testing produces a bias in favour of what might

be called an 'assumption of latent homogeneity': unless and until proven otherwise, it will be assumed that all learners, all test takers, are essentially the same
on all relevant features.

One of those relevant features is language. Whatever the construct or
content area being assessed, all educational assessment is embedded in
language; even vision and hearing screenings depend on linguistic instructions
and responses, and all subject matter testing requires reading or listening and
writing or speaking on the part of test takers. If proficiency in the language of
assessment varies across a test taking population, the assumption that test
takers are essentially the same on all relevant features is violated. The professional standards of testing and measurement recognize this fact in the *Standards
for Educational and Psychological Testing*, a set of standards jointly developed
and adopted by the American Psychological Association, the American Educational Research Association, and the (US) National Council for Measurement
in Education. The section on the testing of linguistic minorities puts it bluntly:
'For a non-native English speaker and for a speaker of some dialects of
English, every test given in English becomes, in part, a language or literacy test'
(American Psychological Association 1985: 73). This simple concession raises a
critical, practical question: to what extent does a given student's score represent
the target construct, and to what degree does it reflect proficiency in the
language of assessment? And even that question oversimplifies matters when
one remembers ELLs are not a single population sharing a single trait; they are
a varied population with varied and constantly changing levels of proficiency.

Additional testing standards have direct implications for those responsible
for the assessment of ELLs.[2] Given that proficiency in the language of the test
influences the meaning of a score, inclusion of ELLs at various and known
levels of proficiency in norming samples would be a logical requirement for
tests that will be administered to ELLs (Standard 2.9). The standard that calls
for full description of validation study samples (1.5) would, therefore, imply
full description of test takers' language proficiencies (and disaggregated
reporting of norms). Likewise, knowing the likely, unspecified and variable
impact of language proficiency levels on test performance would require that
separate reliability estimates be developed for ELLs at various proficiency
levels (2.9). Similar implications follow for various standards relating to
validity and reliability (1.14); test development and revision (3.5, 3.10, 3.13,
3.22); scaling, norming, score comparability and equating (4.3); and principles
of test use (6.7, 6.10). Once one abandons pretensions of latent homogeneity
and seriously acknowledges the recognized impact of test takers' varied and
dynamic levels of language proficiency, one sees that any attempt to implement
standardized assessments in a fair manner demands a great deal more than
most standardized testing programmes can deliver.

The technical discourse on assessment, then, is crystal clear: when ELLs are
involved in assessment conducted in English, the results yielded are not comparable to those of native English speakers and are of uncertain comparability to
those of other ELLs whose level of proficiency in English differs. In other words,
language proficiency constitutes a confounding variable that differentially

influences the scores of students; varying language proficiency levels of ELLs compromise the validity and reliability of tests that seek to measure anything other than English language proficiency itself. Test scores that reflect a combination, in unknown proportion, of a target construct such as academic achievement in a particular subject area *and* second language proficiency in the test language are difficult to interpret at the individual level and, when aggregated into larger sets of test data, introduce errors which preclude making accurate evaluations of the schools or programmes serving the students.

If we seek accurate test-based information on the educational status of a group of students that includes ELLs, then, we have three logical options: (1) recognizing the dilemma, take learning needs and characteristics of ELLs into consideration at each phase of the development process, and gather additional information regarding the performance of ELLs, documenting that evidence and giving our best assessment of what the evidence means in relation to that gathered for non-ELLs (LaCelle-Peterson and Rivera 1994); (2) disregard the dilemma and aggregate the data from ELLs at various levels of proficiency in English with data from others, overlooking the fact that any analysis loses its integrity; or (3) avoid dealing with the dilemma by excluding some or all ELLs from a given assessment programme. Clearly, the first of these options is the best and only defensible option if we seek to remain true to the goals of gathering accurate information on all participants in a given educational programme, and ensuring that the information gathered can be used to support their success. Regrettably, when we look at the treatment accorded ELLs in practitioner-oriented assessment textbooks, in state and local testing policies, and from the perspective of ELLs in classrooms and employment situations, we see that the second and third options are chosen, not on the basis of alternative professional standards or expert opinions, but as a reflection of social and political currents.

Before turning to policy and practice, a contradiction between the theoretical and applied levels within assessment discourse itself bears noting. As part of the general renewed interest in assessment, many excellent new or extensively revised practitioner-oriented assessment textbooks have been marketed. These texts reflect the increased attention to performance and portfolio assessment strategies and have the potential to improve classroom assessment for many students and teachers. Consideration of half a dozen of these otherwise excellent texts, however, shows a glaring gap in their failure to address the influence of variations in language proficiency among students, a relevant factor for one in four or one in five students across the US and thus for many if not most teachers.[3] The texts rightly warn about the possible impact of gender bias and cultural bias on students being assessed and discuss implications for assessment development; each also deals with assessment issues for students with disabilities, per the mandates of federal legislation. Student proficiency in English is, however, ignored. At one level – the theoretical, academic/professional standards-of-record level – assessment discourse clearly addresses the issue of language proficiency and its impact on testing programmes. As the standards of assessment are translated for practitioners, however, language proficiency is ignored.

Assessment Policy: One Size Never Fits

On the ground, among teachers who work closely with ELLs, testing is peren-
nially a hot issue because in practice, testing programmes almost invariably fail
to provide accurate information on the abilities and accomplishments of ELLs.
As a result, tests are seen as 'punishing' ELLs and reflecting poorly on the
teachers and schools that serve them. Given the current emphasis on requiring
accountability for educational outcomes, low test scores – regardless of their
accuracy or inaccuracy – become the grounds for bad publicity, public outcry
and, on occasion, institutional sanction from local or state authorities. State
policies define when language counts in assessment and how so-called LEP
students are tested; in doing so, they reflect an official view of language which
powerfully shapes the educational experiences and prospects of ELLs.

State-level assessment policies begin with defining who is to be regarded as
'LEP'. Because this book is aimed at multinational readership, it bears mentioning that education in the USA is a function of state government, delegated to
local school boards, and not fundamentally a federal responsibility. Though
federal education programmes and policies do exist, the centre of gravity in
educational policy is the individual state.[4] Anstrom provides a succinct
summary of the definition used in federal education policy and the range of
states' definitions of so-called LEP status. Both conceptual and operational
definitions vary, but both alike are concerned with defining the category: who
is in and who is out. Because bilingual education and language minority
students' rights emerged from Civil Rights Era litigation and legislation
(Crawford 1996; Spring 1997), the emphasis is not in the first place educational
(based on how one's linguistic proficiencies might impact one's education), but
rather legal, focusing on whether or not one belongs in a category and therefore
qualifies for (or historically and politically speaking, has a right to) particular
services. And, almost as a precursor to more recently enacted time limits on
welfare benefits, many state definitions have included a time component:
despite excellent research documenting the fact that development of sufficient
proficiency to close the achievement gap between native- and non-native-
English speakers is likely to require 7–9 years (Thomas and Collier 1997), three
years was a common limit, and the recently passed Unz initiative in California
limits services to one year. It bears mentioning, however, that the legal opinions
on which court decisions have been based have, as in other civil rights areas,
included serious consideration of educational issues and evidence based in
empirical research in education. Such consideration is too often lost in the politics of policy formulation with the result that litigation tends to recur.

Assessment as a technology is used to identify ELLs who meet the definition
of LEP, place those who are identified in appropriate programmes, monitor
their progress, evaluate the programmes serving them, and 'exit' them from the
programmes when their English no longer meets the definition of 'limited'
(Zehler et al. 1994). In addition to assessment functions that focus on ELLs *per
se*, the ever-expanding and currently diversifying set of state-mandated and
locally-arranged assessment programmes present questions of definition for

ELLs as well: should they be assessed or exempted? Should their data be aggregated or disaggregated? General assessment policy decisions also shape ELLs' educational experiences and reflect an officially sanctioned ideological construction of their identity. While the rationale for these assessment policies and practices is purely technical, the impact of the policies themselves includes rationing opportunity for ELLs and promoting untenable notions of knowledge, humanity, and society. Assessment policy and practice is complicit in:

- defining ELL students as deficient and uni-dimensional;
- privileging proficiency in the language of power over broader, global, multicultural competencies, and in doing so, positing a monolingual view of knowledge;
- subverting educationally defensible programmes serving ELLs (and thereby compromising the integrity of ELLs' educational experiences);
- reinforcing an anthropology of latent homogeneity;
- promoting a zero-sum view of social and cultural capital.

First of all, assessment policies frame the kinds of questions we ask about learners and their educational needs. Though the intention behind mandates to identify ELLs is good, and takes us a step away from one form of ignorance (in the 'good old days', nobody knew or cared what language you spoke at home), the purpose of identifying students with abilities in languages other than English (one set of questions typically asked in screening for LEP status) is seldom to capitalize on those abilities by creating multilingual learning opportunities, but simply to further screen for those whose level of English proficiency bodes ill for their success. Within this framework, there is little room for celebration but rather a persistent focus on identifying a particular limitation (often read as a deficiency) to be remedied (not that individual teachers and schools do not celebrate their students' and communities' cultural and linguistic richness; indeed, many do so). It becomes a *policy process* of screening to identify those who need 'fixing'. Thus the definition is not only negative but also narrow. It is this combination of negativity and narrowness, I believe, that leads some parents of ELLs to opt out of bilingual or ESL programmes, preferring a general educational placement where their child is not *de facto* defined by a policy having only one relevant learning characteristic; and that one, by definition, a problem.

This narrow concern with second language acquisition privileges the language of power in the USA over the breadth of human experience and the depths of human knowledge and represents both a narrow conception of the educated individual in general and a limited view of the experiences and potentials of particular students. In the decades-long struggle over the rights of ELLs to freedom of speech and appropriate education, assessment policies serve as a reminder that, at the end of the day, the language of power will not be diminished. Transitional bilingual education programmes and some so-called special alternative instructional programmes allow for partial education in ELLs' native language only as a concession on the way to what really counts:

knowledge packaged in, expressed in and assessed in English (maintenance or two-way bilingual programmes, in contrast, value both the students' native and second languages). Performance in English is the criterion by which knowers and their knowledge will be judged, and assessment is the ultimate instrument of judgement. It matters not, in this scheme, that a Central American student grew up amidst mountains, traversed mountain ranges to arrive in the USA, and can discuss mountain geography in colloquial Spanish.[5] Recognizing the pictorial representation of a mountain and recognizing its English definition on a multiple choice test is the act which certifies the knower. Policies remind us that documenting what students know is not the primary function of assessment programmes, and that knowledge only counts in one language: English.

At a more mundane level, assessment policies work in many cases to subvert educational programmes designed to serve ELLs. Under common transitional models of bilingual education, for example, students who have been identified as ELLs and as LEP are placed in programmes in which literacy and other abilities are fostered initially through native language instruction, while English is introduced as a second language. Over the course of two to four years, the amount of instruction provided in English increases, while native language instruction and support decreases. Whether a student remains enrolled in such a programme depends on her or his level of English proficiency. Such practices ignore the fact that it is facility with academic uses of language *in content areas* that remains the greatest obstacle to success for ELLs, not their measured level of English proficiency *per se* (Thomas and Collier 1997). Assessment, in this common scenario, is used as a means of legitimating minimal service to students rather then as a trigger to maximal services. In other cases, 'exit assessment' is avoided altogether to facilitate termination of services: under California's Unz initiative, the calendar serves as the assessment instrument.

General assessment policies also subvert the education of ELLs. Some states address the problem of inappropriate testing in the second language by exempting (or, it could be argued, excluding) ELLs from general statewide assessments for a specified period of time. In New York State, for example, ELLs were historically exempted from statewide testing programmes for twenty months from entry into New York schools (a maximum of two years of instruction with one summer break in between).[6] This policy applied to all students, including those placed in transitional or maintenance bilingual education programmes, in either of which literacy is promoted through the native language before reading is begun in English. Despite the clear inappropriateness of giving standardized reading or other tests in a language other than the language of instruction, students in these programmes were required to take an English-language reading examination in the third grade, regardless of how recently they have started working on reading in English. Students experienced tremendous frustration, building-level and district-level administrators faced sanctions over what appeared to be low performance on the part of their students, and teachers felt pressure from superiors and from the students and families they serve. Not surprisingly, over time, teachers in some programmes began to abandon the programme model in favour of preparing for the test by introducing English reading and test-like exercises earlier in the programme: a clear and unfortunate case of assessment driving instruction. The 'snapshot' nature of state and local testing programmes further undermines the education of ELLs (and other students) and promotes short-sighted instruction. While testing students at a given level in reading, in another level in math, at yet another in science and so on makes sense from a monitoring perspective, it frames educational experience as a series of discrete hurdles rather than as an ongoing, incremental expansion of knowledge and ability. All students, and ELLs in particular, would benefit more if their own progress over time were tracked.

General assessment policies also tend to ignore the limitations of testing as a technology, and in doing so have the effect of limiting or distorting our knowledge of ELLs' abilities. As such, they pose obstacles to individuals at the adult end of the educational pipeline as well as at the beginning, and in doing so, deny society the benefit of ELLs' full participation. Students who are native speakers of languages other than English are among those groups which are underrepresented in the teaching profession in the USA. Standardized teaching tests, in English, are one of the final hurdles to entry into the profession in most states (again, each individual state has its own certification requirements). As a teacher educator, I am aware of several cases in which entry to the profession was delayed or denied for new teachers for whom English is a second or other language. In each case, the candidate's academic work (all completed in English) at the university level was very strong, and her or his performance in the classroom in student teaching was excellent. Candidates whose ability to write well in English was already documented and whose teaching knowledge and skills had been proven in action were screened out by a standardized assessment of 'teaching skills' (see Garcia and Pearson (1994) for an overview of the research on the influence of format and test-taking situations). (Ironically, one of these individuals – a native speaker of Spanish – aspired to be a Spanish teacher.) The consequences for the individual are obvious, the injustice (let alone illogic) of the situation is clear, and the broader social consequence are deplorable.

Taken together, assessment policies that identify and place ELLs in particular programmes, those that include ELLs as part of statewide monitoring efforts, and those that screen for professional certification re-enforce a notion of latent homogeneity which has its roots in the nomothetic, normative and distributive assumptions of the mental measurement movement. Language is treated as a discrete skill rather than as the medium of learning and of expressing knowledge in all content areas. ELLs are treated as if having limited proficiency in English were a temporary condition that, once taken care of, places one back in the general pool of test takers. If a more deeply rooted sense of cultural identity is conceded to exist, the possibility of biculturalism or multiculturalism is not. ELLs are viewed as having a 'treatable language deficiency' and/or as 'on the way' to complete assimilation. The cultural values and assumptions that are embodied and embedded in the substance of assessments constitute a view of the world, of society, of the individual and of knowledge that cannot be negotiated, only conformed to more or less successfully. The movement toward performance assessments may or may not improve this. While the more contextualized uses of language may help ELLs, the increased complexity of the language use as well as questions of cultural content and cultural sensitivity on the part of raters and judges remain causes for concern (Zehler et al. 1994). Indeed, development of rating systems may prove to be the greatest potential threat to equity; in the mid-1990s, one assessment developer reported in private conversation that data collected for some newly developed performance assessments of early language development were going to be re-scored *because* students in bilingual programmes scored 'too high' on them: assumptions easily override data.

Implications and Prospects

The policies discussed above and the mindset they support both find expression and meet resistance at the local level. Not surprisingly, policies that emphasize categorization of students promote programmes that segregate those categorized. Policies that privilege the development of language proficiency over a broader set of learning goals promote a preoccupation with language learning in place of a more balanced educational programme. Student needs are interpreted within a one-dimensional frame: if a group of ELLs are excelling in their bilingual or ESL programme, the response is to 'exit' them rather than to screen them for 'giftedness' and implement a gifted component within the bilingual or ESL programme; if an ELL experiences difficulty in reading, the difficulty tends to be interpreted as a 'problem with English' rather than requiring referral to a reading specialist. Indeed, until recently local educational policies frequently prohibited students from receiving 'multiple services,' reflecting a categorical mind set that saw students as fitting into one or another of a set of mutually exclusive 'need' categories.

Nonetheless, parents, teachers and community advocates continue to press for better policies and practices that reflect the whole set of abilities and learning needs of ELLs. Just as strong federal and state lobbying efforts by advocacy groups have led to better state (the California initiative excepted) and federal educational policies for ELLs (including the increased attention to meeting the needs of ELLs in general educational policies and programmes), local efforts have and will continue to lead to better educational outcomes. Assessment remains an area of immense concern, however, because of the power that test scores have in public debates and because current assessment reforms fail to respond to what is known about ELLs and assessment from research and as reflected in standards. The conceptual space in which progress may be made might just be found in technical assessment discourse.

While much has been made of new assessment proposals and technologies, a potentially more important conceptual shift in the field has received little public notice. In an important step away from a nomothetic conceptualization of measurement as a pure and objective science and toward a recognition of the social embeddedness of all assessment systems, the concept of validity has been redefined with a focus on consequences of test-score use (Messick 1989).

Validity had, in the past, been thought of as the degree to which a given test measured what it set out to measure, as if the target trait or construct had an unproblematic and independent existence, and as if a good test could measure that trait as easily as a thermometer measures temperature. Messick has argued, and the argument has been widely conceded, that we must recognize that the meaning of a test score or other assessment artefact is not inherent, but is relative to the use to which it is put. If we follow this reasoning and consider the consequences of test use as a primary criterion in determinations of validity, we will begin to ask better questions of our tests and other assessment devices, both those used specifically with ELLs and our general testing programmes.

In a broader sense, it could be argued that a consequentialist or (dare one hope?) pragmatic conceptualization of validity, and of assessment in general, opens the door to a bottom-up, culture-based review of assessment practices and policies. Examining the consequences of assessment policies and practices highlights the limitations of current conceptualizations of language, language learning and language learners. While some gains can be made by tweaking the existing system (providing testing accommodations such as time extensions and additional reference resources), the real change would come through a reconceptualization rooted in consideration of the learning needs and experiences of actual students, schools and communities. Rather than building on the assumption that people and their experiences are the same unless and until proven otherwise, such an approach would be grounded in assumptions of manifest heterogeneity, starting from the view that each learner presents a unique profile of abilities, accomplishments, characteristics and needs. And rather than viewing language or any other domain as discrete, isolated and utilitarian, such an approach would build on an integrated model in which language is recognized as the mediator of knowledge and facilitator of learning.

An assessment system rooted in these assumptions would be able to meet the goals of ensuring that the information gathered about any particular individual was both accurate and adequate. Rather than assessing in order to categorize students for assignment to pre-established curricular and instructional programmes, assessment might be used to tailor instructional programmes to learners' individual needs and to connect learners and groups of learners (regardless of their status as ELLs or non-ELLs) in mutually beneficial learning experiences. While this may sound somewhat far-fetched, the conceptual underpinnings in psychology and measurement are present, and the political and social determination to accomplish systemic and sustainable change is widely touted. Assessment can and must be part of any meaningful transformation of schools and (again, dare we hope?) of society. Continued study of the ways in which assessment shapes educational outcomes and, more importantly, shapes our thinking about people and possibilities, will play a crucial role in any such developments.

When the two-hundred-year history of measurement is written in the middle of the next century, it will have to deal with the resurgence of the 'bell curve' mentality in the 1990s, but will, I hope, also document a reconceptualization of assessment ideas, assessment policy and educational practice for ELLs and for all students. The stakes around assessment have always been high for ELLs; as Mercado and Romero (1993) point out, testing has, historically, served the contradictory purposes of safeguarding and violating the rights of ELLs. As the next century unfolds, one or the other of those contradictory consequences of assessment will win out. We do well to remember that the stakes for all learners, not just ELLs, are high and rising. Indeed, as Fraser (1997) points out, the broader standards-based reform movement (which relies on assessment as a key technology) could, in the best case, deliver on its promise of expanding and enriching the academic and intellectual prospects of all students through implementation of higher standards informed and enforced by expanded and improved assessment programmes. However, lacking real and meaningful commitment to the ideal of equalizing opportunities for success, the movement will instead serve as a smokescreen covering a reassertion of the school's sorting function. The sorting-and-ranking mindset is deeply rooted in the history of testing and measurement (Gould 1981), and must be overcome if we are to realize the full promise of all of our students' lives. At least in the USA, the educational fate of ELLs may well be viewed as a bellwether for us all, as a portent for the prospects of the democratic ideal itself.

Notes

1   The matter of definitions is thorny; see Anstrom (1996) for a discussion of the range of estimates of students at various levels of English proficiency. The differences between estimates of so-called LEP students can be traced to differences in definition, for although US federal legislation provides a common conceptual reference point for defining what is meant by 'limited-English-proficient students' (LEP students), operational definitions vary greatly from state to state. The federal definition focuses on students for whom English is not the home language (or, in the case of Native Americans, where a language other than English has major influence in the home environment) and whose level of proficiency in English precludes their having an equal opportunity to learn in classes taught solely in English. While this definition is conceptually clear, it invites a range of operational definitions in educational settings. Individual states operationalize the definition in a variety of ways, often in terms of a cut-off score on one or more tests of English proficiency. There is neither a standard set of proficiency tests nor a common cut-off score. Because of the arbitrary nature of definitions, policies developed with the same goals in mind and following the same principles may, in fact, differ from one another due to differences in definitions.
2   The standards discussed here are easily understood to apply to standardized tests. The same issues must be addressed in the development of 'performance' or 'authentic' assessments, to the degree that such tasks rely on student processing of longer written passages, the linguistic burden is higher and the degree of the material's cultural familiarity even more important.
3   The disjuncture or contradiction between technical standards and practitioner-oriented materials bears further investigation. While the texts examined should be lauded for their clarity, respect for teachers and contribution to the movement to put assessment back in teachers' hands (a potentially important step toward reassertion of teacher autonomy), they virtually ignore the impact of diversity in language and language proficiency that the teachers will certainly experience in their classrooms. Treatment of possible issues of gender and ethnic bias are generally addressed at greater length, but often at a fairly superficial level.

4   The US Constitution makes no mention of education, and therefore education is 'reserved' to the states. The federal role in education has increased since the Second World War, but is still quite limited in scope; fundamental decisions regarding curriculum frameworks and standards and assessment policies are state-level matters. The centrality of the states in educational policy predates the recent, post-1980 trend to reduce the federal role in social policy, deferring to the states.
5   This example comes from an actual meeting with a group of ESL teachers who were, I am sorry to report, deriding their students' purported lack of knowledge.
6   Assessment policies in New York have recently been changed; this paragraph reports on practices under past regulations.

References

American Psychological Association (1985) *Standards for Educational and Psychological Testing*, Washington, DC: American Psychological Association.

Anstrom, K. (1996) 'Defining the Limited-English Proficient Student Population', *Directions in Language and Education* 1(9), Washington, DC: National Clearinghouse for Bilingual Education.

Crawford, J. (1996) *Bilingual Education: History, Politics, Theory, and Practice*, 3rd edn, Trenton, NJ: Crane.

—— (1999) 'What Now for Bilingual Education?' *Rethinking Schools* 13(2).

Fraser, J. (1997) *Reading, Writing, and Justice: School Reform as if Democracy Matters*, Albany, NY: State University of New York Press.

Garcia, G. and Pearson, P. (1994) 'Assessment and Diversity', in L. Darling-Hammond (ed.), *Review of Research in Education* 20, Washington, DC: American Educational Research Association.

Gould, S. (1981) *The Mismeasure of Man*, New York: Norton.

LaCelle-Peterson, M. and Rivera, C. (1994) 'Is it Real for All Kids? A Framework for Equitable Assessment Policies for English Language Learners', *Harvard Educational Review* 64(1).

Liu, K., Thurlow, M., Erickson, R., Spicuzza, R. and Heinze, K. (1997) 'A Review of the Literature on Students with Limited English Proficiency and Assessment', *Minnesota Report 11*, Minneapolis, MN: National Center for Educational Outcomes.

Liu, K., Thurlow, M., Vieburg, K., El Sawaf, H. and Ruhland, A. (1996) 'Resources: Limited English Proficient Students in National and Statewide Assessments', *Minnesota Report 8*, Minneapolis, MN: National Center for Educational Outcomes.

Mercado, C. and Romero, M. (1993) 'Assessment of Students in Bilingual Education', in M. Arias and U. Casanova (eds), *Bilingual Education: Politics, Practice, and Research*, Ninety-Second Yearbook of the National Society for the Study of Education, Chicago: University of Chicago Press.

Messick, S. (1989) 'Validity', in R. Linn (ed.), *Educational Measurement*, 3rd edn, Washington, DC: The American Council on Education and the National Council on Measurement in Education.

Mitchell, R. (1992) *Testing for Learning: How New Approaches to Evaluation Can Improve American Schools*, New York: The Free Press.

Montero-Sieburth, M. and LaCelle-Peterson, M. (1991) 'Immigration and Schooling: An Ethno-Historical Account of Policy and Family Perspectives in an Urban Community', *Anthropology and Education Quarterly* 22(4).

North Central Regional Educational Laboratory (1996) 'The Status of State Student Assessment Programs in the United States: Annual Report', Oakbrook, IL: North Central Regional Educational Laboratory and Council of Chief State School Officers.

Mark *LaCelle-Peterson*

Spring, J. (1997) *Deculturalization and the Struggle for Equality*, 2nd edn, New York: McGraw-Hill.

Stiggins, R. (1997) *Student-Centered Classroom Assessment*, 2nd edn, New York: Merrill.

Thomas, W. and Collier, V. (1997) *School Effectiveness for Language Minority Students*, Washington, DC: National Clearinghouse for Bilingual Education.

Thurlow, M., Liu, K., Weiser, S. and El Sawaf, H. (1997) 'High School Graduation Requirements in the U.S. for Students with Limited English Proficiency', *Minnesota Report 13*, Minneapolis, MN: National Center for Educational Outcomes.

Wiggins, G. (1993) *Assessing Student Performance: Exploring the Purpose and Limits of Testing*, San Francisco: Jossey-Bass.

Zehler, A., Hopstock, P., Fleischman, H. and Greniuk, C. (1994) 'An Examination of Assessment of Limited English Proficient Students', Arlington, VA: Special Issues Analysis Center, Development Associates.

Part II

Technologies of Testing

Editor's Introduction

Ann Filer

Legitimation and Social Control

In this second part of the book, we take a closer look at the role of test technologies in the social structuring of modern societies. As I discussed in the introduction to Part I, functions of assessment in modern societies extend beyond those concerned with grading, selection and accountability. A sociological perspective on assessment allows for explorations of its role in legitimizing the reproduction of social and educational disparities. The term 'legitimizing' is important here, for it emphasizes the point that public perceptions are crucial to the acceptance of systems of assessment. Throughout its history, the outcomes of mass assessment have been economic and social rewards for some, but reduced access to educational and occupational opportunities for many. The mass categorizing and social differentiation of populations have needed to be accepted as broadly socially just, in particular by the *losers* in the assessment stakes. This acceptance has been underpinned by public perceptions of technologies of mass assessment as scientifically neutral and reliable means of measuring learning. Similarly, and crucially, it has to be perceived as a means of drawing conclusions about capacities for future learning. If public unrest is to be avoided, assessment processes need to be accepted as a *meritocratic* means of predicting and selecting individuals for advancement in societies. In making just this point, Armstrong focuses attention on a further function of assessment in societies. He states:

> The education system may fulfil the function of providing a vehicle for advancement within a meritocracy, yet it also serves as a tool for diffusing political dissent by promoting the notion that the privileged deserve to be there.
>
> (Armstrong 1995: 141)

The notion that assessment can serve to diffuse social unrest and political dissent means that we can also consider that it has a function of social control.

To summarize thus far, within a sociological discourse of assessment we can identify functions concerned with:

- social reproduction and the perpetuation of social disparity
- legitimizing particular forms of knowledge, i.e., the cultural capital of the socially powerful
- social control

Myths and Assumptions Surrounding Test Technologies

A sociological discourse of assessment, as well as identifying functions concerned with perpetuating social disparity, also addresses the question of why those functions rarely appear as the focus of public awareness and debate. For example, George Madaus (1994: 79, citing Winner) points out that most Americans do not enquire whether a test may produce a set of disadvantages or inequities along with its professed advantages. Most people are simply not aware of the biases and assumptions of technical elites that underpin test content and processes. In Chapter 3 of this book, writing with Cathy Horn, he makes the point that testing is a *social* technology with social consequences, yet people no more concern themselves with how a technology like testing works than they do how light bulbs or telephones work. From a similar perspective, Broadfoot (1996: 232) argues that the emphasis in public debate on the 'scientific' nature of assessment has consistently disguised the values and power relations, the interpretative and the idiosyncratic in assessment practices. Darling-Hammond provides a useful example of such disguised cultural values and power relations in the manipulation of outcomes in the early development of IQ testing. These tests threw up inequalities in performances favouring urban over rural groups, higher over lower wealth, English speakers over immigrants, whites over blacks, and so on. Quite simply, these differences were taken to reflect and confirm what every intelligent person 'knew'; that these groups were inherently unequal in their mental capacities. However, when girls outperformed boys on a particular test, this clearly reflected a 'flaw', and future test items were 'corrected' to create parity of results for boys. Differences of race, colour or social class did not warrant revision, though, as the validity of those findings seemed patently obvious (Darling-Hammond 1994: 10). It must not be assumed, however, that the kinds of biased assumptions and manipulation of items and scores that we see in early mental testing have been eradicated with more sophisticated understandings and techniques. Mark LaCelle-Peterson in Chapter 2 gives us some prime examples from the testing of language minorities. His account includes the report that newly developed 'performance' assessments (see Introduction to Part I above) of early language development were going to be rescored because children in bilingual programmes scored 'too high' on them. Of course, as I stated in my opening Introduction, test developers are concerned to monitor for bias in their methods and to maintain confidence in systems of assessment and outcomes. However, through Part V of this book in particular, the case is put that there is no place to stand *outside of culture* from which particular groups can set standards and claim to act as disinterested judge (Torrance, see Chapter 9).

Broadly, then, the arguments here are that tests embody hidden values of social and cultural bias and expectations and that the mystique of scientific testing promotes acceptance of outcomes as accurate reflections of abilities and prospects for future success. In Chapter 4, anthropologist Allan Hanson also argues against the common assumption that tests measure a pre-existing reality. Drawing on a wide range of examples from physical, mental and medical testing, he describes ways in which tests actually create what they purport to measure and actually bring into being what they purport to signify. In doing so, he extends further our understanding of test technologies as *social* technologies and their power in shaping our lives.

Suggestions for Further Reading

An overview of the history of intelligence testing and its impact on the English educational system can be found in Chapter 7 of Patricia Broadfoot's *Education, Assessment and Society*.

In *A Fair Test?*, Caroline Gipps and Patricia Murphy examine the evidence for differences, and the reasons for differences, in assessed performance among gender and ethnic groups.

The social and cultural assumptions underlying contemporary testing practices in the USA are challenged by F. Allan Hanson in *Testing Testing: Social Consequences of the Examined Life*. The reasons for the lack of public discussion, the questions that go unasked, and educational assessment as an instrument of surveillance and control are among the issues he addresses.

In the *Harvard Educational Review* symposium 64(1), writers present critiques of testing technologies in the light of proposed assessment reforms in the USA.

References

Armstrong, D. (1995) *Power and Partnership in Education*, London: Routledge.

Bourdieu, P. and Passeron, J.C. (1977) *Reproduction*, London: Sage.

Broadfoot, P. (1996) *Education, Assessment and Society*, Milton Keynes: Open University Press.

Darling-Hammond, L. (1994) 'Performance-Based Assessment and Educational Equity', Symposium: Equity in Educational Assessment, *Harvard Educational Review* 64(1): 5–29.

Gipps, C. and Murphy, P. (1994) *A Fair Test?*, Milton Keynes: Open University Press.

Hanson, F.A. (1993) *Testing Testing: Social Consequences of the Examined Life*, Berkeley: University of California Press.

Madaus, G.F. (1994) 'A Technological and Historical Consideration of Equity Issues Associated with Proposals to Change the National Testing Policy', *Harvard Educational Review* 64(1): 76–95.

3 Testing Technology
The Need for Oversight

George F. Madaus and Cathy Horn[1]

A critically important, but often overlooked, characterization of standardized testing is that testing is a technology. Testing is deeply embedded in the American people's perceptions, thoughts and experiences. It is a familiar, enduring, traditional part of our culture. However, partly due to its ubiquity, testing is generally not thought of as a *social technology* and *a technical craft*. Nonetheless, this is precisely what testing is: a technology embedded in such socio-technical systems as education, government and business. The technology of testing has its 'hardware', such as test booklets and answer sheets, and optical scoring machines that make the testing of large numbers efficient and economical. Increasingly, tests are administered by computers. More importantly however, testing, like much of present technology, is also disembodied knowledge and technical art; it is 'instrumentality, employing special knowledge, that extends human effort beyond that of the unaided mind and hand' (Lowrance 1986: 33–4). And, like other technologies, testing also has a relevant community of technological practitioners who are trained for membership in that community and share a common language, rationale, and set of practices, procedures and methods (Staudenmaier 1985).

This paper will look at testing from the perspective of a social technology. We first show how testing is a technical craft. We then highlight some of the more volatile factors related to the technology, such as power, expertise and isolation. Next, we examine the history of regulating technology in general and testing in particular. Finally, we argue the need for an independent body to monitor testing in the United States and how such a body might function.

Testing is a Technology

The term *technology* often conjures up visions of scientific experimentation and industrial processes and products, but testing fits a generally accepted instrumental definition of technology: something put together for a purpose, to satisfy a pressing and immediate need or to solve a problem (Basalla 1988; Staudenmaier 1988). Ellul has suggested that technology includes any complex of standardized means for attaining a predetermined end in social, economic, administrative and educational institutions (Ellul 1964, 1990). More generally, technology refers to any body of special knowledge and activities, skills, methods and procedures that people use (Lowrance 1986; Winner 1977). Winner has suggested simply that technology comprises all 'artificial aids to human activity' (Winner 1986: 4). All of the foregoing definitions of technology are essentially instrumentalist: technology and technological devices are seen as tools, as means to some end or ends. Testing certainly fits these instrumentalist definitions of technology. During the past two thousand years, tests have been employed as bureaucratic tools to help eliminate patronage, open access to various opportunities, ensure that students acquire certain skills, establish and maintain standards of performance, hold teachers, students or schools accountable for learning, and allocate scarce resources (Madaus and Kellaghan 1992).

People generally do not concern themselves with either how a technology like testing, or for that matter light bulbs, telephones, cars and so on, are made or how they work. They believe such concerns are the province of those who invent, develop, build or repair them (Winner 1986: 5). Instead, most people are primarily interested in the uses of technologies. Thus, once a test is constructed, users interact with it straightforwardly to achieve specific purposes. Because of this emphasis on use, knowing what a test is in a technical sense is not viewed as terribly important. People therefore might shrug and dismiss the question, 'What is a test?' as unimportant. At best, they might go on to describe what tests are for or how they are used. But this 'straightforward use' approach tends to conceal important elements related to the nature of the commodity being used, that is, knowledge about an examinee or institution. Borgmann (1984) speaks to this unrecognized problem. He argues that a defining feature of technologies is this division between the result and the means or device used to produce the result. Using a stereo music system as a prototypical example, he writes:

> Surely a stereo set, consisting of a turntable, an amplifier, and speakers, is a technological device. Its reason for being is well understood. It is to provide music. But this simple understanding conceals the characteristic way in which music is produced by a device...To an apparent richness and variety of technologically produced music there corresponds an extreme concealment or abstractness in the mode of its production...It is the division between the commodity, e.g., music, and the machinery, e.g., the mechanical and electronic apparatus of a stereo set, that is the distinctive feature of a technological device. An object that exhibits this central feature clearly is a paradigm of the technological device.
>
> (Borgmann 1984: 3–4)

Borgmann's description of music and machinery has a similitude with testing. There is a division between the commodity (information) and the device (the test itself); there is concealment or abstractness in the mode of its production, and too often also in the way the information gets used. What Borgmann's example of music and machinery fails to address is the limited nature of use of the device and the commodity produced relative to the situation in testing, where the same information can be used in completely unintended ways by diverse audiences.

Borgmann (1984) has also critiqued the instrumentalist approach to defining technology as inadequate. While he admits that the instrumentalist approach 'is in one way unassailable [and that] any concretely delimited piece of technology can be put forward as a value neutral tool', he goes on to point out that:

> the availability of mere means is itself a remarkable and consequential fact. Historically, it is just in modern technology that such devices become available…A means in a traditional culture is never mere but always and inextricably woven into a context of ends…Putting technology in the context of political purposes is itself naive if one fails to consider trenchantly the radical transformation of all policies that technology may bring about.
>
> (1984: 10–11)

Currently, there is circularity in how tests are used and viewed. Often test results define a problem, such as low standards; tests are then used as a mechanism to drive policy to address the problem and, coming full circle, test results then are used as an indicator of quality to show the problem is solved or has grown worse (or the test results are discounted as corrupted or meaningless).

Both intended and unintended uses of tests produce unintended effects. Edward Tenner, in his book *Why Things Bite Back*, defines these unintended consequences of technology as revenge effects: 'the tendency of the world around us to get even, to twist our cleverness against us, or it is our own unconscious twisting against us' (Tenner 1997: 6). The revenge effects of testing in the United States have been evidenced repeatedly throughout the history of their use; examples include racial segregation in the form of tracking, high school diploma denial linked to high-stakes exam scores, and receipt of public school funding based on student, school, and/or district performance on state or national exams. Although the use of standardized tests was intended to assist in the improvement of public education – and in many ways it has – it also created long-term intractable problems related to misuse or overuse. Unintended test use also highlights Tenner's important point that 'technology alone usually doesn't produce a revenge effect. Only when we anchor it in laws, regulations, customs, and habits does the irony reach its full potential' (Tenner 1997: 9). It is the social and political components of testing that give the technology freedom to create revenge effects. Testing, as a policy tool, has become an end unto itself.

Technology and Power

While we cannot go into great detail on the relationship between testing technology and power, a brief description is in order at this point. The late French philosopher-historian Michel Foucault points to the obvious connection between testing and the exercise of control and power in educational matters.

His book *Discipline and Punish* has ten intriguing pages on the examination as a mechanism of discipline, power and control (Foucault 1979). Foucault's analysis offers a quite different look at the way in which the technology of testing plays a major role in regulating schools and the people in them. He sees the exercise of power not as 'simply a relationship between partners, individual or collective; [but as] a way in which certain actions modify others' (Foucault 1982: 789). He realized that those who control the exam could use results to control the actions of the examinees, as well as the actions of school personnel. In a test, students periodically revealed how their learning is progressing, and the teacher through the exam, defined what was expected. Thus the test guarantees 'the movement of knowledge from the teacher to the pupil, but it extracted from the pupil a knowledge destined and reserved for the teacher' (Foucault 1979: 187). The test is a mechanism, a technology 'that linked to a certain type of the formation of knowledge a certain form of the exercise of power' (1979: 187). Foucault argues that those in control of a test could exercise power over the examinee, who is perceived as an object, and who in turn is objectified. The test not only placed examinees in a 'field of surveillance', it also 'situated them in a network of writing...in a whole mass of documents that captures and fix them' (1979: 189). For the first time, the examinee became a 'describable, analyzable object' (1979: 190), and the test the 'ceremony of this objectification' (1979: 187). The test became a ritualized and 'scientific' method of fixing individual differences, by the 'pinning down of each individual in his own particularity' (1979: 192). Thus Foucault sees born a 'new modality of power in which each individual – [who he describes as calculable man] – receives as his status his own individuality, and in which he is linked by his status to the features, the measurements, the gaps, the "marks" that characterize him and make him a case' (1979: 192). In Foucault's view, this 'new technology of power' – the written exam – marked the moment when the sciences of man became possible (1979: 193).

The written exam or test also made it possible for the first time to accumulate student marks, organize them, rank them, classify them, form categories, determine averages and fix norms. It was the beginning of a:

> comparative system that made possible the measurement of overall phenomena, the description of groups, the characterization of collective facts, the calculation of the gaps between individuals, their distribution in a given 'population'.
>
> (1979: 190)

In other words, the documentation provided by a test gives those in charge of it the ability not only to objectify individuals, but also to form, describe and objectify groups. This in turn makes possible a bureaucratic mechanism of programme, or school-level, accountability.

Although Foucault does not push the argument any further, our position is that it is not the exams *per se* that control the actions of teachers, students and administrators. Rather, it is the coupling of the device and its outcomes with important rewards or sanctions which gives those who control the testing technology real power over the action of others.

Technology affects the nature of our lives and our society in profound ways. Certainly we would argue this is especially true regarding testing. Borgmann points out that if technology – and here we would submit testing – is a 'mere instrument...the inquiry of *what guides* technology becomes a task in its own right' (Borgman 1984: 11, emphasis in original). Similarly, Winner (1986: 6) is careful to point out that technology is much more than merely a set of aids to human activity and that technologies are 'powerful forces acting to reshape that activity and its meaning'. In Winner's view, the problem with technologies lies not so much in the fact that technologies are shaping our lives, but that they are doing it in uncontrolled ways with most of us sitting on the sidelines allowing this reshaping to occur without our participation or even conscious awareness of what is happening. Winner calls this passivity 'technological somnambulism'.

This failure to appreciate the power of technologies to shape human life, this technological somnambulism, has led to the prevalent, but mistaken, attitude that technology in general, and testing in particular, is 'fundamentally neutral as regards [its] moral standing' (Winner 1986: 6). Thus, testing is seen as being employed in a range of moral contexts, used well or poorly, used for good or bad purposes. In this view, it is the particular use in a particular context that determines a test's moral standing. This emphasis on use rather than on the technology itself is captured perfectly in the dictum, 'Guns don't kill people, people kill people.'

Because testing is so entrenched in our culture, and so taken for granted, most people fail to consider how it reshapes our social, educational, business and moral life; how these institutions 'are transformed by the mediating role of technology' (Winner 1986: 9). Like all technologies, tests can be 'judged not only for their contributions to efficiency and productivity and their positive and negative environmental side effects, but also for the ways in which they can embody specific forms of power and authority' (Winner 1986: 19). Winner describes the moral dimension of a technology apart from a particular use, in language that is arguably applicable to testing:

> Indeed, many of the most important examples of technologies that have political consequences are those that transcend the simple categories of 'intended' and 'unintended' altogether. These are instances in which the very process of technical development is so thoroughly biased in a particular direction that it regularly produces results heralded as wonderful breakthroughs by some social interests and crushing setbacks by others. In such cases it is neither correct nor insightful to say 'Someone intended to do somebody else harm.' Rather one must say that the technological deck has been stacked in advance to favour certain social interests and that some people were bound to receive a better hand than others do.
>
> (Winner 1986: 25–6)

In terms of Winner's deck of cards metaphor, the entire test development process – what we decide to measure, the cultural background and specialized training of the people involved in test development, the material chosen for inclusion, the format of the individual items used, the language selected, the directions given, the validation process and so on – might stack the testing 'deck' in favour of certain groups in our society, and unintentionally assure that other groups are dealt a weaker hand. Testing, like 'every technology, is a human artefact, an artificial construction whose design reflects a limited set of prior technical constraints and a limited set of values within a particular world view' (Staudenmaier 1985: 192).

In addition to the basic proposition that testing is a technology, there is an additional characteristic of technologies that must be recognized and addressed. It is that technological endeavours tend to be directed by elites who isolate themselves from those who are not members of the elites, to the detriment of both groups.

Elitism and Isolation

The movement toward standardization and conformity in the United States came around 1815 when the Army Ordnance Department drew up 'a system of regulations for...the uniformity of manufacture of all arms ordnance' (quoted in Smith 1987: 42). The individuality of the skilled craftsman yielded to uniformity, and standard work regulations replaced the village practice of negotiations over working conditions (Staudenmaier 1990). Over several decades, the Ordnance Department developed the administrative, communication, inspection, accounting, bureaucratic and mechanical techniques that fostered conformity and resulted in the technology of interchangeable parts and the eventual manufacture of a host of mass-produced products in the twentieth century (Smith 1987). One result of these scientific and technological revolutions of the past 150 years is that practitioners of technologies eventually form their own communities with their own specialized vocabularies and internalized value systems. In the early days of our republic, scientists and technicians could speak almost as easily to lay people as to each other. With that rise of standardization in the nineteenth century, however, highly specialized vocabularies for the phenomena being studied began to evolve along with highly specialized groups associated with various technologies and social techniques (Gleick 1987). Today, technical specialization with its specialized vocabulary and techniques has changed the relationship between lay people and various technologies (Ellul 1964).

This formation of technological elites and technical and professional communities is a two-edged sword. It can enhance the members' accomplishments and facilitate communication among them, but it can also isolate them from those outside the community and even alienate non-members. This isolation and alienation can be due in part to a tendency for these communities to resist attempts by non-members to have any role or influence in the communities' activities. Staudenmaier associates this latter tendency with the concurrent development of science, technology and laissez-faire capitalism in nineteenth-century Western society. He suggests that:

One takes a short step indeed from the claim that true science and technology must be allowed to operate free from irrational or self-serving outside influences to the claim that scientific and technological practitioners must be allowed to operate free from any challenge or critique from those outside their domains of expertise...Whether applied to the market, to science or to technology, laissez-faire's iron law – 'never interrupt the working of the method by outside critique' – resides in Western consciousness at the primordial level of symbol and rhetoric.

(Staudenmaier 1990: 3)

In a similar vein, Boulding has suggested that members of professional communities inadvertently cut themselves off from their counterparts in other disciplines:

When the possessors of a certain form of specialized knowledge become a self-conscious group, with a professional organization, professional journals, and organized departments in universities, communication is unquestionably facilitated within the discipline...The very organization of a discipline, however, often tends to cut its practitioners off from other disciplines. Consequently, when problems arise from many different disciplines, we are extremely ill equipped to handle them.

(Boulding 1970: 146)

It is certainly true that a gulf has developed between the testing community, teachers, administrators, parents and the general population. The testing community's language and value system do not coincide with the language and value systems of many groups affected by testing and others critical of testing. Consequently, in testing – as in other important technological areas – 'there is almost no middle ground of rational discourse, no available common language with which persons of differing backgrounds can discuss matters of technology in thoughtful, critical terms. Conversations gravitate toward warring polarities and choosing sides' (Winner 1986: 11). An example of one side of such polarization in debates about testing is the work by Barbara Lerner entitled *The War on Testing: Detroit Edison in Perspective* (Lerner 1979). Arguing in favour of testing, Lerner asserts that:

The attack on tests is, to a very considerable and very frightening degree, an attack on truth itself by those who deal with unpleasant and unflattering truths by denying them and by attacking and trying to destroy the evidence for them.

(1979: 1)

On the other hand, O'Meara compiled a list of intemperate attacks on testing that include:

carelessness, hatred, favoritism, labor unrest, unprogressiveness, defective art, dishonesty, discontent, poverty, fraudulence, laziness, a generator of mental defectiveness and physical degeneration, serfdom, radicalism, suffering, death, strikes and war.

(O'Meara 1944: 10)

As Merton observed, 'Technical man is fascinated by results, by immediate consequences of setting standardized devices into motion...Above all, he is committed to the never-ending search for the 'one best way' to achieve any designated objective' (Merton 1964: vi). Too often, the technical elite thinks in terms of what is useful and efficient rather than what is good or just (Merton 1964). Often, however, 'little account is usually taken of long-term effects' (Ellul 1990: 69). Staudenmaier argues that, in fact, the technical elite expects society to respond immediately to the newest iterations of a given technology, ignoring those potential long-term consequences that may result. In Chicago, for example, standardized tests are used to advance or retain students in the eighth grade as a way of ending age-based social promotion. The argument is that academically unprepared students (as defined by a test) should not move to the next grade level. The revenge effects, however, have been seen in a washback on teachers of failing students who are overloading already crowded classrooms, as well as in the narrowing of curriculum to prepare students for these high-stakes exams. The world of standardized testing, however, asks society to change quickly to 'take full advantage of the improvements made possible by advancing technology' while ignoring 'the possibility that some of the technological changes might not be improvements' (Staudenmaier 1985: 144). Partly because of this, serious criticism of a socio-technical practice meets with strong opposition or defensiveness. Winner describes what happens:

A typical response of engineers, for example, is to announce that they are merely problem solvers. 'Tell us the problem,' they demand. 'We will find a solution. That's our job. But you may not presume to question the nature of our solution. You are not a member of a technical profession and, therefore, know nothing of relevance. If you insist on raising questions about the appropriateness of means we devise, we can only conclude that you are anti-technology.'

(Winner 1986: 11)

When the testing community defends testing in the face of strong attacks, they understandably fall back on the limited perspective of their specialized vocabulary, their values such as the objectivity and rationality of science, and their techniques – techniques that themselves embody values. Both sides pick and choose their grounds of attack and defence. However, the technical elite often overlook the fact that a highly technical psychometric defence of a test is itself very limited and based on a narrow set of technical values. For example, in discussions about test bias, some within the testing community argue that group differences themselves do not constitute evidence of bias. However, their techniques for identifying bias often fall back on predictive validity models, models that are themselves based on allocative, meritocratic, efficiency values rather than on a developmental efficiency view of education (Haney 1981). Closely related is the argument by some in the testing fraternity that tests should not be used to put school children in special placements unless there is evidence that these are more beneficial than regular placement; an argument whose proponents fail to extend the logic to regarding college admission tests apparently because of implicit views about the nature of higher education (Haney 1981).

Ellul (1990) points to a dilemma faced by important technical elites, a dilemma that is applicable to the testing community. Technical experts follow their consciences, are competent and honest, do not talk at random or take risks. But they do have opinions based on the science of their discipline. Science, however, is becoming less and less absolute and univocal; convictions often derive from opinions, which in turn are partially shaped by personal values and the values embedded in the science itself. Recognizing this, experts who are asked to give their opinions to policy makers and to a public that has little or no understanding of the technical issues often offer arguments to help policy makers and the public accept a project, to calm their fears or to interest them in a new programme. Thus, their science becomes 'the platform from which they proclaim orientations that are accepted as truths and that will finally shape opinion...[By] engaging in technological discourse, [technical elites] end up as its slaves and have to follow the common path of progress' (Ellul 1990: 196).

Whenever criticism is raised that requires people – either the testing elite or the critics of testing – to reorganize their conceptions of the world, it provokes hostility and defensiveness (Gleick 1987). Joseph Ford, a physicist at the Georgia Institute of Technology, uses a Tolstoy quote to illustrate what happens:

> I know that most men, including those most at ease with problems of the greatest complexity, can seldom accept even the simplest and most obvious truth if it be such as would oblige them to admit the falsity of conclusions which they have proudly taught to others, and which they have woven, thread by thread, into the fabric of their lives.
>
> (Quoted in Gleick 1987: 38)

It is critically important to develop methods of discourse between the testing community and its critics so that the increasing complexity of testing issues – technical and social – and the underlying values associated with various positions can be revealed and understood. As Bellah and his associates aptly point out:

> Complexity is real enough, but it should not be a cover beneath which undemocratic managers and experts can hide. Our culture or our institutions may lead us to believe that the big issues are beyond us; but then we need

to change those assumptions, and a social science that takes its public responsibility seriously can help us do so.

(Bellah et al. 1991: 20)

It is because of that public responsibility that a monitoring board for publicly funded, high-stakes testing is essential: an organization that monitors, audits and evaluates the planning, development, implementation and impact of governmentally sponsored high-stakes tests.

Conditions that Trigger Intervention

Regulation, monitoring, oversight or auditing govern an almost limitless range of things, including a vast array of consumer products such as automobiles, toys and cat food, financial products and services, industrial practices, particularly those involving safety issues, and commercial practices such as advertising and labelling. Professional behaviour is subject to licensing by governmental authority and to various codes of practice established by governmental and private entities. Certain types of personal behaviour such as wearing seat belts or smoking are also subject to regulation. The overseers are many: government at all levels, professional organizations, private groups, and advocacy groups. Their actions are varied as well; they regulate behaviour, evaluate products, set standards and enforce compliance with them, audit, inspect, monitor and investigate. Why are so many things the objects of such activity? In this section, we briefly sketch why so many things have been subject to governmental or private oversight and why other things like testing have escaped such oversight. (See Derthick and Quirk (1985), McCraw (1984), McGarity (1991), Spulber (1989) and Wilson (1980) for more detailed treatments of the growth of regulatory bodies. Also see Bellah et al. (1991) for a treatment issues around regulation in our present-day economy.)

Despite the impressive range of objects that are the focus of regulation, historically, Americans have resisted intervention into private activities. This resistance is an inherent part of a social and political system based on personal freedoms, private property rights, belief in free market forces and the increasing dominance of Lockean individualism in American life (Bellah et al. 1991). Interestingly, and often overlooked, the technology of testing is also an intervention into the private life of individuals. Those who take tests for whatever reason must publicly reveal a part of themselves through their test performance. Further, the test score then objectifies them (see the discussion on Foucault above). Nonetheless, regulation of the technology itself has been opposed in the past by those in the testing community on the grounds that the government should not intervene into private business activities. And, in the United States, testing is big business (see Haney et al. (1993) for a discussion of the business side of testing).

A helpful starting point in describing why so many things in our society are regulated is Freund's comment that the appropriate objects of governmental administrative power include actions recognized as legitimate but attended with peril or liable to abuse (Freund 1928). Freund's interpretation suggests that activities are likely to be regulated if they are hazardous, presumably to persons and perhaps to their property, or if some persons are likely to abuse their positions of power at the expense of others. Sandman (1989) clarified the discussion by another necessary ingredient in bringing an object or activity under regulatory scrutiny: outrage. He suggests that something is more likely to be the object of a governmental or private intervention if both hazard and public outrage are present. Sandman proposed a simple 2 × 2 matrix illustrating the possible combinations of hazard and outrage (see Figure 3.1).

Cells 1 and 4 of the matrix are straightforward situations: with high hazard and high outrage, intervention occurs; with low hazard and low outrage, it does not.

Testing in Relation to the Hazard and Outrage Dimensions

As has been argued in the previous section, testing as a technology is fraught with peril for some people, and even the best-constructed test can be subject to misuse and abuse by a diverse array of users. Nonetheless, peril, abuse and misuse are not among the first words to come to mind when most people, especially policy makers, think about testing. The perils and potential for abuse inherent in testing are simply not as dramatic or as obvious as those associated with other products or activities. To oversimplify, educational and psychological testing technology probably falls in cell 2 of Sandman's matrix (Figure 3.1). The hazards, particularly for certain groups of test takers (such as minorities, women, the handicapped) in certain contexts (such as high-stakes uses of results), are high. However, there is an insufficient level of *generalized* outrage to prompt policy makers to take effective action to address overseeing the testing enterprise – an exception being the so-called 'truth-in-testing' legislation described below.

One reason the potential for abuse and misuse is not readily apparent and hence does not cause generalized outrage, as was the case with boiler explosions,

Figure 3.1   Sandman's hazard/outrage matrix

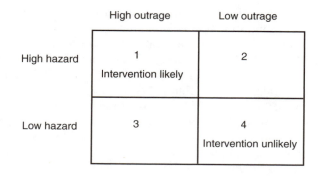

Source: Sandman (1989: 48)

the hazards of patent medicines or the thalidomide disaster (Quirk 1980), is that much of the testing technology is hidden from view by the very nature of its psychometric underpinnings. Testing is not highly visual or glamorous, and its side effects are not immediately visible. Testing is rarely the focus of media attention – although much attention is given to reporting results, particularly bad results – and is typically poorly understood when it is. In some respects, the arcane algorithms, psychometric underpinnings and hidden scoring routines of testing are analogous to credit checks, bank loans, the triggering of an IRS audit, econometric modelling, census projections and so on, all of which are dependent on computer modelling and computerized decision procedures (for a detailed treatment of the issues surrounding the ethics of modelling see Wallace (1996)).

These commercial financial modelling services at their heart, are, like testing, based on hidden algorithms. It is these algorithms, controlled by a technical elite, which influence the lives and destiny of people. Many people simply are not aware of the control these hidden systems can exert on their lives. This is particularly an issue, for example, when performance levels are used to classify individual test performance. The mode of arriving at classifications, like failure, needs improvement, proficient and advanced, is opaque, is not understood by the general public and is accepted as accurate. Finally, calls for confirmatory external evidence about the accuracy of the classifications are largely absent. Consequently, these classifications become an *ipse dixit*. Testing, then, must actively explore institutionalized ways to monitor its products and their use particularly in the political policy sphere.

A Brief History of the Attempts to Monitor Testing

Currently there is a serious and rapidly growing disparity between the burgeoning policy uses of testing technology in education (and their intended and unintended outcomes) on the one hand, and institutional means for evaluating and improving these uses on the other. While policy makers and test users can turn to extensive commercial, not-for-profit and governmental infrastructures that have evolved over the past ninety years to assist them in test development, administration, scoring and reporting, there is no analogous infrastructure for independently evaluating a testing programme before or after implementation, or for monitoring test use and impact.

Although the nation has never had such an oversight organization, it is an old idea. Between 1925 and 1975 there were at least four calls for an independent monitoring body from a variety of sources: Giles Ruch in 1925 (quoted in Buros 1972); Oscar Buros in 1938 (Buros 1972); the APA's Committee on Ethical Standards in 1950 (Adkins 1950); and the Project on the Classification of Exceptional Children in 1975 (Hobbs 1975). The latter drew a comparison between testing regulation and food and drug regulation: 'Poor tests or poor testing may be as injurious to opportunity as impure food or drugs are injurious to health' (1975: 238). None of these proposals was implemented.

In 1979, New York enacted a 'truth-in-testing' law that allowed admissions test takers to see their answer sheets and the key of correct answers.[2] This information is usually insufficient, however, for examinees to evaluate the soundness of decisions based on tests, particularly given their typically limited resources and expertise in the technology of testing. Furthermore, truth-in-testing laws do not enable examinees to evaluate the adequacy of a test as a measure of what it purports to measure, or to question how the technology is used. Ironically, although the New York law provided some measure of oversight protection for college-age test takers, it provided no oversight to protect the rights and interests of younger test takers, who are of course not nearly as able to look out for their own interests as are young adults.

Test standards developed by the major professional organizations concerned with testing – The American Educational Research Association (AERA), the American Psychological Association (APA), and the National Council on Measurement in Education (NCME) – are the professions' attempt to assure the quality of tests and appropriate use. The three organizations have developed the Joint APA, AERA, and NCME *Standards for Educational and Psychological Testing* (American Educational Research Association 1985), hereinafter referred to as the *Standards*. The 1985 *Standards*, currently under revision with a release date sometime this year, are a direct descendent of previous editions that began in the 1950s.[3]

The widely recognized *Standards* appear to have had some influence on the developmental work of the larger test publishers. However, due to their ambiguity they have been used in completely contradictory ways by opposing parties in litigation.[4] The principal weakness of the *Standards* is their lack of any means of enforcement. The reluctance of the three sponsoring organizations to deal with their enforcement has, over the years, limited their usefulness and has assured that the *Standards* have had very limited impact on test use.

The review of previous efforts to establish standards for testing technology and to organize some kind of general oversight agency regarding testing indicates that they have had limited success. Despite repeated calls to establish an ongoing institutional entity to monitor educational testing in the United States, no such organization existed until recently. (In August 1998, the Ford Foundation provided a grant to establish an independent monitoring body, which is discussed in detail later in this chapter.) At least four separate calls for some kind of consumer protection agency or standards bureau regarding testing (the Ruch, Buros, APA and the Hobbs proposals) came to naught. Widely recognized professional standards regarding testing appear to have had some influence on larger test publishers and via litigation, but because such standards generally lack any means of enforcement, they appear to have had very limited impact on practices of test use. Indeed, because standards regarding testing have been so regularly promulgated without much serious attention to how such standards affect practice, such standards must be seen as having a symbolic value, independent of their practical implications. Among such symbolic values of standards are their role as beacons to which people involved in testing can point as models of excellence or at least passable practice; their function as one of the accoutrements of the aspirations for professional recognition of people involved in testing; and even as a tactic for a trade group to help reign in questionable practices of others in the business and to help fend off outside intervention. Thus it seems clear that if standards and monitoring are to have a stronger role in reforming testing practices, some form of more active and independent monitoring is needed.

Why Create an Independent Monitoring Body at this Time?

Over the past few years, a variety of factors, including changes in statute and case law, national and state policy initiatives, and plebiscites have both transformed educational testing and increased the need for oversight. All have altered the uses of testing technology, in some cases fundamentally, and all have the potential to affect profoundly both educational systems and individuals, particularly students currently ill-served by the educational system; economically disadvantaged students, students with disabilities, students for whom English is a second language, and students from ethnic minorities. These changes also raise difficult equity and technical questions, placing policy makers, educators and even researchers in uncharted territory. Perhaps at no time in the past half-century have questions and consequences surrounding educational testing been as widespread and serious. Consider just a few recent examples of how the testing landscape is changing.

State Reforms

Assessments continue to be a central focus of state policy initiatives, and statewide assessments are increasingly linked to serious consequences for individuals or institutions. During the last decade, the number of such high-stakes testing programmes has increased dramatically. Today, as has been shown, it is commonplace for state agencies to build or buy tests used to make very important decisions about individuals and institutions. In the field of education alone, high-stakes tests include those used for the certification or recertification of teachers, promotion of students from one grade to the next, award of a high school diploma, assignment of a student to a remedial class, allocation of funds to a school or district, award of merit pay to teachers on the basis of their students' test performance, certification or recertification of a school or district, and placement of a school system into 'educational receivership'. The use of test results for such purposes in education is widespread, and has grown significantly in the 1980s.

Kentucky's far-reaching reforms, for example, centre on an assessment and accountability system that imposes sanctions and rewards on educators for changes in the test scores of their students. These reforms have been intensely controversial. Most recently, the Kentucky PTA urged lawmakers to hand over management and oversight of statewide testing to an independent agency (Harp 1997). Two years ago, Minnesota adopted a state basic skills test that students must pass in order to graduate from high school. New York, in an effort to extend high standards to all students, has recently adopted a policy that will require that nearly all students pass high-level Regents examinations. North Carolina adopted a system of end-of-grade tests for grades 3 through 8 and end-of-course tests for the high school grades as a means of holding schools and school systems more accountable for student learning. But in an instructive though cautionary example of what can happen once such testing programmes are introduced, one North Carolina county decided that if the new state tests were good enough to hold schools accountable, it would also hold students accountable by requiring them to pass the new tests as a requisite for grade promotion and for earning high school course credit.[5] Virginia and Massachusetts have also implemented tests linked to high standards in the elementary, middle and high school levels as eventual promotional gates. In Virginia, results of the inaugural Standards of Learning exams indicated 97 per cent of schools failed (see Portner (1999) for further discussion of results). The Massachusetts Comprehensive Assessment System (MCAS) tested fourth, eighth, and tenth graders in English, mathematics and science/technology, and saw similar though less severe results to those in Virginia. Among fourth graders, for example, 81 per cent, 67 per cent and 52 per cent failed or needed improvement in English, mathematics and science, respectively. Many of these initiatives are undertaken with the intent of lessening educational inequities, but their effects in this respect remain uncertain.

Federal Statutory Changes

Recent changes in federal statutes will alter markedly the uses and effects of testing in K-12 education. The reauthorization of Title I requires that states use Title I assessments that are linked to high standards applied to all students and requires disaggregation of scores for many groups of students with special needs. The recent reauthorization of IDEA mandates the inclusion of students with disabilities in statewide systems of standards and assessments.

The Hopwood Case, Boston Latin Case, and California's Proposition 209

The 5th Circuit Court struck down affirmative action admissions policies in *Cheryl J. Hopwood* v. *State of Texas*. Four white plaintiffs claimed that the defendants discriminated against them by favouring less qualified black and Mexican American applicants – as defined in part by their test scores – for admission to the University of Texas School of Law through the use of a quota system. As a result of the decision, African American admissions to the School of Law dropped from 65 in 1996 to 5 in 1997, none of whom enrolled. Mexican American admission dropped from 70 to 18 (Fields 1997).

In a similar case, this time at the secondary school level, Julia McLaughlin, who is white, was denied admission to Boston Latin public school even though her grades and entrance exam scores were higher than those of many minority candidates who were accepted. Boston had reserved 35 per cent of the student slots for African-Americans and Hispanics. The McLaughlin family sued in federal court, and the judge ordered her admission and directed the Boston school board to revise its admissions policy for the city's prestigious exam schools (Hendrie 1996).

As a result of the passing of Proposition 209 in California, the University of California (UC) was banned from any consideration of race or ethnicity in college admissions. Even though there was a stay pending litigation, the effect was nonetheless felt. At the undergraduate level, the UC applicant pool declined by 7.7 per cent for blacks and 5.8 per cent for Latinos. At the UC Boalt Hall Law School, the number of blacks dropped by 81 per cent, and Hispanic admissions fell by 50 per cent (Locke 1997; UCLA Office of the Chancellor 1997; UC Berkeley Office of the Chancellor 1997). In practice, abandoning affirmative action in selection is likely to increase the reliance placed on test scores for admissions.

Immigration

Immigration is of course a long-standing issue for educational policy, but recent trends have heightened its importance. Recent immigration has forced schools in many areas to cope with large numbers of students born outside of the United States whose native languages are other than English. Moreover, in many locales the immigrant population is highly diverse, making it impractical for schools to locate staff conversant in all of the relevant languages and precluding testing in all native languages. Policies for addressing these issues in assessment systems are currently in flux, and research evidence provides only limited guidance.

Implications For an Independent Monitoring Body

Evaluating testing programmes does not mean waiting for a perfect test; there is no such thing. Rather, evaluating and monitoring testing programmes means providing critical feedback for the improvement of classrooms, schools, school systems and the tests themselves. In August 1998, the National Board on Educational Testing and Public Policy (NBETPP), housed in the School of Education at Boston College, was created as an independent monitoring system for assessment in American education. The NBETPP does not intend to regulate, accredit, license, control, restrain, limit, supervise, direct or enable testing. Instead, the Board, at one time or another as part of its activities, hopes to monitor, evaluate, review, audit, examine, investigate, assure, oversee, rate, approve, arbitrate, check, criticize, weigh and inspect varying aspects of publicly funded, high-stakes testing programmes.

From a review of other social interventions, the concept of the Board was influenced in a number of ways. First, the Board must be independent of political control. For this reason, the NBETPP should not be a government agency, nor a commission controlled by political appointment. Second, while rejecting a politically controlled agency, the Board must also be independent of the professional organizations that developed the *Standards*. A review leads to the conclusion that monitoring by professional organizations can be heavily tilted toward the views and values of the profession. Third, the NBETPP, if it is to succeed, must have a high degree of trust among all parties, including test developers, sponsors, users, examinees, and the public. It must be seen as impartial, thorough and, above all, fair. The credibility of the Board is crucial. To accomplish this is no easy task; balancing the legitimate views and values of all these parties will be no mean feat. Fourth, the Board must have clear criteria for accepting a particular monitoring function and develop understandable operating procedures for carrying out an audit. Finally, the Board must have clear criteria for accepting a particular monitoring function and develop understandable operating procedures for carrying out an audit.

The NBETPP does not function as a regulatory body, but instead hopes to foster best test practice through the use of research-based information for use in policy decision making. The component parts of the National Board will include board members who represent varying constituencies in American society and encompass a wide range of opinions and interests; a permanent staff that will provide broad expertise in testing and public policy; and a technical panel that will furnish specialized testing and measurement skills. Together, these constituent groups will enable the Board to address apposite testing and public policy issues; to gather, generate, synthesize, and disseminate evaluative information; and to help inform the broader public about testing practices and choices.

Conclusion

Tests, like computers or airplanes, are a technology, with a well-developed technological community and technical underpinnings arcane to lay people. Testing is a complex technological system with its own infrastructure akin to transportation, power, communications, computing or manufacturing systems. It creates both intended and unintended consequences. For some to argue, as they are currently doing, that the issue of high-stakes testing is one for the policy makers to decide, that it is essentially a political issue and not a technical one, is to lose sight of the fact that policy decisions have technical implications, and that technical decisions have policy ramifications.

One way to force a rise in social awareness around the issues of high-stakes testing is through the establishment of a permanent, independent monitoring body. Although a substantial history of oversight boards regarding testing exists, none to date has been successful in establishing a strong role in monitoring and reforming technological practices. The NBETPP hopes that, through their work, important positive contributions of educational testing can be enhanced and the negative consequences diminished. The desire is that testing can better serve as a gateway to the 'development of the talents of all our people' (National Commission on Testing and Public Policy 1990: x).

Notes

1   Special acknowledgements are owed the Ford Foundation for their generous support. We would also like to thank Amelia Kreitzer and Ken Newton for their work on

developing the concept of test monitoring and to Arnold Shore, Walt Haney and Dan Koretz, colleagues on the NBETTP, for their assistance in developing the National Board.

2   California enacted a very watered-down version of the New York bill in 1980.

3   Also, the three organizations have issued the *Code of Fair Testing Practices in Education*, hereinafter referred to as the *Code* (American Educational Research Association 1988). There are other standards and codes that are applicable to the evaluation of tests and testing programmes such as the *Ethical Principles for Psychologists* (American Psychological Association 1981); *Ethical Standards of the American Educational Research Association* (American Educational Research Association 1992); the *ETS Standards for Quality and Fairness* (Educational Testing Service 1987); the *Standards for Teacher Competence in Educational Assessment of Students* (American Federation of Teachers 1990); and the *Guidelines for Computer-Based Tests and Interpretations* (Committee on Professional Standards (COPS) 1986).

4   The courts are poor arenas in which to argue issues of test validity. As one court observed, 'The translation of a technical study [of testing] into a set of legal principles requires a clear awareness of the limits of both testing and the law' (Guardians Association of New York v. Civil Service Commission of New York City 1980: 169).

5   The NAACP Legal Defense and Educational Fund has already approached the Center for the Study of Testing, Evaluation and Educational Policy (CSTEEP) about studying this new use of the North Carolina tests, because of the Fund's concern about the disparate impact and due process implications of the new requirements.

References

Adkins, D.C. (1950) 'Proceedings of the Fifty-Eighth Annual Business Meeting of the American Psychological Association, Inc., State College, Pennsylvania', *The American Psychologist* 5: 544–75.

American Educational Research Association (1992) 'Ethical Standards of the American Educational Research Association', *Educational Researcher* 21: 23–6.

American Educational Research Association, American Psychological Association, and the National Council on Measurement in Education (1985) *Standards for Educational and Psychological Testing*, Washington, DC: American Psychological Association.

American Educational Research Association, American Psychological Association, and the National Council on Measurement in Education Joint Committee on Testing Practices (1988) *Code of Fair Testing in Education*, Washington, DC: The Joint Committee on Testing Practices.

American Federation of Teachers, National Council on Measurement in Education, and National Education Association (1990) *Standards for Teacher Competence in Educational Assessment of Students*, Washington, DC: American Federation of Teachers, National Council on Measurement in Education and National Education Association.

American Psychological Association (1981) 'Ethical Principles of Psychologists', *American Psychologist* 36: 633–8.

Basalla, G. (1988) *The Evolution of Technology*, New York: Cambridge University Press.

Beaton, A.E., Martin, M.O., Mullis, I.V.S., Gonzalez, E.J., Smith, T.A. and Kelly, D.L. (1996a) *Science Achievement in the Middle School Years: IEA's Third International Mathematics and Science Study*, Chestnut Hill, MA: Center for the Study of Testing, Evaluation, and Educational Policy, Boston College.

—— (1996b) *Mathematics Achievement in the Middle School Years: IEA's Third International Mathematics and Science Study*, Chestnut Hill, MA: Center for the Study of

Testing, Evaluation, and Educational Policy, Boston College.

Bellah, R.N., Madsen, R., Sullivan, W.M., Swidler, A. and Tipton, S.M. (1991) *The Good Society*, New York: Alfred A. Knopf.

Borgmann, A. (1984) *Technology and the Character of Contemporary Life: A Philosophical Inquiry*, Chicago: University of Chicago Press.

Boulding, K.E. (1970) *Beyond Economics: Essays on Society, Religion and Ethics*, Ann Arbor, MI: The University of Michigan Press.

Buros, O.K. (ed.) (1972) *The Nineteen Thirty-Eight Mental Measurements Yearbook*, Highland Park, NJ: Gryphon (originally published in 1938 by Rutgers University Press under the title *The Nineteen Thirty-Eight Mental Measurements Yearbook of the School of Education*).

Committee on Professional Standards and Committee on Psychological Tests (1986) *Guidelines for Computer-Based Tests and Interpretations*, Washington, DC: American Psychological Association.

Derthick, M. and Quirk, P. (1985) *The Politics of Deregulation*, Washington, DC: The Brookings Institution.

Educational Testing Service (1987) *ETS Standards for Quality and Fairness*, Princeton, NJ: ETS.

Ellul, J. (1964) *The Technological Society*, New York: Vintage Books.

—— (1990) *The Technological Bluff*, Grand Rapids, MI: Williams B. Eerdmans Company.

Fields, C. (1997) 'Harvard Scholars Convene Civil Rights Think Tank', *Black Issues in Higher Education* 14(5): 8–11.

Foucault, M. (1979) *Discipline and Punish: The Birth of the Prison*, Harmondsworth: Penguin.

—— (1982) 'The Subject and Power of Critical Inquiry', in H.I. Dreyfus and P. Robinson (eds), *Beyond Structuralism and Hermeneutics*, Chicago: University of Chicago Press, 777–95.

Freund, E. (1928) *Administrative Powers over Persons and Property: A Comparative Survey*, Chicago: University of Chicago Press.

Gleick, J. (1987) *Chaos: Making a New Science*, New York: Viking Penguin.

Guardians Association of New York v. Civil Service Commission of the City of New York 633F. 2d232 (1980, US Court of Appeals, 2nd Circuit) (1980) New York: Civil Service Commission.

Haney, W. (1981) 'Validity, Vaudeville and Values', *American Psychologist* 36: 1021–34.

Haney, W., Madaus, G. and Lyons, R. (1993) *The Fractured Marketplace for Standardized Testing*, Boston: Kluwer Academic Press.

Harp, L. (1997) 'State PTA Asks for Independent Testing Agency: Group Says Current System Failing', *Lexington Herald-Leader*, July 27.

Hendrie, C. (1996) 'School Ordered to Admit Student Challenging Quota System', *Education Week*, 4 September.

Hobbs, N. (1975) *The Futures of Children*, San Francisco: Jossey-Bass.

Lerner, B. (1979) *The War on Testing: Detroit Edison in Perspective*, Princeton, NJ: Educational Testing Service.

Locke, M. (1997) 'UC Law School Admits Fewer Blacks, Hispanics', *New York Times*, 15 May: A3.

Lowrance, W.W. (1986) *Modern Science and Human Values*, New York: Oxford University Press.

Madaus, G.F. and Kellaghan, T. (1992) 'Curriculum Evaluation and Assessment', in P.W. Jackson (ed.), *Handbook of Research on Curriculum*, New York: Macmillian, 119–54.

McCraw, T. (1984) *Prophets of Regulation: Charles Francis Adams, Louis D. Bradneis, James M. Landis, Alfred E. Kahn*, Cambridge, MA: Belknap Press of Harvard University Press.

McGarity, T. (1991) *Reinventing Rationality: The Role of Regulatory Analysis in the Federal Bureaucracy*, New York: Cambridge University Press.

Merton, R.K. (1964) 'Foreword', in E. Jacques (ed.), *The Technological Society*, New York: Vintage Books, v–viii.

National Commission on Testing and Public Policy (1990) *From Gatekeeper to Gateway: Transforming Testing In America*, New York: Ford Foundation.

O'Meara, J.F. (1944) 'A Critical Study of External Examinations and of Their Influence on Secondary Education', unpublished master's dissertation, University College Cork.

Portner, J. (1999) 'Massive Failure Rates on New Tests Daze Va', *Education Week*, 20 January.

Quirk, P. (1980) 'Food and Drug Administration', in J. Wilson (ed.), *The Politics of Regulation*, New York: Basic Books.

Ruch, G.M. (1925) 'Minimum Essentials in Reporting Data on Standard Tests', *Journal of Educational Research* 12: 349–58.

Sandman, P.M. (1989) 'Hazard Versus Outrage in the Public Perception', in T. Covello, D. McCallum and T. Pavola (eds), *Effective Risk Communication*, New York: Plenum, 45–9.

Smith, M.R. (1987) 'Army Ordnance and the "American System" of manufacturing: 1815–1861', in M.M. Sokal (ed.), *Psychological Testing and American Society 1890–1930*, New Brunswick, NJ: Rutgers University Press, 21–45.

Spulber, D. (1989) *Regulation and Markets*, Cambridge, MA: MIT Press.

State of the Union Address (1997), *The New York Times*, 5 February (reprint of President Clinton's 1997 address).

Staudenmaier, J. M. (1985) *Technology's Storytellers: Reweaving the Human Fabric*, Cambridge MA: MIT Press.

—— (1988) *Technology and Faith*, Kansas City, MO: National Catholic Reporter (audio tape).

—— (1990) 'Science, Technology and Empowerment: Who Gets a Say?' in *Technological Development and Science in the 19th and 20th Centuries*, Eindhoven: Technische Universiteit Eindhoven.

Taylor, F.W. (1914) *The Principles of Scientific Management*, New York/London: Kegan Paul, Trench.

Tenner, E. (1997) *Why Things Bite Back: Technology and the Revenge of Unintended Consequences*, New York: Vintage Books.

UC Berkeley Office of the Chancellor (1997) *UCLA's Data Simulating the Potential Impacts of SP-1 and Proposition 209*, Berkeley, CA: UC Berkeley, 6 September.

UCLA Office of the Chancellor (1997) *UC Berkeley's Estimate of the Effects of Regents' Policy SP-1 and Proposition 209*, Los Angeles, CA: UCLA, 6 September.

Wallace, W.A. (1996) *The Modeling of Nature: Philosophy of Science and Philosophy of Nature in Synthesis*, Washington, DC: The Catholic University of America Press.

Wilson, J. (1980) *The Politics of Regulation*, New York: Basic Books.

Winner, L. (1977) *Autonomous Technology: Technic-Out-Of-Control as a Theme in Political Thought*, Cambridge MA: MIT Press.

—— (1986) *The Whale and the Reactor: A Search for Limits in an Age of High Technology*, Chicago: The University of Chicago Press.

4 How Tests Create What They are Intended to Measure

F. Allan Hanson

Contemporary society is awash in tests. Some nursery schools require the toddlers who would attend them to pass an entrance examination. This is the beginning of an endless torrent of tests that will probe every corner of their nature and behaviour for the rest of their lives. A faculty member at Columbia University spoke of a friend who was planning to begin graduate studies after having been out of school for several years. The professor asked whether she was anxious about the Graduate Record Examination, a standardized test required for admission to graduate school. 'Well,' came the response, 'I'm an American. I was born to be tested.'

In *Stories in an Almost Classical Mode*, Harold Brodkey writes of his childhood:

> but I did well in school and seemed to be peculiarly able to learn what the teacher said – I never mastered a subject, though – and there was the idiotic testimony of those peculiar witnesses, IQ tests: *those scores invented me*. Those scores were a decisive piece of destiny in that they affected the way people treated you and regarded you; they determined your authority; and if you spoke oddly, they argued in favor of your sanity.
>
> (Brodkey 1988: 121, my emphasis)

Even more than Brodkey, Victor Serbriakoff was invented by intelligence tests. Told by a teacher at age 15 that he was a moron, he quit school and worked for years as an unskilled labourer. At age 32 he happened to take an intelligence test, which indicated that his IQ was a towering 161. His life changed totally. He tried his hand at inventing and received patents, he wrote books on his favourite topic (not surprisingly, intelligence), and he became chairman of the International Mensa Society, an organization with membership restricted to individuals with IQs over 140 (McGarvey 1989: 37).

The other side of the coin is less publicized, but surely the humiliation and sickening sense of inadequacy brought on by poor performance on tests have left wounds that fester in millions for years. Virtually everyone recalls good or bad experiences with tests – standardized or classroom tests in school, aptitude, lie detector or drug tests in the armed forces or in connection with a job – and can trace the effect of those experiences on their lives. In a very real sense, tests have invented all of us. They play an important role in determining what opportunities are offered to or withheld from us, they mould the expectations and evaluations that others form of us (and we form of them), and they heavily influence our assessments of our own abilities and worth. Therefore, although testing is usually considered to be a means of measuring qualities that are already present in a person, in actuality tests often *produce* the characteristics they purport to measure. The individual in contemporary society is not so much described by tests as constructed by them.

Testing and the Orders of Simulacra

To develop this proposition, it is necessary to recognize first and foremost that tests are representational devices. The result of a test is important not in itself but only insofar as it indicates something else, which we may term the 'target information'. The point of giving a standardized intelligence test, for example, is not to ascertain whether the subject can answer the particular questions and solve the particular problems that appear on the test. Instead, that is taken as a measure of the subject's ability to cope with any number of questions and problems of those kinds, and that in turn is taken as an indication of the subject's intelligence. Phrasing this representational relationship in the terminology of semiotics, the test result is the signifier and the target information is the signified.

Because signifiers and signifieds are not the same thing, testing inevitably involves a gap between the immediate results and the target information that the test is intended to provide. The gap varies in width with different kinds of tests, but passage across it is never a matter of simple one-to-one correspondence. Changes occur there, changes that are poorly understood and, in fact, seldom even recognized. If we look at them closely, we will begin to understand how tests do not simply measure independently existing realities but, instead, literally create them.

A useful way to analyse those changes is by means of Jean Baudrillard's ideas about the 'orders of simulacra' (1983: 83–102). Baudrillard distinguished three kinds of relationship between signifier and signifieds. In the first order of simulacra, the signified has priority and the signifier is some kind of copy of it. An Elvis lookalike, for example, is a signifier of Elvis Presley. The original Elvis, the signified, obviously came before any Elvis lookalike and serves as the model that an Elvis lookalike strives to look like. In the second order, the signifier is a functional equivalent or replacement for the signified. Robots in automated factories, for example, are signifiers of human workers in this sense. In the third order of simulacra, the signifier is a code or blueprint for the signified. Now it is the signifier that has priority, appearing before the signified and constituting it. Examples are a recipe as signifier of the dish made from it, or a particular constellation of DNA as signifier of a plant, animal or human being. The evolutionary development of signification is from the first to the third order of simulacra.

Conventional notions about testing conceptualize it very much along the lines of Baudrillard's first order of simulacra. We usually think of the measurements involved in testing human beings as similar in principle (if more complicated in practice) to measuring various properties of, say, steel rods. The rods already have definite length, thickness, tensile strength, ductility and so on, and the measures simply enable us to identify and express those pre-existing characteristics in standardized units such as feet and inches, pounds per square inch and so on. In the same way, the human knowledge, capabilities or tendencies that are the target information (signifieds) of tests are conventionally thought to exist prior to testing. The test results (signifiers) identify just what or how much of it there is, as expressed in standardized units such as personality types or IQ points. But I argue that we gain deeper insight into testing and its social consequences when we view it in terms of Baudrillard's second and third orders of simulacra, which feature the growing priority of signifiers (test results) over signifieds (target information). This will reveal how tests condition, change and even produce the various human characteristics they are intended to measure.

The Future Orientation of Testing

Why is testing so predominant in contemporary society? It is used, of course, to assess at what proficiency level people have completed a course of study or how well they have mastered a skill. But of equal importance with the evaluation of past accomplishments is the use of testing to predict future behaviour. In its future-oriented applications, testing is an instrument of social efficiency. Instead of wasting time and energy in a cumbersome process of trial and error, testing enables prediction of who will do well and poorly in what parts of the race before it is run. Test information about people's intelligence, personality, moral character and habits enables placement of them in positions where they can be optimally effective both in terms of their contribution to society and their sense of personal achievement and self-worth.

The future-oriented character of testing is bound up with the fact that it is, as already discussed, a representational device. For most tests, while the immediate results pertain to the present, the target information concerns the future. Prenatal tests such as amniocentesis, for example, provide information about the genetic state of a fetus. But that information is used to say something about gender and other physical characteristics to be exhibited later, after birth. The immediate results of aptitude tests are taken to signify something about how well a person is likely to perform in future school or occupational settings. Drug testing by urinalysis reports on whether an individual has ingested particular substances within a few days (or, in the case of marijuana, several weeks) prior to the test. The result is taken as an indication of whether or not this individual is a drug abuser. Particularly when drug testing is done in a pre-employment context, that conclusion is used in turn to represent further target information: whether the individual will be a reliable employee.

The passage across the gap from immediate results to target information is negotiated by representation: in one way or another, test results represent – are signifiers of – target information. Although people tend to think of the representation involved in testing in terms of Baudrillard's first order of simulacra, reflection on how testing is used makes it clear that it actually belongs to the second and third orders. To begin to see this, remember that as one goes through the second and third orders of simulacra signifiers become increasingly prior to signifieds. They take on a reality which is more palpable than the things they represent; they become (to borrow a term from contemporary social theory) 'hyperreal'.

As the term is used here, 'hyperreality' refers to a situation in which a signifier so dominates or enhances the process of representation that it becomes more impressive, memorable and actionable, and therefore more real than what it signifies. I recently heard a radio baseball commentator describe 'what might have been the greatest catch I ever saw'. He qualified it thus because he saw it in a minor league stadium that lacked a huge screen that could flash instant replays of the catch, reproducing it several times, stopping the action at critical junctures, displaying it from various angles. Instant replays are, of course, representations or signifiers of actual events. But they are hyperreal because they allow richer experience of events than mere observation of the real thing. So deeply have these representations become embedded in our expectations that the commentator remarked how, having seen the catch only once, as it actually happened, it did not seem quite real.

Test results are equally hyperreal. Unlike the more complex and ephemeral target information they presumably signify, test results are distinct, explicit and durable. Partly this is because they are *written down*: they are concrete records that are storable, retrievable and consultable. They bear the same relation to the aptitude, ability or other personal qualities they report on that the instant replay bears to the catch in baseball. The one is a signifier or representation of the other, but it is more palpable and scrutable than a fleeting event or an abstract, immaterial quality. The signifier is therefore hyperreal, taking on a greater reality than what it signifies. Test results, however, differ from instant replays, but are even more hyperreal because the gap between signified and signifier in tests is wider. Seeing actual events and seeing instant replays both involve visual images, but test results are expressed in a form that is different – and drastically pared down – from what they signify. Consider, for example, the compression and transformation that is necessary to get from the rich complexity of intelligence to the single IQ score that supposedly represents it.

Perhaps most important, test results take on a greater importance and more palpable reality than the target information they signify because test results are *actionable*. The abbreviation of test results constitutes an operational advantage when, as commonly happens in contemporary society, many people vie for limited rewards and those charged with making the selection have no extensive knowledge of the candidates and time only for a rapid review of their credentials. Decision makers for scholarships or fellowships, admission to selective colleges or other competitive programmes often know the candidates only as the bearers of certain academic and extra-curricular records, test scores and assessments in letters of recommendation. Their work would be vastly complicated and perhaps unmanageable if all the applicants were to present themselves on their doorstep as complete human beings with full and nuanced ranges of interests, talents, penchants and problems. In evaluating people for a position in which intelligence is deemed to be an important criterion; for example, it is faster and simpler to make a decision between two candidates when told that one has an IQ of 125 and the other 110 than when given detailed, richly textured accounts of their respective cognitive capabilities. Nor should we overlook the security factor involved. Resting decisions on explicit and readily comparable test scores makes it possible to claim that the best selection was made on the basis of the information available, should decisions work out badly or there be troublesome protests or lawsuits.

Tests are therefore outstanding examples of Baudrillard's second order of simulacra. Test results are signifiers of intelligence, skills and so on, but the preceding paragraphs have shown that decisions are made and actions taken on the basis of the test results rather than what they signify. As with other second order simulacra, signifiers stand in for or replace signifieds.

But there is more. The hyperreality of test results is powerful enough that tests literally *construct* human traits rather than simply measuring them. In this sense, tests belong to Baudrillard's third order of simulacra, where signifiers precede and constitute signifieds. In human testing, the constituting process works in two ways: by selection and by transformation.

Selection

Testing often acts as a gatekeeping device that allows only those candidates who meet certain pre-established criteria to pass. Sometimes the gate that is guarded is the opportunity for life itself. Prenatal tests such as amniocentesis can identify the gender of fetuses, and some parents couple the test result with abortion if the gender is not to their liking. This may have a dramatic impact on the sex of fetuses that are carried to term. Philadelphia medical geneticist Dr Laird Jackson reports that, 'virtually all of the babies ultimately born to his [East] Indian patients are males. For other patients, the relation of males to females is about 50–50' (Kolata 1988: 38). Notice that the constituting effect of selection is in the aggregate. It does not alter the gender of any particular fetus, but it has a profound effect on the demographic makeup of the affected population.

Gender selection achieved by the above method is quite likely to produce the desired outcome: it is highly probable that a fetus reported by amniocentesis to be male will be born and grow up looking like a male. This is less likely for tests that measure human habits, personality characteristics or mental abilities because, in them, the gap between immediate test results and target information is wider. Therefore, using them as gatekeeping devices may produce a pool of individuals with characteristics more or less different from those one had intended to select.

Consider pre-employment drug testing. The target information desired by the employer is whether or not a prospective employee is a drug user who might show up for work in an impaired condition, be excessively absent and unreliable, or steal from the company in order to support an expensive drug habit. The immediate result of urinalysis indicates whether the individual has ingested drugs during a certain period prior to the test. For heroin and cocaine, this is a matter of a few days. Because applicants know they will be tested if they are hired, all but hardcore addicts will be able to curtail their use of these most destructive drugs for a brief period and thus escape detection. This is considerably more difficult for users of the less addictive marijuana, because its traces persist in the urine for several weeks. Therefore, drug testing may deny employment to some individuals who use marijuana on occasion but who would have become reliable employees, while not identifying other individuals who use more dangerous, debilitating and expensive drugs on a regular basis.

Transformation

While the selective effect of testing is felt in the aggregate and does not change the properties of individuals, testing also works in other ways to bring about actual transformations of individual subjects. The sheer act of measuring something may change it. In physics, the Heisenberg uncertainty principle holds that the outcome of experiments on subatomic particles is affected by the experiments themselves, and probably everyone has had the experience of blood pressure rising simply because it is being taken. A similar effect – more subtle but more lasting and pervasive – often occurs in the mental testing of human beings.

One transforming capacity of tests is played out in the negative, in that tests inhibit changes or developments in individuals that would otherwise take place. In schools, tests enable teachers to identify early deviations in learning, making it possible to correct these with small interventions. This is similar to how in the political realm, constant surveillance facilitates early detection of dissident or revolutionary stirrings so that they may be nipped in the bud. So too in the realm of thought: regular testing enables early identification and correction of deviant or independent thinking. One must not, of course, ignore the beneficial results of this; it enhances the learning process by identifying things that students do not understand and preventing them from going off on unproductive tangents. Nevertheless, it is also a marvellously efficient means of thought control, and it comes at a price. Often it is not possible to be certain in advance that a tangent will be unproductive. In all areas of social life – political, artistic, intellectual, technological, economic – as well as in biological evolution, change often originates in minor deviations that, if allowed to develop, may open up hitherto unrealized potentials. By inhibiting aleatory exploration in thinking, testing encourages stagnation of the status quo and impedes the process of change.

The other side of the coin – how testing produces rather than prevents transformations in individuals – encompasses numerous examples. One of the most interesting of these concerns lie detector tests by polygraph. When skilfully done, these tests may so disorient people that they come to distrust their own memories and confess to crimes that they did not commit. To understand how this can happen, it is necessary briefly to review how a polygraph test works. Sensors attached to the subject's body record on a strip of graph paper physiological processes such as rates of respiration, heartbeat, blood pressure and perspiration. In a test used to investigate a specific crime – say, a murder – the subject is directed to answer yes or no to ten or twelve questions. Most of them are innocuous ('Is your name John?' 'Is today Wednesday?'), but the set contains one or two 'relevant' or 'hot' questions, such as 'Did you kill Bjorn Faulkner on the night of January 16?' The theory is that lying provokes physiological reactions that may not be perceived by ordinary observation but are detectable by the sensitive measurements of the polygraph machine. A guilty individual is expected to 'hit' on a hot question (to show a greater reaction to it as compared with responses to the innocuous ones) while an innocent person will not. To 'run a chart' is to go through the set of questions once, with the subject hooked up to the machine. A thorough polygraph test often takes well over an hour. It involves running several charts, between which the blood pressure cuff and other attachments are removed or loosened and the examiner interviews/interrogates the subject.

A particularly effective technique for eliciting a confession is to run a chart and pin it to the wall. The polygraph examiner then points to the response monitored for the hot question, and asks why the subject hit on it. (In fact the response may indicate deception only very slightly, if at all. But subjects normally have no knowledge of how to read polygraph charts, and so have no way to interpret what they are shown apart from what the examiner says.) The examiner then leaves the room, allowing the subject to study the chart alone. The examiner returns and runs another chart, asking the same questions in the same order. The subject knows full well when the hot question is coming and worries that the chart might again indicate deception on it, a worry that subsides after the question has been asked and answered. The new chart is pinned on the wall and, sure enough, the subject did hit on the relevant question again, even more this time. And now a distinctive 'peak of tension' pattern (responses building up over a few questions prior to the hot one, climaxing on it, and then relaxing on subsequent questions) starts to appear. The subject is again left alone to stew over the chart, after which the examiner returns and runs yet another chart: same questions, same order. The subject is increasingly nervous about the course that events are taking, and when this chart is pinned on the wall the peak of tension pattern is unmistakable, even to untrained eyes. Ultimately the subject, confused and bewildered by a pattern of physiological responses that objective scientific measures make obvious, concludes that his or her own memory must be blotted out or playing tricks, and confesses. What else could one do? After all, the subject is there alone, a single person relying on memory that, as everyone knows, can be fallible. How much can that count against the growing suspicion of a trained examiner and the scientific evidence of a precise machine, recorded so obviously that even the increasingly distraught subject can see it more clearly with each new chart?

One examiner told me how, working on the basis of a strong police presumption that a woman was guilty of a certain crime, he succeeded in extracting a confession after about forty-five minutes of work with the polygraph. He then discovered, however, that she was unable to supply certain factual details about the case that the perpetrator would surely know. He concluded that she was in fact innocent, but it took him hours to convince her of that and to persuade her to retract the confession.

The transforming capacity of tests works on individuals before taking them as well as after. Because people covet the rewards that are available to those who pass through the gates guarded by tests, many spare no effort to remake themselves in ways that will improve their test performance. For many students, learning is less a matter of acquiring the information covered in their courses than becoming skilful at cramming and other techniques to get high grades on tests. Kaplan courses and the Princeton Review are designed explicitly and exclusively to raise scores on standardized tests. Nor are students the only ones who put test performance ahead of the acquisition of knowledge. Teachers often 'teach to the test' with the goal that their students' performance on aptitude and minimum competency tests will make them (the *teachers*) and their school look good. Jacques Barzun has suggested that the preoccupation with doing well on standardized tests has literally moulded the way young people in America think (Barzun 1991: 32–7). They have better developed cognitive abilities to recognize random facts than to construct patterns or think systematically, he argues, because the former skill is favoured and rewarded by the multiple-choice format of standardized tests.

Constructing Categories

In all of the above cases, as in many more, tests transform people by assigning them to various categories (gifted, slow learner, honest, guilty, drug user and so on), and then they are treated, act and come to think of themselves according to the expectations associated with those categories. But that is not all. Tests also define or act as constitutive codes for the categories themselves. The process is visible in the tests that were in vogue in sixteenth- and seventeenth-century Europe for identifying witches. One of these was to 'swim' a witch: to tie a suspect's right thumb to left big toe and left thumb to right big toe and then cast the wretch into a river or pond. A witch, it was believed, would float, while an innocent individual would sink.

Numerous suspects were revealed by this and other tests to be witches, and that served as an important wedge for inserting the belief in the existence of witches into the public mind. The process works by a reversal of logic. Ostensibly, the reasoning proceeds deductively: there are witches; witches float; this individual floats; therefore, this individual is a witch.[1] In its impact on society, however, the logic runs in the opposite direction: this individual floats; witches are said to float; therefore, this individual is a witch; therefore, witches exist.

The category-constructing capacity of tests is particularly evident in the realm of intelligence. It is a realm of immense social importance, because in our society intelligence is universally counted among the critical attributes for success in almost any human endeavour. Although psychologists debate precisely what intelligence is, a particular view of it is widely held in the popular mind. This conventional view, seldom precisely articulated, focuses on general mental ability; perhaps it is best stated as the ability to learn. This is often fleshed out by associating the general ability called 'intelligence' with three attributes: (1) it is a single thing; (2) it comes in varying quantities, such that different people have different amounts of it; and (3) the amount of intelligence possessed by each individual is fixed for life.

The conventional view of intelligence derives largely from practices of intelligence testing. First, the idea that intelligence is a single thing is rooted in the fact that the results of intelligence tests are often expressed on a single scale, such as IQ, even when the test itself consists of several distinct parts. Where there is a single score, it is easy to conclude that some single thing must exist to which that score refers. The second attribute – that intelligence is quantitative, and that some people have more of it than others – derives from the practice of reporting intelligence test scores on numerical scales. Only quantitative phenomena may be expressed in numbers, and when those numbers vary from one person to another, so must the amount of intelligence that the numbers represent. Finally, the notion that the amount of intelligence possessed by each individual is fixed for life stems from the belief that intelligence tests measure not so much what one already knows as one's ability to learn. It is widely assumed that how much an individual actually learns depends on opportunity, motivation and ability. Opportunity and motivation may vary at different times in the individual's life, but sheer ability to learn is generally considered to be a constant. It is hardwired in the person. Hence, the amount of each individual's intelligence is considered to be fixed by heredity.

It can easily be argued that the conventional view of intelligence is mistaken. A logician might point out that it stems from the fallacy of misplaced concreteness: the error of assuming that where there is a name (in this case, 'intelligence') and a number, there must be some unique, pre-existing phenomenon to which the name and number refer. And, in addition to problems in logic, the conventional view of intelligence as a single thing seems to be wrong substantively. Numerous psychologists (including Alfred Binet, who invented the first intelligence test) have maintained that what we call 'intelligence' is really a variety of different abilities, some of them possibly only distantly related to others. The notion of intelligence as multifaceted continues to be fruitfully developed today, particularly by Howard Gardner and Robert J. Sternberg. Gardner's theory of multiple intelligences stipulates several quite distinct kinds of intelligence: linguistic, musical, logical-mathematical, spatial, bodily-kinesthetic and 'the personal intelligences' (capacities to deal effectively with one's inner feelings and social relationships). Sternberg advances a 'triarchic' theory that distinguishes three aspects of intelligence: components (the nature of the thinking process); experience (learning from and reasoning on the basis of experience); and context (adapting to and shaping the environment) (Gardner 1983; Sternberg 1988: 58–70).

If one is working in the realm of psychological theory, it is eminently sensible to highlight the shortcomings of the conventional view and to conceptualize intelligence as plural or multifaceted. But if one is exploring the workings of concepts and practices in society, as we are in this chapter, then it is important to recognize that the conventional notion of intelligence is not mistaken. There really is a single thing out there to which the conventional concept of intelligence refers. As we observed with tests for witchcraft, in social life logic sometimes runs in reverse and, in so doing, becomes a creative mechanism. In the present case, what for the formal logician is a fallacy (of misplaced concreteness) is in the logic of social life no fallacy at all but an actual constructive process. We might call it (with apologies for the neologism) 'the concretion of displaced cephalicy'. When it becomes widely assumed that there must be some real thing called 'intelligence' to which the results of intelligence tests refer, that thing is literally called into being. This signals, however, a crucial difference between the conventional view of intelligence and the social analysis of it that I am proposing. The conventional understanding is that 'intelligence' exists first as a thing in itself and intelligence testing comes later as a means to measure it. My contention, on the other hand, is that the concept of 'intelligence' is a product of intelligence tests. As such, intelligence is an outstanding example of this essay's thesis that tests create what they are intended to measure.

We can observe the nature of this creative process most clearly by engaging in a thought experiment of constructing a new test and imagining its consequences. Let us call it, simply, the New Intelligence Test, or NIT. It is intended especially to excel current tests by paying more attention to the practical aspects of intelligence used in everyday life, and to sample more widely from the scope of intelligence as conceptualized by proponents of the multifaceted view. The NIT consists of nine sections:

1   A name recall scale tests ability to remember the names of persons to which the subject has just been introduced.
2   A mathematics section tests the subject's ability to do problems of arithmetic and algebra.
3   The first impression scale invites a panel of ordinary people to evaluate the personableness of subjects by simply looking at them.
4   In the exposition of ideas section, the subject is given five minutes to read a page from Rousseau describing his distinction between self-love (*amour de soi*) and selfishness (*amour-propre*), and thirty minutes to present a clear and accurate written account of it, with original examples. (To avoid subjects learning of this problem in advance and studying for it, different forms of the test will feature other, analogous tasks in this section.)
5   The small talk scale evaluates subjects' ability to carry on an interesting conversation with someone they have never met.
6   A bullshitting scale assesses skill at participating in a discussion with two other people on a topic about which the subject knows nothing.
7   In the follow-the-directions scale the subject is told once, at the speed of ordinary conversation, to do a task that consists of six distinct steps, and is evaluated on how well the task is accomplished.

8   The adult sports scale evaluates the subject's ability to play golf or tennis, with suitable adjustments for male and female subjects.

9   Finally, the SES scale is a simple rating of subjects according to parental socio-economic status. A composite score is generated from the results of the NIT's nine sections.

What ability or human capacity is tested by the NIT? An operational definition of intelligence used by numerous psychologists is that intelligence is that mental capacity which is measured by intelligence tests. On that precedent, one would say that the NIT tests the skills or wits used in taking the NIT, no more and no less. This is certainly nothing inconsequential, for were the appropriate studies to be done, it would doubtless turn out that high NIT scores correlate positively (probably more positively than IQ scores) with desirable social outcomes such as success in the university, high income, and election to public office. But it is also obvious that what the NIT tests is not a single quality or capacity of persons. It is rather a set of distinct qualities, which have been measured by the several sections of the NIT and combined into a single score for convenience in reporting NIT results. In that sense our thought experiment is in line with the view of intelligence as multifaceted.

But assume now that the NIT were to catch on in a big way: that it came, for example, to be widely used for college and graduate admissions and for hiring and promotion purposes by law firms, government and corporations. In such an event, the composite of different abilities measured by the NIT would not remain static. People would spare no effort in preparing for the test, in the hope of achieving the rewards awaiting those who excel on it. They would bone up on arithmetic and algebra, they would master techniques for remembering the names of strangers, they would practise bullshitting, they would take golf and tennis lessons, they would groom themselves to appear more likeable on first sight. High school and college curricula would shift in the direction of more training in the areas covered by the NIT (if they did not, irate parents would demand to know why their children were not being taught something useful). Kaplan and Princeton Review would explode into the marketplace with courses that promise dramatic improvement in one's NIT scores. One side effect would even be to swell the public treasury as people report inflated income in order to improve their children's showing on the NIT/SES scale; and then have to pay taxes on it.

All of this dedicated effort would have a palpable effect. Although the NIT obviously measures several quite different abilities, people would knit them together as they strive to improve them all in order to raise their NIT scores. They would begin to imagine these several abilities to be one. They would name it…perhaps 'NITwit'. Given its importance for success in life, it would be valued as a thing of great significance. People would worry about how much of it they possess; they would envy evidence of its abundance in their contemporaries and look for promising signs of it in their children.

Not only would a new mental category swim into the social consciousness. The empirical amount of it possessed by individuals would literally increase as, in preparing for the NIT, they hone their skills at following directions, playing golf, expounding on ideas, small talk and the rest of it. And, of course, as individuals increase these skills, NIT scores would go up. There would be rejoicing in the land as today's average NIT scores exceed those achieved in the past or by test takers in other countries...until, perhaps, an apogee is passed and national consternation about declining NIT scores sets in. Given all these transformations and developments, it is fair to say that NITwit would become a new, singular, personal trait, an objective reality literally constructed by NIT testing. Perhaps the ultimate development (and the ultimate absurdity, but it unquestionably would happen) would be when rival tests are marketed that claim to measure NITwit faster, cheaper or more accurately than the NIT.

What happened in our thought experiment has been the experience of 'intelligence' in the real world. Because of intelligence tests, several different abilities (to do mathematical problems, to comprehend texts, to compare shapes, to sort ideas or objects into classes, to define words, to remember historical events, and to do all of these things rapidly) have been lumped together to form a new, unitary mental characteristic called 'intelligence'. It is, moreover, a quality of great importance because intelligence tests serve as the basis for offering or denying educational and career opportunities and other social rewards. Given this importance, intelligence has become a target for special effort and training, with the result that people increase their overall proficiency in it. Precisely as with NITwit in our thought experiment, intelligence has been fashioned into an objectively real personal trait by the practice of intelligence testing.

Transforming the Individual

Perhaps the most pervasive (and least recognized) social consequence of testing as a third order simulacrum is its role in a transformation that has been taking place over the last few centuries in the concept of the individual. One source of this transformation may be found in changes in how much is known about individuals. In one of the most perceptive analysis of testing yet written, Michel Foucault has argued that the contemporary concept of the individual is a product of the development and extension of examinations in the seventeenth and eighteenth centuries (Foucault 1979: 184–94). He does not mean, of course, that prior to that time there were no individuals. Obviously there were, for people had individual names, they could tell each other apart, and it was possible to identify an individual as the same person upon encounters at different times or in different places.[2] Foucault is referring instead to the concept of the individual as a complex, dynamic being with specified physical, mental, political and other properties. He means the individual as an object of study and detailed knowledge, for whom it is possible to define ranges of the normal along various physical and psychological dimensions, to explain the nature and processes of normal development and behaviour, to diagnose deviations from the normal and to intervene with the aim of correcting or treating those deviations. Obviously, all of this requires that there be a rich corpus of knowledge about individuals, and prior to the seventeenth and eighteenth centuries so little information about individual persons was systematically gathered and recorded that discourse about the properties, development and pathologies of the human individual was not possible. This changed with more systematic examination of patients in hospitals and students in schools, and with the keeping of retrievable records of those examinations and of information about individuals gathered in other contexts such as the military. Foucault's contention is that these developments invented the individual as a describable, analysable object.

If the testing practices of the seventeenth and eighteenth centuries gave birth to the individual as an object susceptible to description, analysis and treatment, its mature form is largely a product of the testing practices of the twentieth century. Today's individual is much more richly textured and finely grained than its ancestor of two and three centuries ago, a being with normalities and pathologies then undreamed. One of Foucault's central propositions is that power is exercised over the individual through interventions licensed by knowledge (guidance, treatment, punishment, rehabilitation and so on). If so, the contemporary individual is subject to even more coercion than its predecessors. The rich panoply of tests that are routinely deployed today to probe all aspects of our physical and mental makeup, the decisions and interventions that are taken on the basis of test results, and the asymmetrical relation of power between test givers and test takers conspire to produce an individual who is suspended within an increasingly total network of surveillance and control.

Particularly in the mental sphere, contemporary tests are future-oriented to a degree far surpassing previous ones. This too has its effect on the person of the late twentieth century. It creates an individual who is less real than hyperreal: not so much a present as a potential or deferred being, defined less by what it is than by what it is likely to become. It is not difficult to imagine, furthermore, that increasingly refined prenatal testing technologies and genetic engineering could be used to produce infants with physical attributes, behavioural propensities and other qualities that are socially approved or parentally desired. This is already happening in a relatively crude form when parents determine the gender of their offspring by means of selective abortion on the basis of prenatal tests such as amniocentesis. And what goes now for sex might in the future go for sexual preference. No sooner did news break of research findings indicating a possible link between homosexuality and a certain condition of the brain than the prospect was raised 'that the new discovery could lead to...a test that would detect a budding homosexual in the womb early enough for the fetus to be either whisked out in an abortion, or somehow changed with the proper cocktail of hormones' (Angier 1991: E-1).

Genetic 'fingerprints' (the individual's unique genetic profile) are already being recorded for members of the armed forces and prison inmates, in order to facilitate identification of military personnel who may be killed in combat or malefactors who might leave traces of blood, semen or other bodily substances at the scene of some future crime. Simple to perform and extremely accurate, genetic fingerprinting promises to be a powerful technique for registering and identifying every individual in the population. It could well become as common-place as social security numbers and photo drivers licences are today.

As the mapping of the human genome proceeds and new knowledge is developed about the role of genetic factors in ever-widening sectors of life, routine genetic fingerprinting has great potential to be expanded into a potent instrument for acquiring still more knowledge about individuals: what diseases they are likely to contract, how and when the feebleness of old age may set in, the probability of developing various sexual orientations and other personality characteristics, behaviours and life styles. This will propel the transformation of the individual still further along the path we have already charted. The individual of the future will be more thoroughly known and minutely recorded than the individual of today. Most new knowledge from genetic research will pertain to probable future conditions, making tomorrow's individual still more hyperreal, known more for potential developments than present realities. Finally, expanding knowledge will certainly subject the future individual to increased surveillance and, very likely, to greater control. The caring professions will use new knowledge to extend the range of the normal and abnormal, and are likely to seize opportunities to diagnose hitherto unknown pathologies and to intervene in the life of individuals for their treatment. Law enforcement and social welfare agencies, schools, employers, insurance companies and others will certainly welcome increased information about the probable futures of individuals, for it will assist them in making rational and informed decisions about suspects, applicants and other persons in the interest of public safety, efficiency or profitability.

These projections may appear bleak. Especially, to base diagnoses and decisions as to what opportunities are to be offered to or withheld from the individual on future probabilities rather than on present certainties is to constrict equal opportunity and to undercut social justice. What is to be done? We do not have the option of turning the clock back, for these developments stem from the expansion of knowledge and it has never been possible to reverse that process. Nor should we want to, because if the growth of knowledge about the individual has created new opportunities for coercion, it has also encouraged human liberation. The seventeenth and eighteenth centuries produced both the coercive dream of society built on surveillance and control and also a liberal dream of individual rights, freedom and dignity based on the social contract and enshrined in documents such as the American Declaration of Independence and Constitution and the French Declaration of the Rights of Man (Foucault 1979: 169). It follows that by fostering both domination and autonomy the historical development of the individual is laced with contradictions and tensions. The contradictions offer us, as participants in the formation of our own destiny, toeholds for intervening in the process. If we seek to stimulate the growth of personal autonomy and to slow the spread of institutional coercion, it is not so much an effort to reverse the course of history as to influence the trajectory of the individual's and society's future development. One technique available to us in this effort is to apply knowledge for liberal causes:

to study the concealed social consequences of practices such as testing, and to regulate them so as to minimize their coercive effects.

Notes

1   Of course, this is not a proper use of deductive logic because it succumbs to the fallacy of affirming the consequent. Even if all witches float, that does not rule out the possibility that people who are not witches might also float for other reasons. The proper form would be: all witches float; this individual is a witch; therefore, this individual floats. But the logic of social life is governed by imperatives other than those of formal reasoning. In the present case, the proper logical form would not be of much use in devising tests to determine if someone is a witch. What I want to stress here is that the reasoning supporting the test of swimming a witch is deductive in the broad sense that it moves from general assumptions to conclusions about particular individuals.
2   The last property, however, is intriguingly thrown into question in Daniel Vigne's film *Le retour de Martin Guerre*.

References

Angier, N. (1991) 'The Biology of What it Means to be Gay', *New York Times*, 1 September, E-1.

Barzun, J. (1991) *Begin Here: The Forgotten Conditions of Teaching and Learning*, Chicago: University of Chicago Press.

Baudrillard, J. (1983) *Simulations*, New York: Semiotext.

Brodkey, H. (1988) *Stories in an Almost Classical Mode*, New York: Knopf.

Foucault, M. (1979) *Discipline and Punish*, New York: Vintage.

Gardner, H. (1983) *Frames of Mind: The Theory of Multiple Intelligences*, New York: Basic Books.

Kolata, G. (1988) 'Fetal Sex Test Used as Step to Abortion', *New York Times*, 25 December, A1, 38.

McGarvey, R. (1989) 'Confidence Pays', *USAir*, June, 37.

Sternberg, R.J. (1988) *The Triarchic Mind: A New Theory of Human Intelligence*, New York: Viking.

Part III

Classroom Contexts of Assessment

Editor's Introduction

Ann Filer

When we think about 'assessment', we generally conjure images of tests and examinations, grades and scores. However, research into the classroom contexts of assessment broadens our understandings of practices to include a range of day-to-day, often moment-to-moment, judgements made by teachers. We can include in this the vast range of informal, formative and diagnostic judgements which teachers make of students' work, attitudes and responses and of their social and emotional behaviour generally. Research in this area shows that such assessments can be as important in their consequences as can overt assessment practices. However, they are much less readily available for observation, or their effects for scrutiny (see for example Torrance and Pryor 1998). Research in this field relies on detailed observations of classroom life and assessment processes and takes as its prime focus the perspectives, interpretations and actions of pupils and teachers. It therefore includes consideration of the wider contexts of professional and pupil identities and orientations, and of social and cultural identities and biographies beyond the school (see for example Filer and Pollard 2000; Filer 1993a, 1993b, 1995).

Meanings and Interpretations in Classroom Assessment

Researchers investigating new systems of national testing in England and Wales in the early 1990s produced overwhelming evidence of poor comparability of results where assessment tasks were presented to seven-year-olds by teachers (see for example Shorrocks et al. 1992; Abbott et al. 1994). Some of the many contextual factors affecting scores concerned variations in teacher attitude to test situations, teacher interpretations of test materials and of students' responses and the influence of other students. Lack of comparability of results was one reason why these national assessment classroom *tasks* were subsequently replaced with externally marked paper and pencil *tests*.

Now although these national assessment tasks were new, the lack of agreement of scores really should not have surprised anyone. Theoretical understandings established over a period of some thirty-five years, in the USA and in the UK, have consistently shown ways in which assessment results contain within them a measure of the social context. Social context in such cases can relate to the test content itself, to the testing process or to the interpersonal processes surrounding tests. Thus Mehan, for example, investigating the social features of testing of young children in US schools, described classroom assessments involving adult–child interaction as: '...interpretive, interactional processes which should be approached and studied as such' (Mehan 1973).

Some of these important issues of interpretation, meanings and expectations which pupils and teachers bring to assessment situations, are addressed in the next two chapters in this book. In Chapter 5, Barry Cooper and Máiréad Dunne demonstrate ways in which children from different socio-economic backgrounds interpret national test items. Their findings indicate a social class effect whereby faced with 'realistic' mathematics items some working class children fail to demonstrate competencies that they have in other contexts. In Chapter 6, John Pryor and Harry Torrance show the difficulty of creating common understandings between teachers and young pupils, even where teachers attempt to embed assessment in the familiar contexts of everyday stories. They make the point that it is not easy for teachers to recognize and interpret pupil responses; therefore, pupil responses should not be used as an unproblematic source of information.

Differentiation in Classroom Assessment Practices

What Mehan, and other such studies from both sides of the Atlantic, have shown is that in evaluating pupils' academic skills, teachers inevitably include a measure of other attributes and dispositions. Moreover, subjective and erroneous evaluations of pupils' abilities that teachers make, often informally, can go on to produce a reality that reflects those original evaluations. That is, erroneous evaluations can act as self-fulfilling prophecies in producing socially differentiated outcomes in classrooms. Early studies from the 1960s and 1970s (see below for sources) showed that this was particularly so with respect to differentiation by social class. For example, children *expected* to do well on the basis of appearances and social skills were shown to be subject to more positive teacher attitudes and to be allocated to higher teaching sets. Through the 1980s and into the 1990s, similar studies have been made with respect to race and gender whereby differences in educational outcomes originated in stereotypical expectations of students' performance rather than in academic differences. For instance, adverse relationships and expectations of disruption have been used as criteria for allocating Afro-Caribbean pupils to lower teaching groups and exam sets. Gender based expectations of appropriate roles in classroom discussions, gender based interpretations of identical test scores, different forms of feedback to pupils based on gender, have variously been shown to influence assessment results, allocations to exam sets and exclusion from whole subject areas. Thus *formal*, apparently *objective* assessment results can be products of earlier *informal*, *subjective* assessments and the differentiating processes that those earlier assessments set in motion.

A sociological discourse of assessment, therefore, sees classroom assessment as:

- social products derived in part from a teacher-created context;
- a product of wider fields of social, cultural and gender identity and biography beyond the classroom;
- having a role in racial, gender and socio-cultural classroom differentiating practices.

In the context of the development of more classroom-based 'authentic' or 'performance' testing in US schools, Reardon et al. (1994) call for more research into informal as well as formal classroom processes. The above discussion reflects a valuable legacy of insights and theoretical perspectives, from early American and UK research up to the present, on which to draw for such research. Also, the short-lived experience of national assessment tasks (as opposed to tests) in England and Wales described above, offers insight into problems arising from attempts to grade with a 'true score' that which is essentially 'performance in context' (Torrance, see Chapter 9).

Further Reading

A fuller version and bibliography of the above research into differentiation in classroom assessment practices over the last thirty-five years can be found in *Teacher Assessment: Social Process and Social Product* (Filer 1995).

Though not a recent text, *Assessment, Schools and Society*, Chapter 5 (Broadfoot 1979), provides a more detailed account of UK and US research of the 1960s and 1970s than I am able to present here. Relevant topics include stereotype formation and self-fulfilling prophecies, labelling and the development of pupil subcultures.

Researchers investigating developments in classroom-based 'authentic' assessments in the USA will find a valuable legacy of theoretical perspectives in early American work on classroom processes and interaction. I have found, for example, that writers such as Becker (1952), Mehan (1973), Rist (1970) and Rosenthal and Jacobsen (1968), as well as UK writers within the tradition, provide important sources of insight for investigating current classroom assessment practices (see Filer 1995).

References

Abbott, D., Broadfoot, P., Croll, P., Osborn, M. and Pollard, A. (1994) 'Some Sink, Some Float: National Curriculum Assessment and Accountability', *British Educational Research Journal* 29(2).
Becker, H.S. (1952) 'Social Class Variations in the Teacher-Pupil Relationship', *Journal of Educational Sociology* 25: 451–65.
Broadfoot, P. (1979) *Assessment, Schools and Society*, London: Methuen.
Filer, A. (1993a) 'Contexts of Assessment in a Primary School Classroom', *British Educational Research Journal* 19(1): 95–107.

—— (1993b) 'The Assessment of Classroom Language: Challenging the Rhetoric of "Objectivity"', *International Studies in Sociology of Education* 3(2): 193–212.

—— (1995) 'Teacher Assessment: Social Process and Social Product', *Assessment in Education* 2(1): 23–38.

Filer, A. and Pollard, A. (2000) *The Social World of Pupil Assessment*, London: Cassell.

Mehan, H. (1973) 'Assessing Children's School Performance', in H.P. Dreitzel (ed.), *Childhood and Socialisation*, New York: Collier Macmillan.

Reardon, S.F., Scott, K. and Verre, J. (1994) 'Introduction' to the Symposium: Equity in Educational Assessment, *Harvard Educational Review* 64(1): 1–4.

Rist, R.C. (1970) 'Student Social Class and Teacher Expectations: The Self-Fulfilling Prophesy in Ghetto Education', *Harvard Educational Review* 40(3): 411–511.

Rosenthal, R. and Jacobsen, L. (1968) *Pygmalion in the Classroom*, New York: Holt Rinehart & Winston.

Shorrocks, D., Daniels, S., Frobsher, L., Nelson, N., Waterson, A. and Bell, J. (1992) *Evaluation of National Curriculum Assessment at Key Stage 1*, London: Schools Examination and Assessment Council.

Torrance, H. and Pryor, J. (1998) *Investigating Formative Assessment*, Milton Keynes; Open University Press.

5 Constructing the 'Legitimate' Goal of a 'Realistic' Maths Item

A Comparison of 10–11 and 13–14 year-olds

Barry Cooper and Máiréad Dunne

Introduction

Sociological approaches to assessment have taken a variety of forms. Broadly macro-structural perspectives have focused on the relations between the criteria for assessment, social selection and the wider socio-economic context (for example, Bowles and Gintis 1976). Broadly micro-structural perspectives have focused instead on the ways in which assessment outcomes are constructed within classrooms or testing contexts (for example, Mehan 1973; Newman et al. 1989). Both of these approaches have produced important contributions to our understanding of the origins, the practice and the consequences of assessment. Notwithstanding their different emphases these authors have had many useful things to say about the *relations* between social structure, culture and the processes of meaning construction in the contexts in which assessment actually occurs. Bourdieu's work (for example, Bourdieu 1974) on the nature of assessment practices in French higher education serves as an early example of work of this type. Turning to maths education, there has been a considerable body of research in recent years focussing on the ways in which the contexts within which mathematical problem solving occurs can affect radically both the processes and the products of such cognitive activity (Nunes et al. 1993; Lave 1988). In parallel, there has also been much research on children's 'failure' to take a 'realistic' perspective during mathematical problem-solving when it would seem appropriate to do so (for example, Säljö 1991). Our recent research on maths assessment, on which we will draw here, is intended as a contribution to these relational and contextual approaches to the study of assessment in maths (for example, Cooper 1998b; Cooper and Dunne 2000; Dunne, 1994).

We will draw on our research programme on the assessment of the mathematical knowledge and understanding of 10–11 and 13–14 year-old children in England. This research was partly motivated by a concern that the national testing of children's mathematics mainly via 'realistically' contextualized items might have a variety of unintended consequences, especially for the validity of the assessment of working-class children's knowledge and understanding. Children are often required by 'realistic' test items to make quite subtle judgements about the relevance to the process of solution of their everyday knowledge and experience (Cooper 1992, 1994). There are sociological grounds for expecting working-class children to find it more difficult to make these judgements in ways in which the designers of school maths tests define as legitimate (Holland 1981; Bernstein 1996; Bourdieu 1986). There have also been suggestions that girls might find particular types of 'realistic' items more difficult to negotiate than boys (for example, Boaler 1994). Exploratory empirical work had confirmed that children's confusion about the boundary between the everyday and the 'mathematical' could lead sometimes to an underestimation of their mathematical knowledge when it is tested by 'realistic' items (Cooper 1998a, 1998b). This problem seemed worthy of further research, which we have subsequently been able to undertake in three primary and three secondary schools.[1]

In these six schools, this programme of research has collected performance data on national curriculum tests from more than 600 children, as well as data from some 250 individual interviews in which a sub-sample of the same children have responded to a subset of test items (Cooper and Dunne 2000). We have also collected data on children's social class backgrounds, sex and measured 'ability'. This dataset has enabled statistical analyses of children's comparative performance on 'realistic' and 'non-realistic' items. We have defined 'realistic' items as those which place mathematical operations within contexts including everyday objects, events and people. 'Non-realistic' items, which we have termed 'esoteric', do not. An example of each can be seen in Figures 5.1 and 5.2. Our analyses have shown, for example, that for 10–11 year-olds, both social class and sex differences in performance are greater when 'realistic' rather than 'esoteric' items are used to assess children in the group testing context. These social class differences in performance are large enough to produce substantial differences between the social classes when entered into two simulations of an educational selection process using, respectively, either the 'esoteric' or the 'realistic' scores achieved by these children (Cooper and Dunne 2000). Twice as many of the working-class 10–11 year-old children in our sample win through in a process selecting the top-performing quarter of the sample when scores from the 'esoteric' rather than the 'realistic' subsets of test items are employed as the basis for judging performance (Cooper and Dunne 2000). We have also been able to use a comparison of our qualitative interview data with our test data to show that children's actually existing mathematical knowledge and understanding is not always validly accessed by 'realistic' items in test contexts – and that this results at least partly from the problems some children experience in reading the 'everyday'/'esoteric' boundary in ways defined as 'legitimate' by the test designers (Cooper and Dunne 1998).

We intend here to examine the responses of children to one 'realistic' test item originally intended as a 'difficult' item for 10–11 year-olds, but which we also have used in our research with 13–14 year-olds. The item (Figure 5.2) concerns an imaginary tennis competition. The 'Statement of Attainment' which this item was intended to assess is: *Identify all the outcomes of combining two independent events.* The marking scheme gave this solution:

Figure 5.1   Finding 'n': an 'esoteric' item

12   n stands for a number.

$$n + 7 = 13$$

What is the value of n + 10 ?

1 mark

Source: SCAA (1996)

Figure 5.2   Tennis pairs: a 'realistic' item

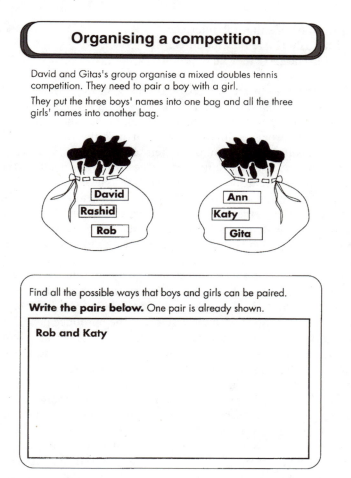

Organising a competition

David and Gitas's group organise a mixed doubles tennis competition. They need to pair a boy with a girl.

They put the three boys' names into one bag and all the three girls' names into another bag.

David
Rashid
Rob

Ann
Katy
Gita

Find all the possible ways that boys and girls can be paired.
Write the pairs below. One pair is already shown.

Rob and Katy

Source: SEAC (1993)

Rob and Katy
Rob and Ann
Rob and Gita
Rashid and Katy
Rashid and Ann
Rashid and Gita
David and Katy
David and Ann
David and Gita

There should be exactly nine pairings, all different. One way to check is as follows:

Are there 3 with Bob? Are they all different?
Are there 3 with Rashid? Are they all different?
Are there 3 with David? Are they all different?

We might note that an 'esoteric' version of the item might have been: *Find the Cartesian product of the sets {a, b, c} and {d, e, f}*. It is an indication of the shift in the climate of opinion in maths education circles since the heyday of 'abstract' algebraic approaches in the 1960s that it is the tennis competition rather than these sets that children meet in their tests (Cooper 1985). It is partly with the consequences for the validity and fairness of assessment of this shift from the 'esoteric' to the 'realistic' as the context for assessment in mathematics that our research has been concerned. In the case of the tennis item, a child has first of all to *see through* the 'noise' of the setting in order to realize the intended meaning of the item which, as can be seen from the marking scheme, concerns a Cartesian product with 'names' acting as the tokens which are to be arranged in pairs.

Several other features of the tennis item and its marking scheme can be noted straightaway. First of all, it is possible that not all children will make sense of the reference to 'mixed doubles'. Second, where they do, they may be misled by the 'realistic' context with the result that they produce just three pairs using the six names rather than the expected nine pairs. After all, these three pairs would form a basis for proceeding with games of tennis and are also the type of outcome children might be familiar with from televised draws for sports competitions (Cooper 1994). The fact that the pair 'Rob and Katy' is given – and in bold type – might help to overdetermine such a response if children believe they should not disturb this pair. Third, children might, and do, respond to the item in terms of 'ways' of producing pairs (process) rather than in terms of the pairs themselves (product). Lastly, it is interesting to note the particular 'esoteric' manner in which the pairs are set out in the model answer. This given arrangement of the names seems to bear no relation to the tennis context. However, a child might also set out nine pairs in a more 'realistic' manner thus:

David and Ann	David and Gita	David and Katy
Rashid and Katy	Rashid and Ann	Rashid and Gita
Rob and Gita	Rob and Katy	Rob and Ann

Here, each grouping of three pairs using all six names could engage in a series of mixed doubles, as long as one pair was willing to act as spectators! We have coded children's responses in our interviews as 'esoteric' or 'realistic' respectively on the basis of whether they have set out nine pairs in one or other of these ways. It should be noted that a child who has produced three pairs, but used each of the six names just once, has his or her response coded as 'realistic'. We will now describe children's responses to and performances on this item, beginning with 10–11 year-olds. Since we have already reported the responses of these younger children elsewhere (Cooper and Dunne 1998), we will summarize their case here before moving on to consider the responses of 13–14 year-olds in more detail.

10–11 Year-Olds

The first point we might note is that many 10–11 year-old children do not respond to the tennis item as if the names are merely 'realistic' tokens representing abstract elements of sets of items. Indeed, when asked in interviews to explain why they had chosen particular sets of three pairs, children referred, amongst other things, to the assumed ethnicity or nationality of the children (Cooper and Dunne 1998). One working-class boy, for example, argued against putting Rashid with Gita on the grounds that 'Rashid and Gita sound like different country names, so that it wouldn't exactly be fair if Rashid and Gita got together, because you've got to give them a chance to meet other people'. Other children, on the other hand, thought they should go together for similar reasons. The crucial point here is that, in the sense of Bernstein's (1996) recognition rules for reading the specialized nature of contexts, these children are not 'recognizing' the intentions of the designers of this item 'correctly'. The marking scheme, with its 'esoteric' setting out of nine pairs, makes no reference whatsoever to such issues as the children's origins or methods of choosing pairs; but children, when accounting for their choices, often do. We have argued earlier that responses of three pairs, as well as nine pairs set out in a tennis-friendly manner, can be seen as 'realistic' responses to this item. Bernstein (1996) has argued that children from working-class backgrounds are more likely than children from middle-class backgrounds to misrecognize the intended nature of specialized problem-solving contexts. With his co-workers he has shown, for example, that when children are asked to sort food items into groups, there are modal differences in the ways in which working and middle class children sort items (Holland 1981). Working-class children were found to more often sort these by reference to the ways the items of food appeared together in their everyday life settings or, in our terms, 'realistically'.

We have been able to explore whether comparable social class differences (and analogous sex differences) appear in the case of 'realistically' contextualized maths test items. For this purpose, we have categorized children's social class by reference to the occupations of their fathers and mothers using the 'dominance' approach set out by Erikson and Goldthorpe (see Appendix on page 108). We have collapsed the underlying categories of the social class schema used by these authors into three broad categories: a service class, an intermediate class and a working class. For the tennis item, we have categorized children's initial responses in the interview context as either 'esoteric', 'realistic' or 'other'(a category which typically involves a setting out of the pairs which mixes elements of an 'esoteric' and a 'realistic' approach). The twenty-eight responses of these 120 10–11 year-olds coded as 'realistic' include four cases where children have not produced pairs but, instead, make various points concerning how they would go about choosing pairs if they were actually undertaking the 'real' task. The remaining twenty-four 'realistic' responses comprise eighteen sets of three pairs, one set of six pairs and five sets of nine pairs.

Table 5.1 sets out the relation between a child's initial response and social class, while Table 5.2 shows the relation between initial response and sex. While there is no evidence in Table 5.2 of any overall difference between the sexes in the nature of the initial response on our chosen dimension, Table 5.1 shows considerable differences between children from the three social class groupings. Working-class children are nearly three times as likely as service-class children to produce 'realistic' pairings (including, we should recall, a set of three pairs using each of the six names). A further breakdown of the data, which we will not reproduce here, shows that this pattern of social class differences holds when boys and girls are considered separately. However, the sex differences are not constant across the three social class groups. Within the service class, girls are more likely to be 'realistic' responders than boys (girls: 16.0 per cent, boys: 11.8 per cent). Within the intermediate class this is reversed, with boys being more likely than girls to respond 'realistically' (girls: 23.1 per cent, boys: 29.4 per cent). Similarly, in the working class, boys are more likely to respond to this item 'realistically' (girls: 33.3 per cent, boys: 42.1 per cent).

Table 5.1 *Response strategy on the tennis item (interview) by class (10–11 years)*

	'Esoteric' pairings	*Other (typically mixed)*	*'Realistic' pairings*	*Totals*
Service class	47	4	8	59
Percentage	79.7	6.8	13.6	
Intermediate class	20	2	8	30
Percentage	66.7	6.7	26.7	
Working class	14	5	12	31
Percentage	45.2	16.1	38.7	
Totals	81	11	28	120
Percentage	67.5	9.2	23.3	

Table 5.2   *Response strategy on the tennis item (interview) by sex (10–11 years)*

	'Esoteric' pairings	*Other (typically mixed)*	*'Realistic' pairings*	*Totals*
Girls	34	5	11	50
Percentage	68.0	10.0	22.0	
Boys	47	6	17	70
Percentage	67.1	8.6	24.3	
Totals	81	11	28	120
Percentage	67.5	9.2	23.3	

Table 5.3   *Marks achieved (1 mark available) on the tennis item in the interview context: initial response (10–11 years)*

	Female		*Male*		*Total*	
	Mean	*Count*	*Mean*	*Count*	*Mean*	*Count*
Service class	0.84	25	0.85	34	0.85	59
Intermediate class	0.77	13	0.82	17	0.80	30
Working class	0.75	12	0.63	19	0.68	31
Total	0.80	50	0.79	70	0.79	120

The distribution of marks awarded for children's initial response to this item in the interview are shown in Table 5.3. There is a clear relation between mark and social class for both boys and girls. Part of this relationship can be 'explained' via the greater tendency of working class children than others to produce three pairs, coded by us as 'realistic', and which gains no mark. What we want to briefly consider now, however, is whether the children who produced three pairs were capable of producing the required nine, had they not apparently misrecognized the demands of the item as more 'realistic' than 'esoteric'. In our interviews, when a child had produced three pairs and seemed to have finished his or her response, we asked whether s/he was sure that all the possible pairs had been found. Given this cue, twelve of the eighteen children who had produced three pairs produced another six, to give nine. Here is an example, an intermediate-class girl, who writes the three pairs thus:

Rob and Katy
Rashid and Gita
David and Ann

MD: Done that one?
Sarah: Yeah.
MD: OK, so tell me how you worked that one out.

Sarah: I put those two names and – so I did those two there can and I did those.

MD: David and Ann, Rashid and Gita, OK.

Sarah: Mm.

MD: OK, see where it says there find all the possible ways that girls and boys can be paired, do you think you've found all the possible ways?

Sarah: No.

MD: You could find some more?

Sarah: Yeah.

MD: OK, let me just do that, so I'll know where you stopped for the beginning. [The interviewer adds a mark at this point to indicate the first response (for later coding).] OK, go on then. [Sarah works at the problem, silently. She then adds six pairs to give:]

Rob and Katy	Gita and David	Katy and David
Rashid and Gita	Gita and Rob	Ann and Rob
David and Ann	Katy and Rashid	Ann and Rashid

MD: OK, so have you finished that one now?

Sarah: Mm.

MD: And you think you've got all of them?

Sarah: Yeah.

MD: OK, do you know? – when you first did it you stopped, after three, why did you stop after three?

Sarah: I don't know.

MD: You don't know, but why didn't you continue?

Sarah: I didn't think that you were supposed to.

MD: OK, that's a good reason, but why didn't you think you were supposed to?

    [The interview continues with Sarah being apparently unable or unwilling to give a reason.]

We cannot be sure why Sarah chose three pairs initially. However, we have shown elsewhere that the relation between the choice of a 'realistic' or 'esoteric' approach and class holds for other items and we have also shown that there is a positive correlation between children's choice of either a 'realistic' or 'esoteric' strategy on tennis and on an item concerning a traffic survey (Cooper and Dunne 2000). We believe it is plausible that children like the one quoted above are, at the level of practical consciousness, captured by Bourdieu's concept of a social class linked *habitus*, misrecognizing the actually 'esoteric' demands of test items because of a cultural predisposition to engage 'realistically' with problems (Bourdieu 1986). We have shown elsewhere that it is working-class and intermediate-class children in our sample who are more likely to fall into the group who initially produce three pairs but then produce nine after the cue

(Cooper and Dunne 1998). The result of this can be seen in Table 5.4, which shows marks achieved *after* children had been cued to reconsider their initial response. This table shows a quite different relation between class and success than Table 5.3. Here, social class differences are reduced and sex differences become greater. Overall success is higher. This tennis item seems therefore to have the potential to underestimate children's actually existing understanding of and skills in 'mathematics'. The children concerned are more likely to be from working and intermediate class backgrounds. For 10–11 year-olds, the item seems to be differentially valid by class. Interestingly, however, while both boys and girls from the working and intermediate classes improved their mark after being offered a second chance, it is girls in these two groups whose scores have improved the most between the two tables.

13–14 Year-Olds: Overall Results

We have shown that, for some children, the intended goal of the problem setters as set out in the marking scheme is not immediately perceived and/or chosen as their own. We will return to this issue of the 'obviousness' or otherwise of the goal of the item below, but first we wish to compare the overall nature of the responses of the older children with those of the younger children. Having had three more years of experience of schooling – and of the culture of school maths – are these older children less likely to read the item 'realistically' as indexed by the 'inappropriate' production of three pairs.

Tables 5.5–5.8 are the parallel tables for the older children to Tables 5.1–5.4 for the 10–11 year olds. Table 5.5 shows a markedly higher frequency of 'realistic' responses from the working-class children than others, as did Table 5.1 for the 10–11 year-olds. In absolute terms, however, the percentage of the working-class children[2] responding in this manner has dropped dramatically between Table 5.1 and Table 5.5 (from 38.7 per cent to 17.3 per cent). Turning to sex, Table 5.6 shows twice as many boys as girls responding realistically. The sex difference is much greater here than it had been amongst the younger children (Table 5.2). Considering the social class distribution of responses for boys and girls separately, as we did for the 10–11 year-olds, we have found that the class differences in 'realistic' responding hold for both boys and girls. Within each class taken separately, boys more often respond 'realistically'. No service-class girls respond 'realistically', though two of the nineteen service-class boys do. Here it is boys, who on our coding of responses, are more likely to fall into the trap of responding 'inappropriately'.

Of the fourteen older children who responded 'realistically', ten produced three pairs and four nine pairs. Of the ten children producing three pairs, four then produced nine after being encouraged to consider their response further. Of the remaining six, one produced the 'super-esoteric' response of 18, two produced six pairs, two produced eight pairs, and one stuck at three. Two of the five girls, and three of the five boys, moved from an initial three to a final nine or eighteen pairs. These five children comprised one each from the service and intermediate class, and three from the working class.

Table 5.4   Marks achieved (1 mark available) on the tennis item in the interview context: after cued response (10–11 years)

	Female		Male		Total	
	Mean	Count	Mean	Count	Mean	Count
Service class	0.92	25	0.88	34	0.90	59
Intermediate class	1.00	13	0.94	17	0.97	30
Working class	1.00	12	0.74	19	0.84	31
Total	0.96	50	0.86	70	0.90	120

Table 5.5   Response strategy on the tennis item (interview) by class (13–14 years)

	'Esoteric' pairings	Other (typically mixed)	'Realistic' pairings	Totals
Service class	31	3	2	36
Percentage	86.1	8.3	5.6	
Intermediate class	25	3	3	31
Percentage	80.6	9.7	9.7	
Working class	40	3	9	52
Percentage	76.9	5.8	17.3	
Totals	96	9	14	119
Percentage	80.7	7.6	11.8	

Table 5.6   Response strategy on the tennis item (interview) by sex (13–14 years)

	'Esoteric' pairings	Other (typically mixed)	'Realistic' pairings	Totals
Girls	51	4	5	60
Percentage	85.0	6.7	8.3	
Boys	45	5	9	59
Percentage	76.3	8.5	15.3	
Totals	96	9	14	119
Percentage	80.7	7.6	11.8	

Table 5.7   Marks achieved (1 mark available) on the tennis item in the interview
context: initial response (13–14 years)

	Female		Male		Total	
	Mean	Count	Mean	Count	Mean	Count
Service class	1.00	17	0.95	19	0.97	36
Intermediate class	0.87	15	0.88	16	0.87	31
Working class	0.86	28	0.88	24	0.87	52
Total	0.90	60	0.90	59	0.90	119

Table 5.8   Marks achieved (1 mark available) on tennis item in the interview
context: after cued response (13–14 years)

	Female		Male		Total	
	Mean	Count	Mean	Count	Mean	Count
Service class	1.00	17	1.00	19	1.00	36
Intermediate class	0.87	15	0.94	16	0.90	31
Working class	0.89	28	0.96	24	0.92	52
Total	0.92	60	0.97	59	0.94	119

Summing up, we can see by comparing Tables 5.1 and 5.5 that, amongst the
older children, fewer within each social class group initially read this item 'realistically'. Similarly, a comparison of Tables 5.2 and 5.6 shows that both boys
and girls, taken separately, were less likely initially to respond 'realistically' at
the older age. Children at 13–14 years of age seem to have a better 'feel for the
game' (Bourdieu 1990). Nevertheless, some children apparently remain
unaware of these rules, and a comparison of Tables 5.7 and 5.8 shows that, as
in the case of the younger children, some older children did succeed in
improving their mark when encouraged to reconsider their initial response. For
some older children, as for some younger children, this item seems to have
underestimated their combinatorial capacities.

13–14 Year-Olds: Three Individual Cases

In the remainder of this chapter, we will examine in depth several older children's accounts of their problem solving in order to bring out more clearly
which features of the item, in interaction with what the children bring to the
situation, produce these problems of invalidity. We will look in detail at some
interview transcripts, concentrating on those where children did recover from
their initial 'choice' of three pairs. We will start with Charlie, an intermediate-
class boy, who almost recovered from his initial three pairs, moving on to

obtain nine pairs, but with one repeat, with the result that he produced eight valid pairs. Now, it is the 'obviousness' of this question's demands that seems clear to some children and not to others. For those for whom it isn't 'obvious' that this is a request for 3×3 pairs, an activity of extended sense-making has to be undertaken in collaboration with the interviewer. In the case of Charlie we can follow his thought processes fairly readily. He began, as did a number of children, by being confused by the wording of the question, thinking that he should address the issue of what process might be used to choose pairs (line 5 of transcript). The interviewer helps him remedy this reading of the question (lines 10–16). Charlie then writes down two pairs, to give as his initial response:

Rob and Katy
Rashid and Gita
David and Ann

In answer to the question why he had chosen Rashid and Gita, he produces an explanation which refers to the way the names are placed on the page (lines 23–24). This works for Rashid and Gita who, like Rob and Katy, can be seen as diagonally related. It does not work for the residual pair David and Ann (line 26). So far, what we see is Charlie apparently undertaking something akin to Popper's (1963) conjecturing and refuting, or in other words, a form of scientific reasoning.

When the interviewer invites him to consider whether he has found all the possible pairs (lines 29–33), his response brings out another aspect of the item which those who consider its demands to be 'obvious' might miss. **Rob and Katy** appear in the item in bold print. They are given, and the bold type seems to lend this pairing some special authority, some fixedness. Charlie asks (line 34) 'What, still having Rob and Katy as that one...and these four?' (pointing, one assumes, to the pair in bold type and then to the other four names). The interviewer, who seems not to have considered this 'problem', comes to understand Charlie's perspective and explains that Rob and Katy can be changed around as well. It might not be stretching the data too far to say that Charlie seems not to believe he has the right to disturb Rob and Katy, defined by the authority of the text as a pair in advance of his thinking. Charlie then adds three pairs to his original three to give:

Rob and Katy	David Ann
Rashid and Gita	Rashid katy
David and Ann	Rob Gita

As he verbalizes these, he also asks, 'and some more?', apparently seeking either instruction or permission from the interviewer to proceed further. His second three pairs form a set which could engage in tennis, but he has reused a pair already chosen (David and Ann). When the interviewer suggests that, if Charlie can think of any more, he should add them, he adds four pairs to give:

Rob and Katy	David Ann
Rashid and Gita	Rashid katy
David and Ann	Rob Gita

David and Gita	David and Katy
Rob and Ann	
Rashid and Katy	

It appears that the interviewer did not notice that, alongside the repeated *David and Ann*, there was also a repeated *Rashid and Katy*. It also seems likely that the interviewer, but perhaps not Charlie, was concerned about the production of *different* pairs (line 52). The final eight pairs have been co-constructed by the child and the interviewer. Later in the interview, Charlie was asked to tackle an item whose structure was very similar to that of the tennis item, shown in Figure 5.3, with his response. While we have not coded this item as 'esoteric', it does seem to be one step further away from everyday life than a tennis competition. This may be one reason why Charlie produces the wanted response of twelve pairs straightaway in this case, and in a systematic fashion. It is also the case that the die/pin item does not seem to invite quite as strongly as the tennis item a response in terms of 'method' as opposed to 'pairs'. However, Charlie has also been encouraged, earlier in the interview, to take the required approach in the tennis item, and he may have drawn on this very recent experience in responding to the die/pin item. It is worth discussing this further, in the light of the analysis of similar combinatorial tasks presented to children by Newman et al. (1989).

1	Charlie:	Does this mean like, er, *you* put, you can *choose them by putting*
2		them in a bag, and you can choose them another way, not in a
3		bag, choose them all different ways?
4	BC:	So what would you need to write down then do you think?
5	Charlie:	Oh right, you can like, muddle them up and like put them in a
6		box and you could pick 'em out together or you could like put
7		them on a table and like close your eyes and like pick two.
8	BC:	Ah-ha!
9	Charlie:	Muddle them up and pick two.
10	BC:	Right, OK, well you're saying that because it says find all the
11		possible ways aren't you?
12	Charlie:	Yeah.
13	BC:	You're thinking of ways, but then it says, so it says find all the
14		possible ways that boys and girls can be paired, then it says, write
15		the pairs below. One pair is already shown, Rob and Katy, so I
16		think what it's actually thinking is
17	Charlie:	just in the bag
18	BC:	write the result down, what the pairs would be.
19	Charlie:	Rob and Katy, Rashid and Gita, and Ann and David, I'm not sure.

Figure 5.3   Die/pin item and Charlie's written response

Here is a dice with faces
numbered 1 to 6.

Here is a drawing pin.

The dice can land with any face up.
The drawing pin can land on its **side**, or on its **top**.

The dice and the drawing pin are dropped at the same
time.

List all the possible ways that the **dice** and the **pin**
can land. One pair has been done for you.

> **1 and top**   6 and siDE
> 2 and sioE
> 2 and top
> 1 and siDE
> 3 and tóp
> 3 and SiDE
> 4 and rop
> 4 and sioE
> 5 and top
> 5 and SiDE
> 6 and top

Source: SCAA (1994)

20 *BC:*   Well, write down what you think they'd be, go on.
21 *Charlie:*   [writes]
22 *BC:*   OK, any special reason why you put Rashid and Gita together?
23 *Charlie:*   Because like, er, Rob and Katy are like diagonals going like
24   that, and that's why I done Rashid and Gita,
25 *BC:*   Right, is it…
26 *Charlie:*   but I didn't know about David and Ann.
27 *BC:*   OK, now, you've got three pairs yeah?
28 *Charlie:*   Yeah.

29	BC:	It says find all the possible ways that boys and girls can be paired,
30		write the pairs below. Do you think there are any other pairs you
31		could get, do you think there are any other pairs you could get if
32		I said, write *all* the possible pairs you could get, do you think
33		there are any others?
34	Charlie:	What, still having Rob and Katy as that one…
35	BC:	Well I'm thinking of all the possible…
36	Charlie:	…and these four.
37	BC:	I'm thinking of all the possible pairs you could get, changing
38		them around.
39	Charlie:	What, changing them around using Rob and Katy as well?
40	BC:	Yeah.
41	Charlie:	Oh! right having 'em going across like that to each other.
42	BC:	Well could you write any more, if I call that your first three pairs,
43		can you think of any others, as many as you can.
44	Charlie:	You could get David and Ann, Rashid and Katy, and Rob and
45		Gita – and some more?
46	BC:	If you can think of some more, yeah, you've got six so far.
47	Charlie:	[Charlie writes some further pairs.]
48	BC:	Right, any more you can get? Do you think?
49	Charlie:	Mm-hm…
50	BC:	Umm, what's that one?
51	Charlie:	David and Katy.
52	BC:	Are you sure you haven't got that one already?
53	Charlie:	Yeah, David and Ann, David and Oh, I've done it, I've got David
54		and Ann twice.
55	BC:	Oh I see right, OK, so take, right do you want to take one of the
56		David and Ann's out then, take
57	Charlie:	Just take that one out
58	BC:	I'll just put a little dotted line through one of your David and
59		Anns, so, right.
60	Charlie:	David and Katy, so I can't get any more.
61	BC:	OK

Newman et al. compared children's responses to several tasks. These tasks included one task in which children had to produce, working with the experimenter, all the possible pairs of cards picturing movie stars, and in which the children were 'trained' by the experimenter to answer the question. Here the 'problem' of finding pairs was made explicit to the children. They did not have to discover it for themselves. Then, in a subsequent 'isomorphic' task, children were given four household chemicals and had to explore, in small groups, what happened when pairs of these chemicals were mixed. Here they needed to discover the 'problem', that is, of finding all the possible pairs, for themselves 'as they began to run out of pairs of chemicals to mix' (1989: 33). Newman et al. describe the contrasting situations in these terms:

In the laboratory setting, we expect the task to be presented clearly to the subject. It is part of the experimenter's job. We conduct pilot studies to find out how to do this effectively; we arrange training on the task and choose criterion measures that let us know whether the subject 'understands' the task that we have constructed. These procedures are certainly socially constructed. In everyday situations people are not always presented with clearly stated goals. They often have to figure out what the problem is, what the constraints are, as well as how to solve the problem once they have formulated it. In other words, in everyday situations people are confronted with the 'whole' task. There is no experimenter responsible for doing the presentation part...This broader conception of the whole task is important to our analyses of the transformation of a task when it is embedded in different social settings. When we look for the 'same task' happening outside of the laboratory, we have to look for how the work of specifying and constraining the task is getting done and who is doing it. This kind of analysis provides us with the basis for arguing that the practical methods of maintaining control in the laboratory veil a crucial process: formulating the task and forming the goal.

(Newman et al. 1989: 33–4)

The key point here is that there is no one problem embedded in the text, but rather a whole range of possible problems which might be constructed by children. Earlier we have referred to Bernstein's concept of recognition rules as one way of making sense of children's use or otherwise of 'everyday' knowledge in responding to test items. What these remarks of Newman et al. remind us is that, within the choice of an 'everyday' or 'esoteric' response mode, there are still other issues for the child to confront. In Charlie's case he had to work through, with the interviewer, several possibilities. Was the item about 'methods' of producing pairs? Was he allowed to disrupt the given pair? It seems likely that without the intervention of the interviewer he would not have resolved these issues so as to produce something like the 'right' goal for the problem, and therefore that he would not have produced more than three pairs. He wrote nothing in the pre-interview group test for this item, and probably had not reached it. We can not therefore compare his two responses, aided and unaided. It does, however, seem quite likely that the work done by the interviewer, with Charlie, in trying to construct the 'right' goal for the tennis problem provided the basis for Charlie to construct the 'right' goal for the die/pin item. Taking responses to both items together, it seems that he can undertake the required combinatorial task with some degree of success, but that this would not have become known as a consequence of his attempting the tennis item in an unaided group testing context.

We will look now at a child who recovered from producing three pairs, in this case fully, to produce nine pairs. In the group test, Emma, a working-class girl, had written nothing for this item, but had attempted subsequent questions. In the interview, she initially wrote:

Rob and Katy
Rashid and Gita
David and Ann

She is worried that her three pairs do not constitute a complete answer, but her worry perhaps concerns 'methods' (lines 8–9 of transcript). As she says, the item asks for 'all the possible ways' as well as referring to 'pairs' (lines 15–16). Her subsequent remark, 'I thought it meant write these pairs below, in the bag', is open to a number of plausible interpretations. One is that she has set up pairs to play tennis, and that this is a 'goal' which has been successfully addressed. Another is that she has read the item as asking her to copy the pairs in the bags, though the diagonal placing of Rob and Katy in the bags makes this less likely. However, whatever her interpretation is, when the interviewer tries to explain what the 'goal' of the item is not, and stresses 'all the pairs' (lines 28–34), Emma quickly responds 'there are loads of other names that you could do' (line 35). The following exchanges make it clear that Emma has now formulated a 'goal' which is broader than that intended by the test designers, one in which she can draw on the whole universe of boys' and girls' names (line 47). The interviewer limits the population (lines 48–9). There is laughter, of recognition. Emma checks her understanding (line 50). She then decides a pair starting with a girl's name is not different from the corresponding pair starting with a boy's (lines 58–62). Only then does she proceed to produce her nine pairs, systematically, thus:

Rob and Katy	Rob and Ann
Rashid and Gita	Rob and Gita
David and Ann	

David and Gita
David and Katy
Rashid and Katy
Rashid and Ann

1	*Emma:*	What have we got to do, explain, 'cos I've never done this one,
2		I've done that one and the others, but I think I've skipped this one.
3	*BC:*	What you don't think you did that one at all?
4	*Emma:*	No.
5	*BC:*	So, you've done three pairs, yeah?
6	*Emma:*	Yeah.
7	*BC:*	What are you worried about now, what you have to
8	*Emma:*	Well, what do you have to do, like find out a way how they can
9		be paired up together?
10	*BC:*	Er, well, it says write the pairs below, have you written the pairs
11		below do you think?
12	*Emma:*	Yeah.

13	BC:	Right, so what, I'm not quite sure what you're thinking of, what are
14		you thinking of exactly?
15	Emma:	Well, it says find all the possible ways that boys and girls can be
16		paired.
17	BC:	Yeah, write the pairs below.
18	Emma:	I thought it meant write these pairs below, in the bag.
19	BC:	Ah, well, what I'm going to say to you is that, if I call this your
20		first answer yeah,
21	Emma:	Mm.
22	BC:	Because you think, you've more or less finished there haven't you?
23	Emma:	Mm.
24	BC:	Do you agree, you think?
25	Emma:	Mm.
26	BC:	Er, what it is, you've found three pairs haven't you?
27	Emma:	Mm.
28	BC:	When it says find all the possible ways that girls and boys can be
29		paired, sometimes people think that means what method you
30		could use, you know, put your hand in, blindfold people, swing
31		them about, that sort of thing, what it actually means is find all
32		the possible pairs, and the answer, the question is do you think
33		you've found *all* the pairs you could make out of boys and girls
34		or do you think there are others that you could do?
35	Emma:	There are loads of other names that you could do.
36	BC:	What, other pairs, OK, if you can think of some more, write
37		them down outside my
38	Emma:	What, just names?
39	BC:	Pairs of names, boys and girls pairs, like those.
40	Emma:	Yeah, but they're just two names ain't they?
41	BC:	Give me an example of what you're thinking.
42	Emma:	They're just names, like David and Katy.
43	BC:	Yeah.
44	Emma:	They're just names and Rashid and Gita, they're just names and
45		Robert and Ann.
46	BC:	Yeah, well, they're pairs aren't they of names, yeah? Two together.
47	Emma:	You could go on for ages though, thinking of names.
48	BC:	Well see how, well, you're only allowed to use the names that are
49		here.
50	Emma:	Oh, only the names that are there.
51	BC:	Oh, I see, you were thinking that you could use others.
52	Emma:	Yeah.
53	BC:	OK, [laughter]
54	Emma:	Shall I do, can you use the same ones that I've put here, or
55		different ones from there?
56	BC:	Well, don't use the same pairs, but you can use names again, but
57		you've got to mix them up into new pairs, yeah?

58	*Emma:*	Mm-*hm.* [thinking] Don't need to do it the other way round for
59		the girls do you, 'cos the girls are like already there look?
60	*BC:*	What you mean you don't have to do Ann and Rob, because
61		you've got Rob and Ann already.
62	*Emma:*	Yeah.
63	*BC:*	I agree you don't. OK, and one more question about this one, if I
64		cover those up
65	*Emma:*	Mm.
66	*BC:*	including the pair they had already, how many pairs do you think
67		you've got altogether.
68	*Emma:*	Nine.
69	*BC:*	How do you know?
70	*Emma:*	Because there's six and you've got three to each one, because
71		there's only three girls, so it's nine.
72	*BC:*	OK, now, when you started you did three, that's the right answer,
73		nine, why do you think you only did three and didn't do nine
74		straight away?
75	*Emma:*	Because I didn't understand what they were saying.
76	*BC:*	Right, a lot of people do this, they do three and then when I say,
77		you're sure, they do nine, so it's obviously not a very good question
78		is it, that one
79	*Emma:*	They didn't explain it properly.
80	*BC:*	Oh, which bit do you think was most confusing, do you know?
81	*Emma:*	This bit where they say find all the possible ways that boys and
82		girls can be paired, write the pairs below, one pair is already
83		shown. Rob and Katy, they probably think, Oh, we'll write those
84		two down so that's three are paired, they're paired up with a
85		person, and then write the way, so it can be paired, like pick it
86		out of a bag or something like that,
87	*BC:*	Yeah.
88	*Emma:*	Because they're not explaining it properly, they're just
89	*BC:*	No.
90	*Emma:*	saying that, that can mean anything.
91	*BC:*	Right, OK, that's very helpful, That was 19, number 13.

Finally, she produces an account of why there are nine pairs to be found, and a critique of the item's construction (lines 75–90). As in the case of Charlie, when she arrived at the die/pin item, she had no difficulty in constructing the require 'goal' and answer. She wrote:

1 and top	1 + side
2 + top	2 + side
3 + top	3 + side
4 + top	4 + side
5 + top	5 + side
6 + top	6 + side

Her understanding of what is required here is demonstrated in the discussion:

Emma: Do I have to write 'and' or can I just…?
BC: No leave it out if you like then we might get in a couple more quickly.
Emma: [she writes]
BC: You're using up that last one, 6 and side, OK, how many of those are there all together are there?
[Interviewer has covered responses with his hand.]
Emma: Twelve.
BC: How do you know that?
Emma: Because there's six on the dice and there's six ways you can go with that, so that's twelve.
BC: OK, right, even though it's covered up, you know it's twelve, good. Number 17.

We will look briefly at one last child from amongst those who recovered from three pairs to produce nine. Mike, a working-class boy, did write something for the tennis item in the group test:

Rob and Katy
David and Gita
Rashid and Ann

He received, of course, no mark. In the interview, he initially wrote the same three pairs, with one reversed:

Rob and Katy
Gita and David
Rashid and Ann

In this case, almost immediately the interviewer began to probe, Mike recognized what the required 'goal' of the problem was (line 6), and produced a further six different pairs (not shown here). There is a suggestion later in the interview that he found three pairs an appropriate response for the incorrect 'goal' he had formulated (lines 16–20).

1 *MD:*   Finished?
2 *Mike:* Yeah.
3 *MD:*   OK so how did you work that out?
4 *Mike:* Easy I just looked at that and just paired them up.
5 *MD:*   See it says here it says find all the possible.
6 *Mike:* Oh all the possible, oh yeah.
7 *MD:*   OK let's do that and you carry on. [child works]
8 *Mike:* That's another one.
9 *MD:*   Is that all of them? [He now has nine different pairs.]
10 *Mike:* Done it.

11	*MD:*	OK so how did you do that then?
12	*Mike:*	It's just don't know really, I just looked at that and just paired
13		them up in different places.
14	*MD:*	And was that easy or?
15	*Mike:*	Yeah easy.
16	*MD:*	So if it was like a real competition, how do you think they would
17		have done it?
18	*Mike:*	They would have just…
19	*MD:*	What like you did in the first place?
20	*Mike:*	Yeah.
21	*MD:*	Yeah so they would have stopped there, have you seen competitions
22		done like that before? No, you don't. OK, that's nineteen good,
23		thirteen now.

Conclusion

In this paper we have discussed children's responses to a 'realistic' maths test item. We have shown that, at both 10–11 and 13–14 years of age, a considerable minority of children experience difficulty in reading the intentions of the test designers in a way which enables them to show their 'mathematical' skills and understanding in its best light. These children, at both ages, are more likely to be from intermediate and working-class backgrounds than from the service class. However, the older children are less likely than the younger children to misread the demands of the item, suggesting that between the ages of 10–11 and 13–14, children do succeed in gaining a better understanding of the peculiar 'rules of the game' which characterize much of school maths. Of course, we must be aware of the danger of overgeneralizing from this case – though much can be learned from it. However, elsewhere, in an analysis of performance on more than one hundred National Curriculum maths items, we have shown more generally that there are greater social class differences at age 10–11 in children's performance on 'realistic' items than on 'esoteric' items (Cooper and Dunne 2000). It is of course likely that some part of this difference is due to problems in the design of 'realistic' items. No doubt some of the ambiguity of meaning children experienced in the wording of the tennis item could be removed. Notwithstanding such remedial action, there will nevertheless remain an underlying problem for children to tackle before they can attend to the 'mathematical' operation embedded in the noise of the everyday context. Should they or should they not import 'everyday' considerations? Does the appearance of children's names, in the context of tennis, imply that these are not merely tokens to be arranged as elements of abstract sets? Test designers need to give further careful thought to just what it is that they are testing. An examination of recent test papers suggests that it seems to have been decided, for the moment at least, that the testing of maths in the English National Curriculum will be via the use of mainly 'realistic' items. Given the interpretative problems that these items can produce – especially for children from intermediate and working-class social class backgrounds – we would urge that further thought be given to their unintended consequences for both the validity and the fairness of the assessment of what children know and, in some contexts at least, can do.

Appendix: Social Class Groups

(Combined from Goldthorpe and Heath (1992) and Erikson and Goldthorpe (1993).)

1. service class, higher grade: higher grade professionals, administrators and officials; managers in large industrial establishments; large proprietors
2. service class, lower grade: lower grade professionals, administrators and officials; higher grade technicians; managers in small industrial establishments; supervisors of non-manual employees
3. routine non-manual employees
4. personal service workers
5. small proprietors with employees
6. small proprietors without employees
7. farmers and smallholders
8. foremen and technicians
9. skilled manual workers
10. semi- and unskilled manual workers
11. agricultural workers

We have collapsed 1 and 2 into a service class, 3–8 into an intermediate class, and 9–11 into a working class.

Notes

1. Funded by the ESRC via grants R000235863 and R000222315.
2. It should be noted that these younger and older children are not matched samples. In particular, the older children have lower mean 'ability' scores.

References

Bernstein, B. (1996) *Pedagogy, Symbolic Control and Identity: Theory, Research, Critique*, London: Taylor & Francis.

Boaler, J. (1994) 'When do Girls Prefer Football to Fashion? An Analysis of Female Underachievement in Relation to "Realistic" Mathematics Contexts', *British Educational Research Journal* 20(5): 551–64.

Bourdieu, P. (1974) 'The School as a Conservative Force', in J. Eggleston (ed.), *Contemporary Research in the Sociology of Education*, London: Methuen, 32–46.

—— (1986) *Distinction: A Social Critique of the Judgement of Taste*, London: RKP.

—— (1990) *The Logic of Practice*, Oxford: Blackwell.

Bowles, S. and Gintis, H. (1976) *Schooling In Capitalist America*, London: Routledge and Kegan Paul.

Cooper, B. (1985) *Renegotiating Secondary School Mathematics: A Study of Curriculum Change and Stability*, Basingstoke: Falmer Press.

—— (1992) 'Testing National Curriculum Mathematics: Some Critical Comments on the Treatment of "Real" Contexts for Mathematics', *The Curriculum Journal* 3(3): 231–43.

—— (1994) 'Authentic Testing in Mathematics? The Boundary Between Everyday and Mathematical Knowledge in National Curriculum Testing in English Schools', *Assessment in Education: Principles, Policy and Practice* 1(2): 143–66.

—— (1998a) 'Assessing National Curriculum Mathematics in England: Exploring Children's Interpretation of Key Stage 2 tests in Clinical Interviews', *Educational Studies in Mathematics* 35(1): 19–49.

—— (1998b) 'Using Bernstein and Bourdieu to Understand Children's Difficulties with "Realistic" Mathematics Testing: An Exploratory Study', *International Journal of Qualitative Studies in Education* 11(4): 511–32.

Cooper, B. and Dunne, M. (1998) 'Anyone For Tennis? Social Class Differences in Children's Responses to National Curriculum Mathematics Testing', *The Sociological Review* 46(1): 115–48.

—— (2000) *Assessing Children's Mathematical Knowledge: Social Class, Sex and Problem-Solving*, Buckingham: Open University Press.

Dunne, M. (1994) 'The Construction of Ability: A Critical Examination of Teachers' Accounts', D.Phil. thesis, University of Birmingham.

Erikson, R. and Goldthorpe, J.H. (1993) *The Constant Flux: A Study of Class Mobility in Industrial Societies*, Oxford: Clarendon.

Goldthorpe, J. and Heath, A. (1992) 'Revised Class Schema 1992', Working Paper 13, Nuffield College, Oxford.

Holland, J. (1981) 'Social Class and Changes in Orientation to Meaning', *Sociology* 15(1): 1–18.

Lave, J. (1988) *Cognition in Practice: Mind, Mathematics and Culture in Everyday Life*, Cambridge: Cambridge University Press.

Mehan, H. (1973) 'Assessing Children's School Performance, in H.P. Dreitzel (ed.), *Childhood and Socialisation*, London: Collier-Macmillan, 240–64.

Newman, D., Griffin, P. and Cole, M. (1989) *The Construction Zone*, Cambridge: Cambridge University Press.

Nunes, T., Schliemann, A.D. and Carraher, D.W. (1993) *Street Mathematics and School Mathematics*, Cambridge: Cambridge University Press.

Popper, K. (1963) *Conjectures and Refutations*, London: Routledge and Kegan Paul.

Säljö, R. (1991) 'Learning and Mediation: Fitting Reality into a Table', *Learning and Instruction* 1: 261–72.

Schools Curriculum And Assessment Authority (1994) *Mathematics Test, Key Stage 2*, London: Dept. for Education and Employment.

—— (1996) *Key Stage 2 Tests 1996*, London: Dept. for Education and Employment.

Schools Examinations And Assessment Council (1993) *Pilot Standard Tests: Key Stage 2: Mathematics*, SEAC/University Of Leeds.

6 Questioning the Three Bears

The Social Construction of Classroom Assessment

John Pryor and Harry Torrance

Introduction: The Social Setting of Classroom Assessment

Over recent years, teachers have been encouraged to improve their classroom assessment skills, especially in England and Wales with the introduction of a formal role for teacher assessment at all stages of National Curriculum Assessment. A particular focus has been placed on the formative role that classroom assessment can play in learning, with teacher questioning and teacher observation of pupils during classroom work emphasized as key elements of good quality teaching and assessing (for example, Alexander et al. 1992; SCAA 1997).

While agreeing that the formative impact of classroom assessment can be significant, we would argue that the process of classroom assessment is by no means as transparent and unproblematic as such claims suggest. Classroom assessment, like other educational encounters, is socially situated and constructed. Teachers are responsible for setting up classroom tasks and eliciting responses from pupils, but these responses are often very ambiguous and hard to interpret. Similarly pupils often have great difficulty in understanding the teacher's agenda and struggle to make sense of what is being asked of them. Claims for formative classroom assessment often assume that teachers can easily recognize and interpret pupil responses, treating them as unproblematic sources of information for pedagogic decision making, but a good deal of research suggests that this is not the case, especially with respect to younger children. Studies have investigated how and why young children make apparently simple 'errors' when questioned, with context and language emerging as particularly important in children's perceptions of the task; it is not necessarily that they didn't 'know the answer', or could not 'answer the question'; rather, they thought they were being asked something else, or had to answer the *implicit* question deriving from the context of questioning, rather than the explicit question and so forth (for example, Donaldson 1978; Beveridge 1982).

Moreover the very activities of classroom assessment can mediate and impact on understanding of classroom processes and subject learning. Teachers' questions and pupils' responses carry meaning about the structure of classroom interaction as well as its content and a number of studies have demonstrated the role that teacher questioning plays in establishing and continually confirming teachers' control of the classroom and in constructing and sequencing the very definition of a 'lesson' (Edwards and Furlong 1978; Edwards and Mercer 1987; Mehan 1979). Thus teachers' questions achieve many purposes and are as much to do with managing the lesson and making it happen as social interaction, as with eliciting particular information from particular pupils at particular times.

So, classroom assessment does not take place in a social vacuum, but is an integral part of what constitutes classroom life. This carries consequences for the validity and reliability of teacher judgements, as well as the developing understandings of pupils. Judgements and understandings are constituted and achieved through interaction and are necessarily a product of the social relations of the participants. The data we present here illustrate these points, but also attempt to go beyond them to explain why one pupil featured seems to get a raw deal – the process of the interaction itself seems to construct his apparent failure. This chapter focuses on the way that teacher–pupil interaction in the context of assessment generates learners' knowledge and classroom identities in the here-and-now. Our concern is less that teachers may draw the wrong conclusions about what pupils know, understand and can do (though the data certainly demonstrate that this is an issue) and more about how classroom assessment can impact on pupils' understanding of schooling and their place within it. In particular, we are interested in the way in which assessment interactions are of crucial importance in establishing the discursive practices which condition not only cognitive inferences about what is an acceptable answer to teachers questions, but also about much wider issues such as pupils' identity in relation to the culture of their class, their school and wider society. Moreover these issues are inextricably bound up with each other. Assessment is not simply a technical activity which can be accomplished without impacting on pupils' perceptions of themselves and their surroundings. The process of assessment carries consequences for its outcomes, both intended and unintended. Thus the chapter argues that classroom assessment itself constitutes a context of learning which in turn both produces and is produced by the understandings that pupils bring to their schooling and the transformations that thereby occur.

The data presented below demonstrate the many different purposes that teacher questioning serves, particularly with respect to managing classroom interaction. Furthermore the teacher's agenda, which seems to meander but becomes more apparent as the interaction unfolds, is by no means explicit at the beginning, and this carries consequences for pupil understanding of the encounter. Thus there is considerable evidence of the pupils misunderstanding the teacher's intentions and of the teacher misunderstanding the pupils' responses, both with respect to the overall purpose of the task and the assessment opportunities embedded within it (is the focus language, maths, or an opportunistic combination of the two?). There are also many examples of the confusing use of language in the teacher's questioning. Finally, there is evidence that one of the pupils (Simon) is wrongly assessed as being unable to count, recognize numbers or estimate, because his anxiety about his place in the 'pecking order' of the group prompts him constantly to bid for attention, irrespective of whether his intervention is appropriate. We return to all these points in our analysis of the data after the transcript.

The Data

The data are presented in two parallel columns. The left-hand column contains a transcription of dialogue derived from both audio and video recording. In italics is the account we constructed of the nonverbal interaction, the 'stage directions'. Pseudonyms are used throughout. In the right-hand column is a commentary constituting our own 'first interpretation' of the action. Further analysis and discussion then follows the transcript. (For discussion of the project from which the data derive see Torrance and Pryor 1996, 1998.[1])

The transcription is of part of a lesson in the reception class of an English primary school. The teacher is working with a 'focus group' comprising three boys: Jimmy, Simon and Seb. The rest of the class is occupied with activities supervised by a nursery nurse. The teacher is attempting to assess early language and maths through the retelling of the story of 'The Three Bears'. The teacher sits at one corner of a square table. Seb is next to her, while directly opposite are Simon and Jimmy. Three teddy bears are in front of the teacher leaning against the wall. The one nearest her, wearing a blue teeshirt, is noticeably larger than the other two, though it has bendable legs and in a sitting position would not necessarily look taller. The difference in size between the other two is confused by the fact that they have fixed legs with the middle bear being designed to stand up and the furthest bear to sit down. Thus the bears might appear to be different sizes to a competent adult familiar with the story of 'The Three Bears', but the actual difference between them is open to interpretation. The three boys each have a large sheet of paper in front of them on the table.

T places three large cardboard tiles with numbers on them behind the teddy bears ...

T   right – now then – we're going to make our own story – you're going to help me to make a book – about bears – and I've got a very famous story here – and there's a <u>clue</u> –

> T initially defines the activity of making a 'story' and a 'book' about bears.

T holds up a book and rearranges three teddies on the table. Jimmy looks across room. Only Seb looks at the bears.

> A clue to what? Holding up the book and rearranging the bears is presumably meant to draw attention to these objects. But what might the word clue signify for these 4–5 year olds?

T   what story do you think this is about...

Simon is making marks on his paper.

T   Simon – would you like to look at the bears –

> This utterance appears to be designed to bring Simon back on task: it is an instruction, not a question.

T opens book as she addresses him.

T   do you know a story =

Simon   >= no<

Jimmy   > yeah (**)<

T	about that number of bears what number what number's that –

T holds up large tile with figure 1 on it.

Cs	one
T	now you have the one

Hands tile to Jimmy revealing the number two.

T	and would you put your pencils down for a minute because we're going to play a game...what number's >that one<
Simon	>umm<

T looks at Seb and puts her finger to her mouth when Simon says 'umm'.

T	do you (*know what that is)
Simon	um – three
T	it's a three you think –

T looks back at Seb.

T	what number do you think it is Seb
Seb	um – two
T	two –

T looks back at Simon.

T	it's a two –

T looks back at Seb.

T	so you have the two

T gives number two tile to Seb; number three tile is revealed. T closes Three Bears Book and places it behind her. T turns to face Simon directly across the table.

T	what number's that one Simon
Simon	err – (*four)
T	it's **a** – <u>three</u>
Simon	three =
T	that one's a three

T hands tile to Simon.

Jimmy	you don't know all your numbers
T	sorry – Jimmy – could you say that again – I didn't <u>quite</u> hear

T grasps the tile while still talking about the bears (three of them) but without a pause starts to ask a question about the number on the tile. 'That' is used to stand both for the quantity three and immediately afterwards for the symbol for one. The question seems to be addressed to the group in general rather than Simon in particular.

There is no acknowledgement of the children's correct answer; 'would you put your pencils down', again, is an instruction, not a question, aimed at reasserting teacher control. The pencils seem to be distracting the children from the task in hand. The declared purpose of this task is to encourage emergent writing – 'to make our own story' – but it has quickly developed into a maths lesson. This shift is further emphasized by the use of the word 'game'. What expectations might this arouse in the children?

An answer is clearly expected and Simon gives one. It is not correct; has he been influenced by the original enquiry about the bears; would he expect to be shown the number three? Does he think the question refers to the bears?

T is correcting Simon's mistake, presumably assuming that he cannot recognize the numbers two and three.

This appears to be some sort of symbolic closure. The lesson is no longer a language activity – the book has been replaced by the number tiles.

T uses the word 'one' in her question while holding up the symbol for three; and, although the recording is unclear, T seems certain that Simon has said a wrong number.

The confusion of one and three is compounded.

Two errors are generalized to 'all your numbers' (note personalizing possessive).

Either T really did not hear or this is another question where locutionary force is different from

Jimmy   he dun't know about (*all
        of) his numbers

T   he doesn't know about all
        the numbers – well we can
        help him   can't we if we
        play a game –

*T drops her gaze from Jimmy, and
turns to pick up largest bear.*

T   <u>now</u> – who would like – the
        big bear

*All three Cs raise hands. Simon is
fractionally quicker than the others.*

Cs   ME

T   who could he be

T looks at Seb.

Simon   > ME <

T   > in our story <

Simon   errr

*T glances at Simon then looks
directly at Jimmy who still has his
hand in the air. Simon picks up his tile
(Number 3) from table, hits his head
with it several times and then hides
his face behind it.*

Jimmy   ME

T   you can have him

T hands big bear to Jimmy.

C   big bear

T   right – OK –

T picks up next bear.

T   who's going to have the
        ><u>middle-sized</u>< bear

*Simon immediately raises his hand. T
glances at Simon and then looks at
Seb.*

Simon   > ME < ME

Seb   > ME< ME

T   right – give him to you

*T hands second bear to Seb…Simon
continues to hit his head with tile. T
reaches for last bear.*

T   right then

T looks directly at Simon and smiles.

T   who's going to have >this
        one < then

Simon   > ME <

ostensible purpose, possibly an example of T
attempting to protect Simon from a harsh peer
assessment.

T accepts the generalized observation as correct and
engages the group to 'help' Simon. This could be seen
as a sympathetic gesture in the context of providing
scaffolding for Simon, but does he think he is now the
recipient of the group's pedagogical condescension?

'Who would like the big bear' seems closer to a
genuine question, and all the children bid, but T's
subsequent actions suggest that she has already
decided to allocate the bears according to the
numbers as distributed. Use of 'he' genders the
biggest bear (also it has a blue tee-shirt – the other
bears have no clothing).

Whose story? The emergent writing lesson or the
Three Bears in the book?

Simon seems frustrated by T's lack of recognition of
his response to her question.

Jimmy already has the tile with the number 1 on it.
It is unclear whether 'big bear' is said by Simon or
Jimmy.

The lesson has taken another turn towards establishing relative sizes as well as recognizing symbols.
Jimmy is not bidding for this bear, either because he
assumes that there will be one bear or, because
having the 'big bear', he has no interest in the
smaller ones. 'Give him to you' indicates that at this
stage 'the middle-sized bear' is male.

Simon is ignored again. The second bear has been
handed to the boy who has the number two tile.
Linking numbers with size now seems to be the
focus of the activity, but Simon wouldn't necessarily
appreciate this, and certainly the 'game' doesn't
seem to be about helping Simon to learn 'his
numbers'.

Neither Seb nor Jimmy bid for the last bear. The
answer to T's question is interpreted procedurally,

Simon holds tile aloft with both hands.
The number is facing away from T.
Neither of the other two children has
their hands up.

T   right

T hands last bear to Simon who rec-
eives it with his left hand whilst still
holding his tile up in his right hand.

Simon   you ain't got any

T   I haven't got any –

T opens her hands showing that they
are empty. Simon places bear on table
and continues to hit his head with tile.

T   I haven't got any – now I'm
            going to read you a little bit
            > out of this book <

Simon   > (**draw) a teddy <

As T speaks she moves some pencils
to one side, picks up Three Bears book,
opens it and shows it to the group.

T   it's a very good story

Simon puts tile down and picks up his
bear. T turns over pages.

T   because it's got pictures to
            help (*us) here look – can
            you see…right who's going
            to help me with this story –
            if I point > to the picture <

Simon   > ME < > ME<

Seb   > ME <

T looks at Seb.

Seb   > me me me <

Simon   > ME <

T   ·> see if you can tell me <

T looks at Seb while she says this;
Jimmy raises hand.

Jimmy   > ME <

Simon   > MEEEE <

T   >once upon a < time there
            were ~

T looks at Jimmy.

Jimmy   three bears

Simon   three bears

T   well done – a big father –

Simon   father

Simon does not have a bear, so this last one must be his. The children now appear to understand the classroom management code, though it is a moot point what they are learning about mathematics (and/or emergent writing) or what the teacher is learning about their capabilities. This bear has the identity of the smallest bear and has been positioned as the last, smallest, and therefore least desirable bear. Nevertheless Simon does bid for it and has a reward of sorts insofar as this intervention is recognized as legitimate. He then initiates a sequence, most unusual in classroom settings, observing correctly that T now has no bears. Does he interpret the object of this 'game' as the acquisition of bears and/or observation of who no longer has them? Either way, he certainly recognizes what no bears looks like.

T picks up book again; closure on the maths, reopening of the language activity. Simon bids for an art lesson!

Simon's bid is ignored: the pencils are moved out of reach.

Interestingly, this action suggests that Simon may also be making a symbolic switch from maths to language.

The book is designed to be shared by an adult and a non-reading child; some words are left out and substituted by pictures.

T appears to be asking Simon but then focuses on Seb.

T's questions follow in quick succession and seem to be designed to keep the group on task rather than to elicit direct answers. Moreover the competitive nature of the interaction is reinforced by the children's response, which T does nothing to diminish. Competition for her favour focuses the children's attention on the task in hand and keeps her firmly in control, as does the classic cueing utterance 'once upon a time there were…'. Finally she settles her attention on Jimmy (again) and cues his response, though Simon tries to usurp him.

'Big' and 'father' are associated, a literary, rather than a mathematical, association.

T – what do you think that picture could be

T holds book up in her left hand pointing with right.

Simon umm =

T = what word

Simon a bear

> T points at a picture of a bear and then associates the picture with a word by specifically asking 'what word?'

T bear – well done – who's got the biggest bear here =

T points first at Jimmy, then at Seb, then back at Jimmy when he speaks.

> Praise of Simon is immediately followed by repetition of the association between the children and the size of the bears which might be interpreted by Simon as diminishing his achievement; he can guess/read 'bear' but he doesn't have the biggest bear.

Jimmy = ME

Simon ME

Both Jimmy and Simon hold their bears above their heads. Seb raises his hand and brings it immediately down to bang his elbow several times against his bear's stomach.

> Simon makes the claim even though his bear has been designated as smallest.

> Seb is outbid by Jimmy and Simon. He covers his unsuccessful bid by pretending to be doing something else, i.e., assaulting his bear.

T well is he fa\ – is that one as big as that one –

T points at Simon's bear then at Jimmy's bear. Simon brings his bear down to the table and puts it alongside Jimmy's bear.

> T uses a masculine pronoun and just seems to stop herself from again naming the biggest bear as 'Father Bear', apparently returning the task to a mathematical one. Simon seems to interpret it as an invitation to make a physical comparison.

Jimmy umm – the big – I'm daddy

T you're daddy bear – OK so you're =

Simon = I'm bigger than him

> Jimmy's statement is very hesitant; he seems uncertain about comparative sizes, but has picked up T's cue and takes on the identity of 'daddy' from his bear.

Simon raises his bear in the air and takes it back to his side of table.

T so Jimmy's the daddy bear right –

T turns back to book, pointing to a picture as before.

> Jimmy's designation is accepted and causes a return to the story. Mathematical comparison is not pursued.

T a <u>middle-sized</u> mother ~

Simon bear =

> The 'middle-sized' bear has now been gendered.

T glances across table towards Simon and Jimmy but immediately turns to Seb.

T = which word could that be

Seb holds up his bear.

> Seb has the middle-sized bear so although it is Simon who completes the sentence, T does not respond to him, but invites involvement from Seb.

Seb (*) mother bear

T mother bear – good – so who's got the middle-sized teddy here

Simon   me

T   do you think so shall we put them all together and measure them – lay them on the table in the middle – let's measure them

Seb places his bear in middle of table.

Simon   let's – I'm bigger than his

Simon places his bear in middle of table and T pushes Seb's bear so they are directly alongside each other.

T   is that one bigger

Jimmy picks up his bear.

Simon   (* need) to change over

T   what would you – which one would you like then

Simon   um – I – um (**) to change over

T   what would you like to > change it<

Simon   > (**) <

T   change over =

Simon grabs at the 'big' bear but cannot move it as Jimmy has both hands on it.

Jimmy   = (*I'm having) that one

T   so you're daddy – right – which one would you like to be then Simon

Simon   > (**) <

T   > which one do you think < this one is then

T puts her finger on 'small' bear. Simon picks up the middle bear.

Simon   I'd um the baby one

T   baby one, so what one must this one be

Simon   (**) mummy one

T   it must be mummy one – right

Simon   I'll have THAT one<

Simon grabs with his right hand at the 'big' bear which Jimmy is still holding.

Jimmy   no you won't…[ ]…

Simon is determined to be noticed by T. He seems to wish to avoid the 'social stigma' of having the smallest bear. (N.B. also that 'size' of the bears was a social construction or at least open to some interpretation.) Whether or not Simon can estimate accurately is unclear, but T seems to think this is the problem.

Seb's movement is desultory and suggests boredom with this activity.

Simon seems to appreciate that he has the smallest bear. The problem is not that he doesn't recognize this, but that he does not want it. He invokes the criterion of fairness to suggest that the bears are swapped round. T is prepared to pursue this agenda possibly in order to assess whether Simon can make a judgement about size.

Jimmy retains ownership of the 'big bear'. T drops the possibility of pursuing the three way comparison and reduces it to two. She confirms that Jimmy is 'daddy'; without unambiguously ascertaining that Simon (or indeed Jimmy) understands the size comparison; however she still seems to be leaving the possibility of Simon having the middle-sized bear.

Simon again seems to be resisting the stigma of association with the smallest bear, which has been compounded by T's question about which one he would 'like to be'. He identifies the small bear which T is touching as the 'baby', not an identity he is likely to aspire to, and picks up the middle-sized bear.

T accepts correspondence of baby one and mummy one with small and middle-sized bear. This vocabulary derives from the picture book, it is still unclear whether any of the boys can use the mathematical vocabulary correctly.

Jimmy defends his bear from physical capture.

In the above sequence, Jimmy is privileged by being handed the 'number 1' tile, and later the 'big bear', which the teacher obviously had in mind all along to associate with the 'number 1' tile. Her intention is unlikely to have been apparent to the pupils. Later, Jimmy's identification of himself as 'daddy bear' allows him to be interpreted as answering a question about relative size correctly, even though he actually doesn't do this explicitly; he claims to be 'daddy', he does not say that the bear he has is the biggest. Seb appears content to acquiesce to the schooled conventions of the interaction without really engaging with the task, while Simon is continually frustrated in his attempts to intervene and receive the teacher's attention. For whatever reason, he has been given the 'number 3' tile and relegated to being third out of three in the group's social dynamics. We shall return to this issue below. In the meantime the interaction continues, and a few moments later the teacher ostensibly moves the agenda on to counting bears. However in doing so she conflates cardinal and ordinal numbers:

T	right now – who can give me some numbers to help me count how many bears	The focus returns to mathematics.
Simon	>ME-ME<	
Jimmy	>ME-ME<	The children again compete for primacy in holding T's attention, with Jimmy and Simon the most competitive.
Seb	>(*me-me)...	
T	– right – <u>number one</u> please – could someone...would you give me number one bear please – give the number one	T cues the desired response by directing her gaze at Jimmy.

T looks at Jimmy whilst saying this. Jimmy throws 'big' bear across the table to her. T picks the bear up placing it in sitting position.

T	thank you – have you got a number one

...T continues to look at Jimmy. Simon picks up 'middle-sized' bear holding it on the table with his left hand, while his right hand hits his head with his number tile.

T	have you got a number one anywhere you can give me to sit the bear on	T mentions the tile with number one on it not as a physical object. She simply asks for 'a number one' while looking directly at Jimmy.

T bounces 'big' bear up and down twice on table. The 'small' bear is now between her arms. Jimmy picks up the tile and hands the tile over to T, who

places it under the 'big' bear. The
bear is resting against the wall on the
corner of table closest to T, in a
sitting position facing outwards
towards the three children.

T   so that's <u>one bear</u> – right –
who's got a number two

*T says this whilst still adjusting big
bear.*

Simon   > me <

Seb   > me <

*Simon stops hitting himself briefly to
hold up his number tile. Seb picks up
his tile. T looks at Seb's tile, glances
briefly up at Simon then back at
Seb's tile.*

T   number two there

*T takes the number 2 tile from Seb,
putting the 'small' bear down in front
of him. She looks at Seb.*

T   where are you going to put
your teddy then – bear

Seb   this

*Seb passes 'small' bear over towards
number 2 tile. T places it on the tile.*

T   does he go there – is he the
next one down

Seb   (*)

*Seb shakes his head. T is still
adjusting the position of the bear.*

T   right Simon – have you got
another number – what
have you got

*T looks directly at Simon and moves
basket on the table further away from
her. There is now space to place the
third tile next to the other two. Simon
stops hitting his head with the tile and
holds it upright so it is facing T.*

Simon   err – (*whole three)

T   good boy you remembered
that time…

'One bear' or the 'number one bear'?

Simon makes another bid for involvement.
He now has the middle-sized bear but it is
unclear whether he knows that he does not
have a 2 on his tile.

Seb who originally had the middle-sized bear
has now been allotted the small bear.

By appropriating the middle-sized bear,
Simon seems to have positioned himself to be
next in turn for T's attention but once again is
thwarted. T continues to engage Seb to establish that the smallest bear does not go with
the number 2 tile.

Four mathematical issues now seem to be in
play – cardinal numbers, ordinal numbers, relative sizes and arrangement by size. They appear
to come to the fore as a result of whatever
linguistic formulation is being employed.

Seb indicates that he knows that according to
the designations already accepted this bear is
not 'the next one down', that is, the taken-for-
granted agenda is arrangement by size.

T indicates doubts about Simon's mathematical capability while praising his correct
answer ('you remembered that time'), once
again diminishing his achievement.

Much later Simon indicates his capacity to count by observing and commenting on how few children remain in the classroom:

The door squeaks – Seb, Jimmy and T look around.

Simon (*) how many've we got there – one two three four five – that's all

Simon turns around and looks at the rest of the classroom. He points to each person in the classroom in turn.

Someone has left the room. Simon notices there are only five people in the classroom (the fifth is the researcher). In a 'naturalistic' context he has demonstrated his knowledge and understanding of number up to five. Moreover he has a notion of that being a relatively small number in the context of the whole class ('that's all').

T there's lots isn't there right – so you've done your bit of writing teddy bear and he eats honey and he puts it behind his back – right Simon – would you do me a picture –

T responds to Simon's comment in desultory fashion. She is more focussed now on the writing of the story.

The lesson continues.

Classroom Assessment is Situated Within Routine Classroom Interaction

In addition to observing this and many other incidents, we also interviewed the teacher about the activity and her response to the video tape-recording. She said she was being opportunistic, trying to assess as much as possible in order to plan future activities:

> I always like to assess as much as I possibly can…social skills to science to the whole lot…[this was]…a quick assessment of what they knew…very, very rough assessment in various different things.

She claimed the assessment had been successful since she was able to make many notes afterwards about the children's attainment. However, what is an opportunistic use of a holistic activity for an adult may be very perplexing for young children. Far from providing them with a flexible and responsive context in which to demonstrate what they know, understand and can do, it may well confuse and constrain them, actively contributing to the social construction of their failure. And, as we shall discuss below, such processes of social construction may well enhance the contributions of some pupils over others.

Both the tiles and the bears were brought to the table by the teacher, so it appears that mathematics was planned as the 'core' of the assessment; yet the idea of making a story is introduced immediately, although not systematically pursued. Moreover, the teacher states that *'we're* going to make our own story' – positioning the enterprise as collaborative, with the children involved in producing rather than reproducing a story. However, by then saying that the children are going to help her make a book, they are immediately repositioned as subordinate to her and are then moved even further back from the act of production by the mention of the 'very famous story' whose title they are to guess. The position is complicated still further by the statement that they are 'going to play a game'. This proliferation of tasks seems to be designed to capture the children's interest and contextualize the activity as something both familiar and attractive, stories and games being part of their pre-school experience. Although both understandable and recognizable as an everyday strategy in many infant classrooms, it certainly complicates the assessment process (see also Walkerdine 1988).

The mathematics alone is very complex, partly as a result of the teacher's lack of differentiation between the different meanings of 'one'. It is used as an ordinal (the first bear), a cardinal (a single bear), and a pronoun. The second sense seems to have been the major focus of the teacher's attention since (in interview later she stated that) she wanted to know 'if they actually, any of them, knew their numbers one to four'. Thus the purpose of the activity is stated as assessment. However, as we argued above and demonstrate below, this cognitive agenda is necessarily situated within, and in many respects overtaken by, the social agendas of both teacher and pupils, where issues of cultural acuity and gender come to the fore.

Assessing Simon

The transcript demonstrates the multifaceted nature of teacher questioning, the struggle of the pupils to comprehend both the nature of the task and the specific cognitive demands of each question, and the social construction and accomplishment of assessment judgements. More particularly, Simon seems to suffer from the gendered competition for attention which the activity promotes. Within the interaction, the teacher appears to interpret his utterances as evidence of lack of understanding, a view she later confirmed:

> Simon hadn't got a clue. He hadn't got a clue what numbers were or letters...Simon was absolutely zilch...

But can we be so sure? Simon recognizes when the teacher has no bears and counts up to five when he notices that the rest of the class have left the classroom. However, these observations were not part of the teacher's 'official' assessment agenda and therefore did not attract her attention. Of course, we have the benefit of hindsight and detailed analysis of the transcript. Our point is not to criticize the teacher, but to highlight the sociologically implicated nature of both the teacher's judgement and the pupil's accomplishments. More particularly, and for whatever reason, Simon received the smallest bear, and his subsequent engagement with the assessment process seems to have been completely coloured by this. Three distinct but overlapping issues are in play here. First, the teacher's agenda emerged as one of engaging each child in turn, according to the size of the bear that they received. Simon received the smallest bear and hence each time had to wait his turn until last. He was not prepared to do this; possibly because he genuinely did not appreciate the differing size of the bears, or understand counting in relation to taking turns, but more probably because he did not comprehend the teacher's implicit agenda (the social rules of the classroom 'game'). Thus he constantly made bids for attention, and in so doing got the answers to the questions 'wrong'. This problem was compounded by a second issue, that of all three boys being relatively new to school and bidding against each other for the attention and favours (largely the same thing in this context) of a female teacher, a surrogate mother. Finally, the problem was further compounded for Simon by competition among the boys for the largest bear. Not only was he given the smallest bear, but in the course of the interaction it was defined as the 'baby' and, by association, so was he. He immediately resisted the association by grabbing the 'middle-sized', 'mother' bear (while also struggling with Jimmy for the 'daddy' bear). Thus, from his actions it might be inferred that he understood relative size, though it may simply be that he was resisting the implication of being the 'baby', irrespective of whether or not he appreciated the different sizes of the bears. More particularly, from the teacher's point of view, his behaviour led her to believe he understood 'zilch'. One might argue about whether or not boys *should* be so competitive over such trivial matters, and indeed about how they learn to take offence at such designations, but given current gender roles and identities, it seems clear that designating one object and, by association, one participant as the 'baby' is unlikely to lead to their dispassionate engagement with the mathematical task at hand.

Whether any learner can ever engage entirely dispassionately with the task at hand is a moot point, implying as it does that there are occasions when a totally socially decontextualized cognitive agenda is in play. This returns us to the competence/performance issue and the implication that competence can be disentangled from the social context of performance. Our argument is that it cannot, although clearly, avoiding obvious pitfalls such as the characterization of one participant in an assessment task as the 'baby', ought to improve the overall validity of the inferences drawn. Furthermore, the data demonstrate that Simon displays competence in another context, one of his own spontaneous choosing, which makes sense to him but which is overlooked by the teacher. However sociologically challengeable the concept of 'mis-assessment' might be, such assessments carry real consequences for real children, Simon amongst them. Our next section seeks to analyse in more depth how such mis-assessments are structured and explore the extent to which such structuration is not arbitrary.[2]

Structuring Achievement: Habitus and Field

The fact that this transcript deals with children at the very start of their schooling highlights the formative nature of the assessment. However, we use this term not in the generally accepted technical sense of having any obvious positive influence on the children's learning, but in the sense of providing a glimpse of the way such interactions might affect children's developing under-standing of the social relations of the classroom, and impact on their own and their teacher's perceptions of their achievements.

Such an analysis need not necessarily be seen in a negative light. While claiming that her primary purpose was an assessment of knowledge and under-standing, the teacher also stated that she had socialization in mind. Discussing the video tape-recording in interview she said:

> I was trying to see, to get them to sit down to do, a, a lot of it was training I think at that early stage as well. To see if they could work in a group cos they weren't used to sitting at tables in a group.

This seems reasonable; indeed, an understanding of learning based on social constructivism or sociocultural theory would emphasize the role of teachers in inducting children into the culture of schooling. However this cannot be seen as unproblematic: socialization is not merely about accustoming children to sitting at tables and working together. More significantly, even at this early age, they are not just passive recipients of social conditioning. Instead they already bring to the situation understandings of purposes and social relations which constitute important aspects of the way that the incident is structured, even though they may be less visible than the intentions of the teacher.

Thus, the three bears that are used as props for the assessment are not just stuffed toys of equal mathematical value. Instead, because of the size relations established and the social meanings of these relations, the boys view them very differently. Throughout the incident competition for the biggest bear acts as a leitmotif in the wider competition of the boys themselves. The connection between what they bring to the event, what the teacher brings to it, the text of the incident itself and its role in shaping future relations is therefore dynamic rather than static. This nexus of relationships and inscribed meaning *creates* the differential achievement of the participants, rather than simply acting as a context in which differential achievement is revealed.

A way of making sense of this might be to look at the transcript in terms of some of the central concepts of Bourdieu's sociological theory, in particular *habitus*, the embodied social structures that individuals bring to interaction and that form the principles for organizing their practice and *field*, the structured arenas of social interaction (Bourdieu 1977). The habitus of the three boys has been constituted during the social life they have already experienced at home, at playgroup and elsewhere. Although they are able to make individual choices about their practices, in any setting the habitus predisposes them to behave in certain ways. In this incident, competitiveness around having the big bear may be seen as an aspect of the habitus of many small boys and can be related to gender relations and the way that masculinity is commonly constructed. Meanwhile, the school constitutes a very obvious field in Bourdieu's sense. It is a structured arena but the structures are not fixed; rather, they are drawn from a series of options. These are certainly mediated by the teacher, but are also constituted by the practices of the boys and developed through interaction with the teacher and each other. Thus, these elements are not separate but are inter-acting, and the power of Bourdieu's analysis lies in its reflexivity, how field and habitus work upon each other. Interaction is not only structured by the practices of individuals, derived from their habitus, and by the field in which this takes place, but also tends to structure each of them in turn. Thus it is forma-tive, looking forward to and influencing the future and providing an explanation of the way that society reproduces itself.

Recognition and Misrecognition

The power of this kind of event to position children in schooling can be seen from what the teacher said about the event, that 'Simon hadn't got a clue'. Yet our reading of the situation strongly contradicts this since, at the end of the transcript, Simon demonstrates his competence in using numbers up to five by counting the people left in the room. Another of Bourdieu's concepts, that of recognition ('reconnaissance') is most important here, in that the power that one has in any setting is dependent not so much on one's knowledge, as on the recognition that this knowledge receives from the group (Bourdieu 1991). Simon receives no such recognition at least in part because the demonstration of his competence has taken place at the wrong time, when the teacher is preoc-cupied with something else. Thus, Simon is a victim of misrecognition, in that the outcome of the interaction is that the teacher positions him as failing.[3]

However this begs the question of why Simon failed to make use of earlier opportunities to show his mastery of number. Here one can only surmise that the very factor that the teacher identified, his inexperience and lack of under-standing of how to work in a group, led him not to appreciate the agenda. He was waiting to 'play a game', but was in fact a participant all along in a game whose rules he did not know. The most important distracting feature appears to have been that the bears were allocated arbitrarily and he received the smallest and least desirable bear. Furthermore the teacher's openness to appro-priating Jimmy's assertion 'I'm daddy', and then to identify the boys with the bears, demonstrates that her own hidden or taken-for-granted agenda is class-room management; the primary pedagogic task at hand. Her agenda and vocabulary are located within a teacherly discourse (keeping the boys 'on board', moving the activity along) which prevents her from being alert to the pejorative meaning of 'baby' for young children (especially, perhaps, within a group of boys) and also, possibly, the attraction of being a 'daddy' in relation to a surrogate 'mummy' (see also Walkerdine's (1988) discussion of the overlap-ping discursive practices of home and school based on a similar 'three bears' incident). The bear now becomes less of a character in a story and more a kind of trophy or symbol of the holder's position. Simon apparently hopes to procure status through his attempt to grab the 'big' bear, perhaps thinking that he will thereby become the 'daddy' of the group.

Another way of looking at this is to use the term 'misrecognition' once more, this time drawing on Bernstein's theorization. Bernstein (1996: 32) states that:

> Recognition rules regulate what meanings are relevant and realization rules regulate how meanings are to be put together to create the legitimate text...[and] at the level of the acquirer, enable that acquirer to construct the expected legitimate text.

In this example, Simon has not recognized what meanings are relevant when he is first questioned and so has a problem with the recognition rule. On the other hand his counting of the people in the room suggests that he may, given suitable circumstances, be able to create legitimate text. Bernstein points out the strong links between children's social background and their orientation to recognition and realization rules. We have no explicit data on Simon's social class, but this is not the key issue for our argument. The example demonstrates that the assessment of Simon cannot be understood as purely cognitive; his social understanding and positioning are also being assessed. Moreover, this assessment is in turn creating a new positioning for him in the social context of the group.

In the transcription Simon becomes increasingly frustrated as he struggles not just to make sense of the language of the interaction, but also to retain some power within the situation. Both the teacher's management of the children and the interaction between the children, particularly Simon and Jimmy, show a jockeying for position. As someone publicly identified with the baby bear, and who does not know all his numbers, he is conscious of and frustrated by his powerlessness. As Delpit (1993) has noted, issues of power are enacted in classrooms through a 'culture of power' whose rules reflect the rules of those who have power. Moreover, 'those with power are frequently least aware of – or least willing to acknowledge – its existence. Those with less power are often most aware of its existence' (Delpit 1993: 583).

Simon seems only too aware of his powerlessness, arising partly from his lack of appreciation of the recognition rule and partly from the teacher's seemingly arbitrary allocation of the bears and number tiles. Her reference to training quoted above shows that she is trying to ensure all children understand the rules of classroom activities, but she tries to accomplish this by implicitly modelling appropriate classroom behaviour rather than explicitly stating what the task is about and how it will be executed. She seems unaware of the way her exercise of power might work in a differential way between the children.

This teacher's pedagogy is very common in primary schools, especially in the early years, and is what Bernstein describes as 'invisible': the boundaries between subjects of the curriculum, between work and play, are not clearly drawn (weak classification) and the control of the teacher is generally implicit (weak framing), though it is no less manifest for that. In addition, the assessment criteria are diffuse and multiple (Bernstein 1978). The invisibility of the pedagogy and the teacher's multiple agenda serve to extend her power. Children such as Simon have little chance of cracking the code, as the way the agenda changes seems arbitrary. Furthermore, the teacher's attempt to invoke a context familiar to the children, (the three bears story) only serves to make what she says more complex and hide what is going on. She never makes her intentions explicit and, although recognizing that the boys are unused to this kind of activity, she apparently sees the issue purely in terms of behaviour. If she can get the group sitting down and working together, she assumes that they will be equally able to infer the purpose of the activity unproblematically, with any differences between them being attributable to differential knowledge and/or ability.

The literature of child development and early years teaching is replete with advice to teachers to avoid intervening inappropriately in children's 'natural curiosity' and 'natural development' (Walkerdine 1988). Elsewhere we have also emphasized the potential benefits accruing from a 'divergent' rather than a 'convergent' approach to classroom assessment where teachers take their cues from the children, albeit in a way which sees mediation and scaffolding as a central part of the process (Torrance and Pryor 1998). Interviews with this teacher suggest that she views her practice in this way. Such pedagogies are intended to be empowering; however in this situation problems with recognizing what constitutes a legitimate text mean that pupils have very little access to power. Thus, although the teacher may feel she is reacting to the pupils' actions, her responsiveness is not transparent, and they therefore struggle to make sense of her actions.

The big issue for the children in the example is to make meaning. They are always struggling to catch up with the teacher's changing agenda, a struggle which embodies the power differentials between them. Delpit (1993: 583) asserts that 'if you are not already a participant in the culture of power, being told explicitly the rules of that culture makes acquiring power easier'. A key issue for teachers then is to be more aware of the sociological issues at stake and therefore to clarify the rules of the game. Furthermore, explicit articulation of procedures and criteria for judgement not only provides a means for children to understand what constitutes legitimate text, but potentially opens up these procedures and criteria for discussion.[4]

Conclusion

Assessment is not an activity that can be *done to* children, but is accomplished by means of social interaction in which the practices of the participants have a critical effect on the outcome. The outcomes of assessment are actively produced rather than revealed and displayed by the assessment process. Moreover, each participant brings to the event understandings not only of the cognitive agenda, but also of the kind of social relations and practices that are legitimate in the circumstances. These understandings are then subject to change as a result of the inferences that are made during the interaction. It may in practice be very difficult to actualize a pedagogy where teachers' primary concern is 'minimizing code mistakes by continuously and methodically stating the code' (Bourdieu 1977: 126). However, by failing to recognize the issue as important, assessment policies and classroom practices are likely to reinforce and perpetuate the poor performance of many school pupils.

Appendix: Transcription Conventions Used for Classroom Interaction

Normal prose punctuation is not used though capitals are retained for proper nouns and the first person singular.

(*)	inaudible (probably one word)
(**)	inaudible phrase
(*Tuesday)	inaudible word, 'Tuesday' suggested by transcriber
–	short pause
disapp\	incomplete word
these	word emphasized
Bold	word pronounced with lengthened vowel sounds
COME HERE	words said very loudly compared to other utterances
=	rapid change of turn speakers
> It's mine <	simultaneous speech
Italics	non-spoken material (stage directions)
T	teacher
C	unidentified child
~	rising intonation, slowing (invitation to other speaker to complete sentence)
…	brief omission from original transcript to shorten it for publication

Notes

1   The data derive from 'Teacher Assessment at Key Stage 1: Accomplishing Assessment in the Classroom', funded by the Economic and Social Research Council, 1993–6, grant no. R000234668. Analysis has also been informed by later work from our subsequent ESRC project, 'Investigating and Developing Formative Assessment in Primary Schools', 1997–9, grant no. R00023860.
2   We use this word in the generally accepted sense. A more specific usage is employed by Bernstein (1996: 169ff), which he contrasts with that of Bourdieu. The exploration of this distinction is outside the scope of this chapter.
3   We should add that the teacher is presumably not deliberately victimizing him. As Grenfell and James (1998: 23) point out, 'Misrecognition relates to the ways these underlying processes and generating structures of fields are not consciously acknowledged in terms of the social differentiation they perpetuate, often in the name of democracy and equality'.
4   In our more recent research project, we have been working with a group of teachers in an 'action research' framework to develop ways of making assessment processes and criteria more explicit (Pryor and Torrance 1999; Torrance and Pryor 1999).

References

Alexander, R., Rose, J. and Woodhead, C. (1992) *Curriculum Organisation and Classroom Practice in Primary Schools*, London: Department of Education and Science.
Bernstein B. (1978) 'Class and Pedagogies: Visible and Invisible', in J. Karabel and A.H. Halsey (eds), *Power and Ideology in Education*, Oxford: Oxford University Press.

—— (1996) *Pedagogy, Symbolic Control and Identity: Theory Research and Critique*, London: Taylor & Francis.

Beveridge, M. (ed.) (1982) *Children Thinking Through Language*, London: Edward Arnold.

Bourdieu, P. (1977) *Outline of a Theory of Practice*, Cambridge: Cambridge University Press.

—— (1991) *Language and Symbolic Power*, London: Polity Press.

Delpit, L.D. (1993) 'The Silenced Dialogue: Power and Pedagogy in Educating Other People's Children', in A.H. Halsey, H. Lauder, P. Brown and A.S. Wells (eds), *Education: Culture, Economy and Society*, Oxford: Oxford University Press.

Donaldson, M. (1978) *Children's Minds*, London: Fontana.

Edwards, A. and Furlong, V. (1978) *The Language of Teaching*, London: Heinemann.

Edwards, D. and Mercer N. (1987) *Common Knowledge: The Development of Understanding in the Classroom*, London: Methuen.

Grenfell, M. and James, D. (1998) *Bourdieu and Education: Acts of Practical Theory*, London: Falmer Press.

Mehan, H. (1979) *Learning Lessons: Social Organisation in the Classroom*, Cambridge, MA: Harvard University Press.

Pryor, J. and Torrance, H. (1999) 'Developing a Framework for Classroom Assessment', paper presented to the annual meeting of the American Educational Research Association, Montreal, April 1999.

School Curriculum and Assessment Authority (SCAA) (1997) *Teacher Assessment in Key Stage 2*, London: SCAA Publications.

Torrance, H. and Pryor, J. (1996) 'Teacher Assessment at Key Stage 1: Accomplishing Assessment In The Classroom (The "TASK" Project)', Final Report to the ESRC.

Torrance, H. and Pryor, J. (1998) *Investigating Formative Assessment: Teaching, Learning and Assessment in the Classroom*, Buckingham: Open University Press.

Torrance, H. and Pryor, J. (1999) *Investigating and Developing Formative Teacher Assessment in Primary Schools: Final Report to ESRC of Grant No. R000236860*, Swindon: ESRC.

Walkerdine, V. (1988) *The Mastery of Reason*, London: Routledge.

Part IV

Assessment as Lived Experience Beyond the Classroom

Editor's Introduction

Ann Filer

The chapters in Part IV continue to examine assessment practices and outcomes from the perspectives of those whose lives they most affect. In Part III, the authors did this from the immediacy of particular classroom assessment situations. Here, we explore some meanings of assessment practices in the lives of individuals and groups and the values and interpretations they bring to them. In doing so, we examine some ways in which assessment practices and outcomes are mediated and contested, drawing on wider sets of meanings than those generated by official policy and practice.

Questioning and Contestation in the Public Arena

Just as systems of assessment have developed differently in different societies (see Introduction to Part I), so also the nature of contestation and pressure for change varies across different national contexts. For instance, until the changes brought about by the 1988 Education Act, assessment procedures in England remained virtually unchallenged for decades (Broadfoot 1996: 52–3). On the other hand, from the 1970s onwards in the USA the expansion of testing has been actively contested by different interest groups questioning the role of assessment in their own and others' lives (US Congress, Office of Technology Assessment 1992: 67). Challenges arise from the inequitable power relations embedded in practices that are ill-understood by those that use them, and from decision-making processes that are remote from the populations they act upon. For example, in the USA, controversy has surrounded the lack of privacy in relation to test results and students' lack of power and control over them. Scores can be used, or misused, by anyone with access to student records, whether or not that person knows anything about a particular test. Further, there is little public discussion and knowledge of a highly technical arena in which there is no unanimity among professionals concerning what is good practice (US Congress, OTA 1992: 69–71). A further key aspect of public contestation in the USA has come from cultural minorities resentful of having their histories and cultural meanings represented in curricula by white governing elites of European descent (Berlak 1995).

Meanings, Interpretation and Mediation

In my Introduction to Part III, I described everyday classroom assessments as, in part, a product of teachers' biographies and experiences of a wider field of action beyond the classroom. Similarly, students engaging in assessment practices draw on a field of action that includes their families, peers and wider communities and within which they shape their identities. Studies that include perspectives that draw on these wider settings reveal the complex and diverse origins of children's classroom responses. For example, studies of children's perspectives on their curriculum in both North American and UK schools show that their responses are not simply a product of teacher questioning or task instructions. Rather, responses are shaped by their awareness of a range of evaluative contexts. Home, community, peers and friends are ever-present contexts within which children locate their classroom meanings and responses. Moment to moment, these contexts influence the content of children's spoken and written responses, the manner of their presentation and their levels of social and emotional involvement or withdrawal from tasks. These studies show pupils shifting and modifying their responses as they shape and protect their sense of self and status through the changing contexts of teacher expectations, classroom relationships and peer appraisal (Filer 1997; see also Maguire 1997; Nicholls and Thorkildsen 1997; Pollard with Filer 1996; Pollard and Filer 1999).

In the following chapter (Chapter 7), I explore with Andrew Pollard the rather more direct potential for families in shaping assessment outcomes in schools. Our longitudinal studies of children's experience in English primary schools show parents variously supporting, acting upon, contesting or ignoring the official and unofficial voices of school assessment. In exploring the nature of families' responses to school assessment, we argue for a greater understanding of the importance of family contexts and parental perspectives as a basis for a more holistic, collaborative and reflexive approach to assessment for younger children. In Chapter 8, and at the other end of the age range for educational assessment, David James, explores the meaning of assessment grades for mature students and their tutors. Fundamental to this is the tremendous impact of grades on the self perception of mature individuals and the centrality of assessment events to their experience through university.

The relationship between assessment practices and communities beyond the school, and the power relations embedded in those relationships, is a very much under-researched area of study in the USA and the UK. Some concerns, for example, relate to the problem of disparities between centralized assessment policies and local cultural or linguistic needs (see for example Chapters 2 and 10 in this book). Research potential also lies in improving understandings of how meanings that attach to assessment practices influence students' sense of self as learners and their achievement outcomes. Concerning young children in particular, research is needed into the value of promoting more collaborative understandings between homes and schools of pupils' achievements, motivations and identities (see the further reading suggestions below).

Further Reading

In *Experience Through the eyes of Quiet Bird: Reconnecting Personal Life and School Life* (Nicholls and Thorkildsen with Bates 1997), teacher, parent and researcher liaise to present the curriculum in ways that were personally meaningful for the child. Through this process, they were able to look beyond easy assumptions of 'lack of ability' in his failure to accomplish routine tasks, and to seek a more holistic understanding of his difficulties.

In her study *Shared and Negotiated Territories: The Socio-Cultural Embeddedness of Children's Acts of Meaning* (1997), concerning three bilingual Muslim girls living in Quebec, Mary Maguire presents their language, learning and social relations, at home, school and in their communities, as inextricably linked in their textual representations.

In *Power and Partnership in Education* (1995), Derek Armstrong explores expectations that parents work as partners with professionals in assessing the special educational needs of their children. Using parents, teachers and children's accounts of the process, he discusses power relations in the assessment process and the relative importance of the views of parents and children themselves.

In *The Social World of Pupil Assessment* (Filer and Pollard 2000), we use longitudinal case studies of children's primary school careers to explore ways in which children shaped their identities as pupils in the contexts of judgements made by teachers and the responses of families friends and peers to the official and unofficial voices of school assessment.

Harold Berlak, in *Towards the Development of a New Science of Educational Testing and Assessment* (1992), explores possibilities for assessment processes that are responsive to the conflicting needs of a multicultural, polylingual society and whereby control is exercised horizontally at the local school–community level as well as vertically at district, state or national levels.

References

Armstrong, D. (1995) *Power and Partnership in Education*, London: Routledge.

Berlak, H. (1992) 'Towards the Development of a New Science of Educational Testing and Assessment', in H. Berlak et al., *Towards a New Science of Educational Testing and Assessment*, Albany, NY: State University of New York Press.

—— (1995) 'Culture, Imperialism and Goals 2000', in R. Miller (ed.), *Educational Freedom for a Democratic Society*, Brandon: Resource Centre for Redesigning Education.

Broadfoot, P. (1996) *Education, Assessment and Society*, Milton Keynes: Open University Press.

Filer, A. (1997) 'At Least They Were Laughing: Assessment and the Functions of Children's Language in their "News" Session', in A. Pollard, D. Thiessen and A. Filer (eds), *Children and Their Curriculum: A New Challenge*, London: Falmer.

Filer, A. and Pollard, A. (2000) *The Social World of Pupil Assessment*, London: Cassell.

Maguire, M. (1997) 'Shared and Negotiated Territories: The Socio-Cultural Embedded-ness of Children's Acts of Meaning', in A. Pollard, D. Thiessen and A. Filer (eds), *Children and Their Curriculum: A New Challenge*, London: Falmer.

Nicholls, J. and Thorkildsen, T. (1997) 'Experience Through the Eyes of Quiet Bird: Reconnecting Personal Life and School Life', in A. Pollard, D. Thiessen and A. Filer (eds), *Children and Their Curriculum: A New Challenge*, London: Falmer.

Pollard, A. with Filer, A. (1996) *The Social World of Children's Learning*, London: Cassell.

Pollard, A. and Filer, A. (1999) *The Social World of Pupil Careers in a Primary School*, London: Cassell.

Pollard, A., Thiessen, D. and Filer, A. (eds) (1997) *Children and Their Curriculum: A New Challenge*, London: Falmer.

US Congress, Office of Technology Assessment (1992) *Testing in American Schools: Asking the Right Questions*, OTA-SET-519, Washington, DC: US Government Printing Office, February.

7 Assessment and Parents' Strategic Action

Ann Filer and Andrew Pollard

Introduction

Over the past decade, research into classroom assessment in England and Wales has been concerned primarily with issues relating to new forms of national testing, in particular those associated with their impact on teachers' work and pupils' learning. One particular focus for attention has been the work of primary school teachers, for whom the Education Act of 1988 brought about the most revolutionary changes (see Chapter 1 in this book). This necessary focus on understanding momentous changes in national assessment practices has meant that comparatively little research has been undertaken into ways in which parents use and respond to new forms of assessment (Hughes 1996, and see exceptions below). As Hughes notes, this is somewhat surprising, since parents have certainly received huge amounts of attention from policy perspectives.

Over the last decade there have been two main aspects of governmental rhetoric regarding parental power through assessment. First, assessment data has been constructed as the currency of an education marketplace whereby parents as 'clients' of the education system are supposedly free to 'choose' successful schools, allowing those less successful in league tables to sink. This exercise of choice has been explored by, among others, Reay and Ball (1998), Allatt (1996) and Gewirtz et al. (1995). However, policy changes to make assessment the key to parental power have not just been about programmes of national testing and league tables of schools' results. In addition to new forms of national testing externally set and marked, teachers themselves have become accountable to parents in very categoric ways. These changes have had particular impact with respect to primary school practice (see Chapter 1). Teachers have been trained in careful observation, reflections and review of 'evidence' in order to match pupils' work and achievements against curriculum specifications and levels. Many primary teachers began to take a pride in their new professional skills. Parents of primary school pupils began to receive reports on their children with more carefully worded and detailed descriptions of attainment than those formerly criticized as 'frequently generalized, laconic statements' (Department of Education discussion paper, Alexander et al. 1992). In Figure 7.1 we offer typical examples of old-style and new-style reporting

Figure 7.1   'Elizabeth's' two Year 2 reports from 'Mrs Major': a comparison of typical old-style and new-style primary school reporting

Albert Park County Primary School

Name Elizabeth Barnes   D.O.B. 3-1-84   Teacher (MRS. MAJOR)

Year 2   1990   Term 1   Key Stage 1.

Personal Development / Special Consideration Elizabeth Barnes   Elizabeth has days when she works hard & is kind to all, but also has days when she is either very boisterous or even aggressive.

Attitude to work Elizabeth has greater capability than she exhibits. She is still attracted to disruptive behavior + will be involved in it sometimes.

Maths _____

Quite capable. Picks up new concepts easily but does not cover as much work as she should.

_____

Science Good basic concepts. Willing to participate in group discussion. Very quick to think through "what if" proposals arising from her work.

_____

English – Speaking / Listening Very well articulated Good vocabulary. Imaginative + mature speech. Elizabeth has to be placed stategically within a group to ensure maximum concentration.

English / Reading _____

Making pleasing progress. Still needs to read at home every night. 10 pages should be about the quantity level to maintain progress levels.

English / Writing _____

Imaginative ideas well in sequence but Elizabeth needs to have more quantity in her work. She unfortunately wastes a lot of time.

ANNUAL REPORT 1991

School Name: Albert Park Co P	
Pupil's Surname: BARNES	
First name: ELIZABETH	D.O.B 3.01.84 END OF KEY STAGE 1

	COMMENTS	P.C.	LEVEL
ENGLISH Speaking and Listening Reading Writing	Elizabeth can participate as a speaker + a listener in group activities. She can describe real or imaginary events. She can follow more complex instructions. She can read a range of material with some independence, fluency, accuracy + understanding. She can describe what has happened in a story + what may happen next. She can produce independently, pieces of writing parts of which show correct use of sentence making. She can sequence her work chronologically. She is beginning to understand the basic structure of story writing. She can spell many common words.	*2* *1* *2*	2
MATHEMATICS Number and Measure Shape and Data Handling	Elizabeth can select the materials + the mathematics to use for a task (Level 2). She can add + subtract objects to 10. She can talk about her own work + make predictions based on experience. She can explore + use patterns in addition + subtraction facts to 10 (Level 2) She can compare objects for weight length + capacity without measuring. She can sort 2D + 3D shapes, state position + recognise the outcome of random events.	*1a* *1*	1
SCIENCE Exploration Knowledge and Understanding	Elizabeth can formulate hypotheses (Level 3). She can record findings in charts + other appropriate forms. She can identify simple differences. She can select + use simple instruments to enhance observations. She can use standard + non-standard measures. She can list + collate observations. She knows there are a wide variety of living things + her own individuality. She is aware that humans produce waste products. She has basic concepts of weather conditions, push + pull, electricity + magnetism, sound + energy. We have studied Earth in Space.	*2* *3*	2

The above are the results of statutory assessment procedures

TECHNOLOGY	D.T Elizabeth has planned + made models. I.T She has used the computer as a word processor.
GEOGRAPHY) **HISTORY**	These two subjects are undertaken as part of the whole class topic for the term. We have studied The History of Transport + The Lives + Times of the North American Indians Elizabeth has difficulty maintaining concentration, which is a pity because at times she has good contributions to make to class discussion. She is usually interested in the topic work. Basic map work has been undertaken
RE	Term 2 We studied "God's Wonderful World". Term 3 We studied "Flowers for Beauty, Food, gardens, shops + special occasions.
ART	Elizabeth has a natural flair for art work. She is very precise in her execution + has good control of the materials.
MUSIC	She has participated in percussion activities. She can nearly hold a more complicated rhythm. She has participated in class productions.
PE	Elizabeth is very well balanced + has well developed large motor skills. She is supple + innovative in small group floor work.

GENERAL COMMENTS ; Elizabeth failed to attain Level 2 reading because she could not meet the necessary requirement in use of the dictionary. She has gained a good assessment in English + Science. Her maths one could also have been Level 2 had she worked more quickly through the school maths scheme. She must endeavour to concentrate in class, + apply herself to the task in hand.

CLASS TEACHER(S) (MRS MAJOR)   HEADTEACHER _____

and readers will no doubt agree that, as well as being more detailed, the latter certainly has an *appearance* of greater 'objectivity'. (See Introduction to Part III and Filer (1993a, 1993b, 1995) on issues of teacher assessment and 'objectivity'.)

However, a longitudinal study of primary school assessment carried out by the authors between 1987 and 1995 revealed that while parents were naturally quite pleased to receive more detailed reports on their children's activities and attainments, they made little use of the information such reports contained. In evaluating teacher perceptions of their children's 'abilities' and achievements, there was no change between old-style and new-style assessment and reporting with regard to what parents used, how they expressed satisfaction or dissatisfaction, or information through which they intervened for change. Notwithstanding changes intended to provide more detailed and objective assessments, to make teachers more accountable and to empower parents, the parents in our study responded to and used information just as they had previously. That is to say, they used less overt indications of their children's progress and teachers' perceptions, such as reading book and maths scheme levels, spelling lists and informal information gathered from teachers, their children and their own observations.

In this chapter, we explore the nature of parental responses to primary school assessments. We draw on findings from the ESRC-funded study 'Assessment and Career in a Primary School'. That study represented the fourth phase in the Identity and Learning Programme, which concerns the development of two parallel longitudinal ethnographies that continue to track the learning and school careers of groups of children from two primary schools growing up in very different socioeconomic circumstances.

The 'assessment' phase of the Identity and Learning Programme (see Filer and Pollard 2000) focused on the classroom, playground and home life of a cohort of predominantly skilled manual working (with some minor professional) home-owning families living in the Easthampton suburb of Albert Park. Albert Park was a busy and thriving suburb on the outskirts of the city, where light industrial development stood among Victorian terrace housing, interspersed with more modern housing estates both privately and council-owned. The study in Albert Park School tracked the assessment experience of a cohort of pupils from the beginning of national assessment in 1989 through to the end of their primary years. This study was undertaken in two parts. The first part, which began in 1989, was Filer's (1993c) part-time PhD project. The second part, an ESRC-funded extension of the PhD, was designed to generate further comparisons with an existing study of pupils' learning and identity initiated by Andrew Pollard in 1987. Our co-direction of this second phase also formalized a collaboration that already existed through the parallel development of the two projects. The existing study, initiated by Pollard, featured a cohort of predominantly middle-class pupils from Greenside School in the same city. Modern growth of the original village of Greenside began in the 1930s with the development of many larger than average semi-detached and detached properties with attractively laid out gardens. It rapidly became the sought-after place to live by many relatively high-salaried middle-class professionals in the city.

Most of Greenside children moved out of state education at eleven and dispersed around a number of private secondary schools in Easthampton. Ten key pupils from each cohort were tracked year on year through their primary school experiences. Through this time they were monitored regarding ways in which they progressively shaped their school identities and careers in the context of judgements made by teachers, families, friends and peers who variously supported, acted upon, contested or ignored the official and unofficial voices of school assessment. We continue to track them through their secondary schools.

We used a variety of qualitative methods in the Identity and Learning Programme. These included classroom observations, pupil and teacher interviews, use of teacher records, reports and other documentation regarding pupils' achievement, samples of pupils' work, photographs and video recordings. Parental interviews and diaries kept by parents represent the main form of data gathering for the analysis presented in this chapter, although the analysis is of course embedded in our wider, more holistic understandings of families, neighbourhoods and classrooms through the study as a whole.

Parental Roles in Assessment Processes

As described above, English education policy has made much of the role of newly empowered parents in their children's education, their partnership with schools, and shared responsibilities for the education of their children. However, research suggests that there were no real gains in parental power and relationships with schools over the 1980s and 1990s. In the case of most schools, the rhetoric of partnership amounts to little more than the expectation that parents attend school events and are passive recipients of information, rather than co-constructors of a shared understanding of their children (Vincent and Tomlinson 1997; Johnson and Barber 1996; Barber 1996; see also Hughes 1996; Hughes et al. 1994). Vincent and Tomlinson argue that schools' 'soft rhetoric' of partnership has, through successive Conservative and Labour politicians, become translated into mechanisms for defining good parenting, directing family life and emphasizing complete parental responsibility for their children's behaviour and achievements. This emphasis on parents as 'responsible consumers' (Vincent and Tomlinson 1997: 369; DfE 1992) can be seen as an aspect of the current discourse of target setting, 'standards' and home–school 'agreements', and in the context of the 'moral panic' about disruptive pupil behaviour (see also Chapter 1 in this book).

Although the role of parents in their children's education has received a vast amount of attention within public debate, we know comparatively little about how parents themselves view their supposedly new roles, or about how they view the assessment initiatives that are supposed to support them. Hughes (1996; Hughes et al. 1994) found in a study of 150 children that parents had learned 'nothing new' from SATs but wanted a closer, more interactive relationship with schools. In a further study, of around 240 children in a variety of schools, parents particularly wanted a more active role in assessment through providing additional information about activities and interests at home

(Desforges et al. 1994, 1996). Teachers in that study, however, were generally not aware of such desires, were unwilling to change practices and in any case generally found parents' wishes inappropriate. Some thought that parents had little to offer in the field of assessment. Overall, the study reflected the results of a study fifteen years earlier (Tizard et al. 1981, 1982) which showed that teachers' sense of professionalism kept them from acknowledging what parents had to offer (Hughes 1996: 108). That parents have knowledge and the potential for contributing to school understandings of their children's achievements is, however, very well established. West et al. (1998) made a study of the educational activities of 107 children in their homes other than those directly associated with school work. They found a range of activities including cooking, music, library visits, writing, art and craft. They found no significant difference in the range of activities undertaken between parents in terms of their social class or mother's educational level. One statistically significant and interesting finding was that state-educated children spent more time writing stories at home than privately educated children. A study by Hirst (1998) confirmed and extended the research of others (for example, Huss 1997; Delgado-Gaitan 1996) in finding that ethnic minority families were involved in extensive home literacy practices and much learning was happening at home. These practices were neither understood, valued nor built on in schools. Indeed, whereas most families in these studies were interested in their children's learning and eager to be involved in home–school collaboration, schools often took a deficit view of the attitudes to education of ethnic minority families.

As described in the introduction, the Identity and Learning Programme has a sample of families drawn from two distinctly different parts of a city in the south of England, and facing very different socioeconomic conditions. In the light of the above, it is worth looking at the way their respective schools viewed the populations of parents of their pupils and their involvements in their children's education. An important consideration in this, as other studies remind us, is that not all teachers within schools share the same perspective. While the following were typical of unofficial staffroom and informal conversation with us as researchers over seven years in the schools, there were of course exceptions to them. By the same token, not all families were seen in the same light. However, at Albert Park, parents *en masse* were generally viewed as active in their children's schooling – but in entirely the 'wrong' way. Many staff held a critical view of parents as very confident, vociferous and challenging to school in relation to their 'rights' with regard to such issues as the wearing of school uniform and selection for sports teams. On the other hand, they saw most parents as lacking concern and less likely to raise issues with regard to academic decisions or outcomes in relation to their children's attainment: 'If their son doesn't get selected for the football team fathers that you never see will be up here like a flash' (teacher at Albert Park).

Further, some staff in the school expressed opinions that, although poverty and unemployment were not great problems for most families in Albert Park, families for the most part exhibited a kind of shallow consumerism, a lack of 'culture' in their recreational pursuits. It is perhaps worth noting that this community represented the socioeconomic group then described as C2s, who were much courted by Thatcherism and then by New Labour. For one teacher, many families had '… plenty of money but not much couth – if that's not being unkind' (teacher at Albert Park).

It is worth noting that in our sample, as well as attending the usual children's local and church organizations of Brownies, Cubs and sporting activities, children were involved with their parents and sometimes with more distant communities in a number of educational activities. These included amateur dramatics, light opera production, music and marching bands, photography, crafts and computer activities. We have no reason to believe that these were exceptional. Certainly in our study, we found parents at Albert Park to be often *apparently* more accepting of teacher assessments and perceptions of their children than those at Greenside School, but as we shall see later in this chapter, the picture was not that simple.

However, if Albert Park parents were criticized for not contesting or raising issues in relation to their children's attainment, the parents at Greenside School came in for some criticism for being *too* active. Though the ethos and the school intake changed somewhat over the time of the study (see Pollard and Filer 1999), many parents in the community of Greenside were perceived by school staff (and indeed among themselves) as 'pushy', and as having unrealistic expectations or putting undue pressure on their children. A parent in our study was denounced, for questioning the reading level attributed to her child, as being '…one who would take over her child's education if she could' (teacher at Greenside School).

As this chapter shows, teachers were often perceived by parents to be on the defensive, even in one case 'unprofessional', when parents questioned their children's levels of achievements or what they were capable of. Parent intervention in their child's education in Greenside School often led to a deterioration, at least temporarily, in home–school relationships.

At a relatively simplistic level, then, our schools seem to reflect other findings that teachers do not consider that parents have much to contribute to the assessment of their children's achievements. Indeed, some of the parental data from Greenside which follows illustrates some teachers' sense of affront to their professionalism when parents question their views of what children are capable of.

Notwithstanding the specific circumstances of our two case study schools, the issues in relation to social class and parental intervention in children's education reflect issues from other research. In spite of the expectation that parents call teachers to account, it is still middle-class parents who are most active in this. This is a reflection of, on the one hand, the cultural capital of middle-class parents and, on the other hand, the unwillingness of working-class parents to question professional knowledge (see for example Crozier 1997; Vincent and Tomlinson 1997). However, as Vincent and Tomlinson point out, explanations such as these regarding differential power relations among teachers and parents have clearly failed to engage the teaching profession. Rather, a working-class deficit model of parental involvement and parenting has grown up over the years whereby some groups of parents are designated as lacking in interest or involvement and failing to provide the kind of home life and discipline that supports their children's education. As Broadfoot and Pollard describe in Chapter 1 of this book, this has intensified in an atmosphere of target-setting and the competition among schools for pupils that will enhance their standing in league tables.

Notwithstanding the relevance of existing studies of social class and school expectations of parental involvement, the longitudinal design of this study enables a more dynamic analysis of parental involvement in their children's education than that offered by an analysis of social class differences. It also at the same time problematizes simple dichotomies of 'problem/uninterested' and 'supportive/active' parents which prevail in both political and practitioner discourse. In illustrating some of the dynamics of home–school relationships, we also hope to offer some insights for supporting an improved 'partnership' between schools and parents and the potential for a less adversarial response to parental intervention and a more collaborative use of parental knowledge and skills in assessment processes in primary schools.

In the following section, we offer a model of 'dimensions' and 'dynamics' of parental strategic action. This has been extended from a similar conceptualization of pupil strategies which we have developed, and it is helpful here to review the key features of this pupil model.

Dimensions of Pupils' Strategic Action

In *The Social World of Pupil Career* (1999), we constructed a four-part typology of pupils' strategic and adaptive responses through their school careers, to a range of curricular and social structures and expectations of the primary schools. These strategies can be summarized as follows:

- *anti-conformity*: some rejection of school career structures, expectations and norms; oppositional learning and social agendas, characterized as deviance.
- *non-conformity*: some indifference and lack of concern about career structures, expectations and norms; little perception of risk because pupils have their own learning and social agendas, characterized as independence.
- *conformity*: reification of career structures, expectations and norms; low-risk conformity to others' learning and social agendas, characterized as adaptation.
- *redefining*: personal identification with career structures, expectations and norms; high-risk strategies for influencing learning and social agendas, characterized by negotiation and challenge.

Dynamics of Pupils' Strategic Action

The 'dimensions of strategic action' do not describe *children*, nor do they represent psychological 'types'. They describe relatively coherent patterns of strategies which pupils adopted. Pupils tended to use particular dimensions consistently, in so far as the *meaning* of the context remained the same for them. However, patterned responses were liable to disruption where, for instance, changing classroom contexts and expectations meant that a pupil's accustomed orientations and strategies became no longer appropriate or viable.

Thus the seemingly static typology of 'dimensions of strategic action' can be extended and used to plot the *dynamics* of strategic action for individual children as derived from longitudinal case study data (Figure 7.2).

Pupils, for example, moved towards greater or lesser conformity in response to a particular pedagogic style or learning context. For similar reasons, a switch might occur from, for example, a redefining position of negotiation and challenge towards anti-conformity and deviance.

The model is also designed to depict the way in which the gaps between conformity and anti-conformity, non-conformity and redefining are potentially sites of tension. Such tension may occur between an individual pupil and a teacher or between individual pupils and their peers as a result of, for instance, a learning stance or expression of identity which contravenes the structural norms or relationship expectations of classroom or playground.

We found that the typology and model also provided a useful analytic framework for characterizing the strategic action of parents as interpreters and

Figure 7.2   A model for plotting the dynamics of pupils' strategic action

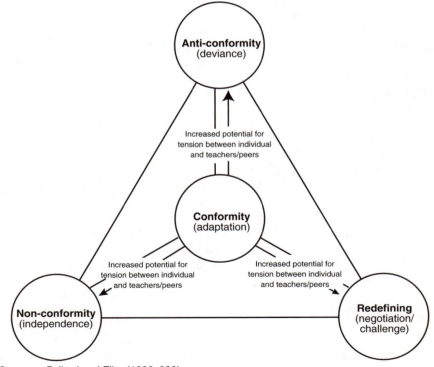

Source: Pollard and Filer (1999: 299)

mediators of their children's assessment and school experience generally. These could be set against simplistic assumptions and caricatures of parents as 'lacking interest' or 'pushy', 'supportive' or 'nonsupportive'. Also, it shows them in dynamic interaction with teachers, just as pupils were in dynamic interaction with a series of teachers.

Dimensions of Parents' Strategic Action

The dimensions of strategic action and orientation which typify pupil adaptation and response to classroom and learning contexts can be extended to characterize the strategic responses of parents as mediators and interpreters of assessment and school experience generally. We can take the characteristics of those dimensions and map them on to a typology of parental strategy as follows.

Redefining: characterized by 'identification', high-risk strategies for influencing a shared agenda, negotiation and challenge

Some parents, while they identified with and supported school assessment procedures and curricular expectations generally, often disputed the school's or a particular teacher's interpretation of satisfactory *levels* of achievement, either for pupils generally or for their own child in particular. In Greenside School, this sometimes happened in the context of anticipating entrance exams for independent schools. Parents were involved in negotiating higher achievement outcomes and school expectations, for instance through requests for extra homework, a focus on some particular area of weakness for their child or for faster progression through maths and reading schemes for their child.

The following are examples of redefining strategies:

Mrs Keel: One thing I have noticed (different) from last year – some of David's spellings – I've noticed they've been quite easy, whereas Ms Luke used to grade them a bit more. I think in that way he needs to be pushed a little bit more (...)

(Albert Park School, Mrs Keel, parent interview,
November 1994, Y6)

Mrs Keel: I went in to see Mrs Hutton to ask her if he could have some more difficult spellings to do, because he was finding them too easy. And so I did go and mention it at open evening, that if he could have some more difficult.

(Albert Park School, parental interview with
Mr and Mrs Keel, July 1995, Y6)

I was disappointed with Mary's progress after she had been back at school for a few weeks. This is because I had been told (and also thought) that she was bright, interested and her attitude was just right and she should 'take off' with her reading at any time and it just hadn't happened. I went to see Miss Scott to talk about this. Anyway, her progress has been a lot better recently and she seems to be more interested again.

(Greenside School, Mrs Inman parent diary, October 1988, Year 1)

(At the above meeting) a somewhat stormy encounter between Mrs Inman and Miss Scott took place, with Miss Scott believing that Mrs Inman was making Mary over-anxious. Nevertheless, following their discussion, Mary received a steady stream of books to take home and more attention at school.

(from Pollard with Filer 1996)

Mary's parents' data show that redefining could be a relatively high-risk strategy for parents. Managed carefully, and in the context of a mutually respectful parent–teacher relationship, it was able to influence outcomes and achievement levels for their children. Where there were many such parents, as in Greenside School, it was also likely to have been highly influential in raising levels of school expectations for pupils generally. Managed poorly, however, it was interpreted as criticism, viewed by teachers as 'deviant' and could lead to antagonistic home–school relations. This brings us to anti-conformity.

Anti-conformity: characterized by 'rejection', high-risk strategies associated with oppositional agendas and 'deviance'

Some parents' *alternative* views or expectations regarding their child's achievements represented a challenge to school assessments. Anti-conformity largely represented a failed interventionist strategy to redefine; parental attempts to negotiate for change interpreted by the school as 'deviant'.

The case of Harriet provides an example:

After a year of schooling, Harriet's reading achievement in relation to the graded reading scheme did not accord with Mrs Morley's estimation of her potential. Mrs Morley's wry assessment of the situation was:

"She is nearly up to the standard she was when she left playgroup last year."
(Greenside School, Mrs Morley, parent interview, July 1998, Reception)

There was a gulf between what Harriet's mother thought she should be reading and school reading level expectations. The level of graded reading books being selected by mother and daughter for home reading lead to accusations that she was 'pushing' Harriet, contributing to strained relations with teachers generally.

Mrs Morley took into school a newspaper article suggesting that 'children respond to more of a structured approach'. She sought Harriet's teacher's opinion on the issue:

Mrs Morley:　　That went down terribly. Mrs Powell interpreted it as I was finding fault with Mrs Long (teacher of Harriet's sister). I

143

never mentioned Mrs Long but there is so much tittle-tattle in that school. I was called in by Mrs Long – did I have any complaints about her teaching? It was awful. So unprofessional.

(Greenside School, interview with Harriet's parents, July 1988, Reception. From Pollard and Filer 1999)

Such patterns of interaction occurred more often in our more affluent middle-class Greenside sample than in Albert Park. This was also reflected in the schools' perceptions of the communities they served. As described above, some of the teachers in Greenside School saw parents as variously 'pushy', 'taking over' their child's education, holding educational ideologies and expectations for outcomes that pressurized their children, as well as themselves as teachers.

Non-conformity: characterized as a measure of 'indifference' and 'independence', with parents holding their own agenda

Some parents expressed a measure of indifference to school agendas for success and attainment outcomes, and this was sometimes an expression of dissatisfaction with the evaluations of school as irrelevant to the cultural norms or educational ideologies of the family. Robert's mother provides a good example of non-conformity:

Though pleased with Robert's early school reports and evidence of his fast developing reading skills, Mrs Osborne expressed doubts about early formal education either institutionalized or in the home:

"I would say he has got on very well, because I think it is very young to be bothered with that. I think it is very young. I mean, I am not a teacher, I know nothing really about education in that sense, but you know, you hear about people teaching them at playschool how to read and mothers teaching children to read before they go to school, and what is the rush really?"
(Greenside School, Mrs Osborne, parent interview, March 1988, Reception)

There was a consistency between Robert's parents' attitude to his early learning as expressed here and their attraction to some elements of the Steiner school of educational philosophy.

(From *The Social World of Pupil Career*, Pollard and Filer, 1999)

Sometimes non-conformity represented an adaptation to a lack of responsiveness on the part of the school to pupil or family concerns for learning; again, a failure to 'redefine'. For instance:

Alison's parents felt that school assessment of her attainment was not in accordance with her ability and that she was frustrated by the pace of school expectations for her. They were asked how they interpreted that situation for their daughter and how it was managed.

Mrs Gough:	Well, what we used to do was, we used to say that she'd have to do what the teacher told her but then what she wanted to do we did at home.
AF:	Ah, right.
Mrs Gough:	The next stage we did at home, so that way she was doing both and she was still getting what she wanted.
AF:	One step ahead of school and doing what she wanted. And does it continue in that way?
Mrs Gough:	Yeah, and now she's ready to go to senior school – now. (Senior school begins in Year 7 – over a year away for Alison).
Mr Gough:	She was ready last year really. I feel she was. She finds some things still menial at school and she helps others, as you're probably aware. But while she's helping others she's not getting ahead herself is she? And we feel that you shouldn't hold anyone back who's got the ability. I know it's difficult in a class of thirty children for a teacher to cater for every individual child, she's got to go with the majority and clever children are a minority in most classes.

(Albert Park School, Mr and Mrs Gough,
parent interview, July 1994, Y5)

Conformity: characterized by 'reification' and adaptation to procedures and curricular expectations, and low-risk strategies in conformity to the agenda of school

Many parents, particularly in Albert Park School, appeared to generally support school assessments and trust teachers to objectively assess and report their child's achievements. For instance:

AF:	So, reflecting on those results, and the sorts of teachers' assessments that you've had over the years generally, have you always felt that they are a reflection of Chris's achievements. Or of Chris's abilities.
Mr Kennedy:	I think, I suppose I'd have to say that the teachers who dealt with him at the time know him best for what he achieves in class. And we can't comment on that, but we've – you know, it's our place to listen to their opinion. At (his brother's) secondary school, I questioned one particular teacher about the way things were done when we visited the school, but not at Albert Park.

(Albert Park School, Mr and Mrs Kennedy,
parent interview, July 1995, Y6)

As we have described, therefore, and as we discuss in greater length later in the chapter, there was nothing fixed or inevitable about parental patterns of response. Neither indeed did surface appearances of conformity or 'good' and 'supportive' home–school relationships always reflect parents' underlying and more complex feelings about teachers' evaluations and expectation of their children and of them as parents. We discuss some of this complexity and its implications for ways in which school assessments could be interpreted and mediated within families in the next section.

Parental Mediation and Interpretation of Assessments

'Conformity' at Albert Park was often strategic in relation to teachers but was contradicted by parents' mediation and interpretation of assessments to their children. Parents' sincere concerns for their children's progress were often mixed with a desire to hold off pressure, on teachers as well as their children, and for good relations at school and home. This meant that poor achievement evaluations made by teachers, or underachievement generally, might be interpreted as 'not important so long as you're trying' or mediated, for instance, 'just like my report when I was a kid'.

Apparent conformity also usually hid ambivalent, antagonistic feelings and oppositional agenda's (anti-conformity) which ran beneath what were, on the surface, supportive home–school relations. The case of Adrian Rowe provides an example of this.

Throughout his primary career, Adrian's failure to apply himself to tasks meant his attainment was well below what teachers and parents knew he was capable of. His parents had frequent contacts and relaxed, supportive relations with teachers. However Mr Rowe explained:

> (I get told) he's been fighting in the playground, or he hasn't done his work, he should have sent some homework in. And sometimes you think I shouldn't be put in that position. And I never feel hostile to teachers or anything, because I'm a professional myself, I deal with children and I know how difficult it is. So I'm not going to go round there saying 'Why haven't you flipping *made* him do his work?' But you do wonder some-times. You think, 'Well, why should I?' I'm a parent and I'm supposed to love him and protect him and care for him and develop him. Why have I suddenly been given this task of actually meting out some discipline? (You think), 'Don't tell me. Just deal with it. Nine to four. School. Deal with it'. I find that a bit disturbing (that) automatically I feel compelled – I must do something about it. Ultimately it makes me an antagonist (and) I'm not comfortable with that.
>
> (Albert Park School, Mr and Mrs Rowe, parent interview, July 1994, Y5)
>
> ...and I think we've got enough on our plate without every minute of the day thinking, Oh he's got to improve. I mean, you can end up putting him under so much pressure.

...and it's not (just) a case of I'm trying to sit him down saying 'do your homework'. (The trouble is) he doesn't know about study skills. He doesn't know anything about setting out conclusions, what do you want to say? What do you want to show? It's no good you just writing a few pages if you mean absolutely nothing by it. I don't think he's been taught that. They haven't been prepared for study. But I'm not going to...I shouldn't be too critical because, you know, they're good teachers, but I look after children with *learning* difficulties and I expect far more from them!

(Albert Park School, Mr Rowe, parent interview, November 1994, Y6)

Dynamics of Parents' Strategic Action

As we have stated above, there was nothing fixed and inevitable about parental patterns of response. As with the children's career strategies, the dimensions of conformity do not describe *parents*. The model of 'dynamics of strategic action' in Figure 7.2 shows the gap between conformity and other strategies as potential sites of tension for, in this case, home–school relationships. Assessment is a two-way process, and parents made assessments of teachers as well. Redefining was not therefore constantly necessary but a strategy that could be used according to the degree of confidence felt in a particular teacher's approach as well as according to any objective measure of attainment. As the data has suggested, parents often attempted redefining, especially in the early years of their child's education. Mismanaged, these attempts could be labelled deviant by the school and antagonistic relations developed. As we have also seen, other failures to redefine came about as a result of unresponsiveness on the part of the school to parental attempts to influence outcomes for their child.

Something of the dynamics of one parent's strategies through her daughter's career through Greenside primary school is set out below. We have described above how Mrs Morley's attempts to 'redefine' teachers' expectations for her daughter were actually realized as strategies of 'anti-conformity' as they became increasingly interpreted by teachers at Greenside as 'deviant'. From those early antagonistic relations with school, Mrs Morley began in Year 1 (age 6) a gradual withdrawal from involvement in her daughter's schooling which culminated by Year 6 (age 11) in an almost complete separation of home and school concerns and experience for Harriet and her mother.

AP: | Tell me a little bit more about how you see her self confidence with maths.
Mrs Morley: | Well really, not being in the classroom, I can't say, and I always find it very difficult to find out exactly what is going on because if you ask too many questions you're labelled anxious. So I can't tell you.

...

At one time I was helping her to chose the (reading) books but that went out of my control completely. And I didn't find the books very good that she was bringing home. It makes it sound as if I am very pushy and anxious but in the end I thought, I can't. I won't do anything at all. Just let it slip.

AP: So really, your policy over the year was to 'keep your head down', in a sense?

Mrs Morley: Yes. I mean, I wish that teachers would appreciate parents who are anxious to find out what their children do. Why don't they? Tell me.

(Parent interview, July 1989, Year 1)

In time Mrs Morley moved to a position of 'non-conformity', adopting a measure of indifference to school agenda and assessments. For instance, Mrs Morley was not confident that Harriet was doing as well in maths as teachers reported. She explained:

Well, you know, they always write really nice reports but I imagine they probably do for most people and I honestly don't think Harriet's got much of a clue in her maths and yet they all say she's got a good grasp. But delve below the surface and she knows very little.

(Mrs Morley, parent interview, July 1993, Year 5)

Some of Harriet's maths improvement in school her mother believed was due to the extra tutoring they now were paying for, but which Harriet was resisting. Although concerned about Harriet's maths, Mrs Morley now expressed a more philosophical perspective on the children's education. She thought that, with a busy family life that did not leave a lot of time for over-close supervision of learning, they were, as parents, probably not 'pushy' enough to see high academic success coming from their children. For the same reason she felt relatively relaxed that (all three children) did less homework than they should have done and she understood their perspective if they wanted a less 'chasing around' and demanding life than they saw their father lead.

(Reproduced from Pollard and Filer 1999)

Conclusion

We have documented the ways in which families variously act upon, contest, challenge, support or ignore the official and unofficial voices of both teacher and standardized assessment. In so doing, we have emphasized the significance of how families interpret and give meaning to assessment outcomes.

The longitudinal nature of the Identity and Learning Programme enables us to trace the *dynamic* development of families' characteristic repertoires of strategic involvement and influence in shaping school assessment outcomes and in mediating and interpreting them with their children. It provides an analysis over time, beyond a simple comparison of the two schools. In so doing, it extends a structural analysis of class-based differences to show how variations both exist and develop. In particular, we would argue that the dynamics of home–school relationships cut across the structural analysis of power inequalities of working and middle classes (Vincent and Tomlinson 1997). In so doing, our analysis problematizes simple dichotomies of 'supportive' or 'problem' families which prevail in public and political discourse and among practitioners.

We see greater understanding of the importance of family contexts and parental perspectives as a basis for a more holistic, collaborative and reflexive approach to assessment. Assessment policy in England has, for some years, been based on misconceptions of 'what parents want'. There is plenty of evidence that parents are more sophisticated in their understanding of what is important in education, and potentially more willing *partners in learning* than their positioning as 'consumers' allows. Unfortunately, whilst government policy remains driven by the ideology and discourse of performance (see Chapter 1), then teachers are likely to remain within its yoke, and parents will remain as clients.

However, like the many other studies we cite here, our study shows the enormous potential of parents for facilitating children's learning in more holistic ways. In particular, parents may be more able than teachers to sense emotional issues in learning, to notice changes in attitudes over time, and to monitor motivation, interest and commitment in different subjects or areas of skill development. Personal interest, individual attention, deep knowledge and sensitivity are all on the parent's side as a teacher of their child. But this potential must also be harnessed into an active, collaborative partnership between parents and their children and teachers. In this, mutual understanding of motivations, perceptions and the strategic and dynamic nature of home–school relationships is a precondition. The analysis offered in this paper is a contribution to this goal.

References

Alexander, R., Rose, J. and Woodhead, C. (1992) *Curriculum Organisation and Classroom Practice in Primary Schools: A Discussion Paper*, Department of Education and Science, London: HMSO.

Allatt, P. (1996) 'Consuming Schooling: Choice, Commodity, Gift and Systems of Exchange', in S. Edgell, K. Hetherington and A. Warde (eds), *Consumption Matters: The Production and Experience of Consumption*, Oxford: Blackwell.

Barber, M. (1996) *The Learning Game*, London: Golancz.

Crozier, G. (1997) 'Empowering the Powerful: A Discussion of the Interrelation of Government Policies and Consumerism with Social Class Factors and the Impact of This Upon Parent Interventions in Their Children's Schooling', *British Journal of Sociology of Education* 18(2): 187–200.

Delgado-Gaitan, C. (1996) *Protean Literacy: Extending the Discourse on Empowerment*, London: Falmer Press.

Department for Education/Welsh Office (1992) *Choice and Diversity: A New Framework for Schools*, London: HMSO.

Desforges, C., Hughes, M. and Holden, C. (1994) 'Assessment at Key Stage One: Its Effects on Parents, Teachers and Classroom Practice', *Research Papers in Education* 9: 133–58.

—— (1996) 'Parents, Teachers and Assessment at Key Stage One', in M. Hughes (ed.), *Teaching and Learning in Changing Times*, Oxford: Blackwell.

Filer, A. (1993a) 'Contexts of Assessment in a Primary Classroom', *British Educational Research Journal* 19(1): 95–107.

—— (1993b) 'The Assessment of Classroom Language: Challenging the Rhetoric of "Objectivity"', *International Studies in Sociology of Education* 3(2): 193–212.

—— (1993c) 'Classroom Contexts of Assessment in a Primary School Classroom', unpublished PhD thesis, University of the West of England.

—— (1995) 'Teacher Assessment: Social Process and Social Product', *Assessment in Education* 2(1): 23–38.

Filer, A. and Pollard, A. (2000) *The Social World of Pupil Assessment in a Primary School*, London: Cassell.

Gewirtz, S., Ball, S. and Bowe, R. (1995) 'Markets, Choice and Equity in Education', Buckingham: Open University Press.

Hirst, K. (1998) 'Pre-School Literacy Experiences of Children in Punjabi, Urdu, and Gujerati Speaking Families in England', *British Educational Research Journal* 24(4): 415–29.

Hughes, M. (1996) 'Parents, Teachers and Schools', in B. Bernstein and B. Brannen (eds), *Children, Research and Policy*, London: Taylor & Francis.

Hughes, M., Wikeley, F. and Nash, P. (1994) *Parents and Their Children's Schools*, Oxford: Blackwell.

Huss, R.L. (1997) 'Teacher Perceptions of Ethnic and Linguistic Minority Parental Involvement and its Relationships to Children's Language and Literacy Learning: A Case Study', *Teaching and Teacher Education* 13: 1–30.

Johnson, M. and Barber, M. (1996) 'Collaboration for School Improvement: The Power of Partnership', in D. Bridges and C. Husbands (eds), *Consorting and Collaborating in the Education Market Place*, London: Falmer.

Pollard, A. and Filer, A. (1999) *The Social World of Pupil Career: Strategic Biographies through Primary School*, London: Cassell.

Pollard, A. with Filer, A. (1996) *The Social World of Children's Learning: Case Studies of Pupils from Four to Seven*, London: Cassell.

Reay, D. and Ball, J. (1998) 'Making their Minds Up: Family Dynamics of School Choice', *British Educational Research Journal* 24(4): 431–48.

Tizard, B., Mortimore, J. and Burchell, B. (1981) *Involving Parents in Nursery and Infant Schools*, London: Grant McIntire.

Tizard, B., Schofield, W.N. and Hewison, J. (1982) 'Collaboration Between Teachers and Parents in Assisting Children's Reading', *British Journal of Educational Psychology* 52: 1–15.

Vincent, C. and Tomlinson, S. (1997) 'Home–School Relationships: "The Swarming of Disciplinary Mechanisms"?', *British Educational Research Journal* 23(3): 361–77.

West, A., Noden, P., Edge, A. and David, M. (1998) 'Parental Involvement in Education In and Out of School', *British Educational Research Journal* 24(4): 461–84.

8 Making the Graduate

Perspectives on Student Experience of Assessment in Higher Education

David James

Assessment and Student Experience at 'Robbins University'

Assessment is at the heart of the undergraduate experience. Assessment defines what students regard as important, how they spend their time, and how they come to see themselves as students and then as graduates. It follows, then, that it is not the curriculum which shapes assessment, but assessment which shapes the curriculum and embodies the purposes of higher education.

(Brown and Knight 1994: 12)

Brown and Knight's assertion above is well-supported in the literature (for example Heywood 1989; Ramsden 1992; Stefani 1998; Thomson and Falchikov 1998). It also emerged as a dominant theme in a series of interviews carried out between April 1991 and November 1994 as part of a PhD study investigating mature student experiences in higher education (James 1995, 1996). The twenty-one interviewees were approximately a third of one year's intake. All were over 25 years old on entry, pursuing a number of related social science degree courses at 'Robbins University' (RU) in the UK. The institution was one of those that came into being after the expansion proposals of the 1963 Robbins report, although in a modern UK context would now be referred to as an 'older university'. As well as giving a very clear general impression of the *centrality* of assessment events in student experience, students' descriptions of being assessed seemed to fall into two areas. First, many of their comments were about the utility of feedback on assessed work, which in most cases fell below their expectations. Second, their comments indicated that a number of major effects were associated with the act of being assessed. These included serious consequences for students' self-perception and levels of confidence.

There is only the space here to give a small number of examples from the data that illustrate these two themes. With regard to comments on assessed coursework, most of the mature students interviewed referred at some point to the variability in the length, scope and utility of such comments from different tutors. Disappointment with the brevity and content of comments from some tutors was widespread (though not universal) in the first year and the early part of the second year of study: Maurice refers to the 'six words you usually get', while Theresa, Bruce, Mike and Sophia contrast full and useful feedback with 'the sort of one-liner that tells you nothing'; 'one sentence which will be illegible'; 'just [a] ten word sentence'; or 'just a couple of sentences' respectively. For many, the focus of their disappointment was the lack of information on which to base decisions about what they should do differently if they wished to raise the level of their marks in assessed work. For others, the concern was in identifying what they should *continue* to do to achieve high marks. Laura and Sandra provide examples of each of these. Laura described how examination scripts from the end-of-first-year examinations were never discussed or made available so that students could use them to improve their technique. Such opportunities had been a regular feature of life in the small adult residential college she had attended while completing her Diploma in Higher Education before coming to university. She said she realized that this would be 'impractical' where one or two tutors were marking hundreds of scripts, but that it made for a rather impersonal setting in which to learn. Sandra spoke about a coursework assignment of hers which had gained a (very high) grade of 80 per cent and the comment 'Excellent, could be shorter':

Sandra: You think Oh, it would be nice to know why it was excellent, then perhaps I could do it again! As I haven't got any idea why it was excellent, I'll never be able to, but there you go. It took two and half months or something to get the essay back anyway, so I wasn't going to send it back for further comments.

David: Right. Have you ever felt you've been in the dark a bit too much about what's expected?

Sandra: Oh yes, absolutely, 90 per cent of the time. Absolutely, that is the single greatest problem on this thing.

(Sandra, second interview)

In several cases, students did approach tutors in attempts to get more information about a mark. Maurice wanted a 'second opinion' on a piece of work which gained a lower mark than he had expected. He felt he had been 'given the benefit of the doubt' in order to resolve a disagreement with a tutor about whether he had sought and obtained prior agreement on the topic as the assignment had required. The result was a small increase in his mark. However, he still felt this left him in ignorance of underlying criteria used in marking. Theresa felt unable to pinpoint what it was that had led to a mark of 57 per cent (her first mark below 60 per cent) on a particular assignment, and went to see the tutor concerned. She felt that the discussion they had left her with no clues whatsoever about improvement.

Other concerns about feedback centred on its *timing* and *frequency*. Sophia was working on the sixth of the eight first-year essays before she had any feedback at all, and insisted that feedback should come much earlier, especially in the first year, 'so that you can either get confident, or get help for how to do it better'. Several students argued that assignments should be shorter and more frequent in the first year, on much the same grounds.

All the interviewees had recent experience of study in other institutions and arrangements (including full-time and part-time Advanced Level GCE,[1] Access courses,[2] Diploma in HE courses, various professional qualifications and Open University courses). Many of their comments about being assessed in their university course were made with reference to these other settings. All students knew from personal experience what is was like to receive *useful* commentary on marked coursework, and their remarks strongly suggested that they valued it for its role in helping them to *develop* their capacities in relation to academic work. Well over half of the students interviewed felt that some or all of the feedback they received during their first year fell short of providing this opportunity.

There were, then, strong and shared perceptions amongst these students about the inadequacy of some of the feedback they received on assessed work, and importantly, about the implications of this for their own development. This contrasted with the declared intentions of tutors and with what might be expected from the structure of arrangements for first-year assignments. This is important enough. However, its significance increases when we consider another aspect of the students' accounts: namely, the role of assessment in changes in students' self-perception.

In answer to my questions about how they saw themselves at various times during their studies, many students spoke at length about their 'self-confidence' during different periods, and about connections between this and assessment events, often without any prompting. Theresa described her self-confidence as having reached a peak at the point where she completed her part-time GCE Advanced level examinations which secured her place at the university. Since beginning the degree course, her confidence had progressively declined. Crucially, she saw the causes of these trends as being linked with readjustments to her expectations about the likely classification of her final degree result. A first essay had gained a mark of 74 per cent, but subsequent grades showed a gradual decline from this point. The regularity in this pattern was quite unusual, but the feelings she described were by no means untypical amongst the students interviewed:

Theresa: [my self confidence is] probably lower than its ever been. That last essay did it, because the first two I had back I thought OK this is good, you know you're doing well kid, hang on in there...So I felt good about myself for a while, for a week. And then I got the other one back, and I thought I just don't know the game, this is a game...you know, I'm not playing it right. I'm so dependent on other people's assessment of my work for my own feelings, which is crazy, and I hate that I should be dependent on other people, because they're only assessing a piece of paper, not me. But it always feels so bloody personal... sorry I didn't mean to swear.

David: Well, one invests a lot of effort, time and so on.

Theresa: Yes, it's like a direct criticism of me as a human being, which I know that's not rational, and that's rubbish, but...that's why I get upset I think.

(Theresa, second interview).

Theresa had felt 'devastated' when her assignment came back to her with a mark of 57 per cent, and had 'cried for three days' before arranging to see the tutor who had marked the work. Assignment grades had become a ruling definition for Myra, too. Pressures on her course had combined with stresses at home and in her part-time job, resulting in visits to her doctor and some six weeks away from both study and work. At the end of this period, she had tried to take stock and to readjust her expectations of herself so as not to lead to further difficulties. Interpreting numerical grades on assessed coursework was central in both the generation of her difficulties *and* in her strategy for coping with them. In particular, she resolved to try not to allow assessment grades to obscure all the (many) other dimensions and achievements (as mother, worker, etc.) in her life, claiming that what she had allowed to happen was 'ludicrous'.

It is instructive to compare the many testimonies of this nature with examples of the opposite effect. In her third interview, Doreen had been describing how she had maintained minimum self-expectations with assessed work as a strategy to cope with the potential impact of low grades on her confidence:

David: ...So were you often pleasantly surprised?

Doreen: I got some fantastic results. I got nominated for an award for one of my essays – I didn't get the award, but I got nominated.

David: That's pretty good isn't it?

Doreen: Yes, and I got all firsts, and I think sixty-eight was the lowest in social work, when I moved into the social work bit, but I did I mean the second year wasn't that bad but then the minute I moved into third year, then everything seemed to be upped, and then I got this nomination for an award, and then...people started treating me differently, which was quite interesting.

David: Who did?

Doreen: The people on my course.

David: Your peers, your fellow students?

Doreen: Yes, Yes.

David: What, how did that change?

Doreen: All of a sudden I was some sort of intellectual, very interesting, I was quite fascinated by it really, and so [people would say]... 'Oh well ask Doreen' and all these compliments and all that sort of stuff. It was quite interesting how it was affecting my confidence and my personality and my ability to do better maybe, and all that sort of stuff. It was very interesting little period.

David: How did it affect you, tell me, tell me how it affected you.

Doreen: My work?

David: Yes how did…you just said something about it affected the way you saw yourself as well.

Doreen: Yes definitely, because it was confidence, to me it was all about confidence it was about thinking 'somebody's telling me I can do well'. But at the same time, interestingly enough, when I was told I was had been nominated for this award, I said 'what me? Are you sure you've not got the wrong essay?' and I was decrying myself. And then I said 'what did I do?' because as far I was concerned I did exactly the same formula as for everything else. So…how is that reflected in my…is it me, or is it just 'cos it happened to be at the right time with the right person reading it. So I was interested…[but] still the feedback wasn't there.

David: Right, but the mark was there?

Doreen: The mark was there, but still, you know, they said it was about your style, the style it wasn't about content as such, it was about style. And then I still, I read it yes but I thought well I don't understand, I still don't understand.

David: So you really don't know?

Doreen: No. I wish I did, it would have been so good if someone could have sat down with me and said something about…

David: Why it was so good?

Doreen: 'You could have done this, maybe this could have been a bit better, and this is why, you know, because you put it in this way, or this is how your paragraphs…'

David: So this was in the third year?

Doreen: Yes.

Doreen's account incorporates the earlier point about the utility of feedback for developmental purposes as well as providing a graphic illustration of the impact of grades on self-perception. The extract is also of interest in relation to earlier interviews with Doreen herself. Along with some of the other (mature) students, she had felt that her entry to the university must have been the result of a 'fluke' or a mistake of some kind, and she felt that the university was not really for 'people like her'. Like several students who had gained entry via Access courses, Doreen had noticed that GCE Advanced level qualifications were a constant point of reference amongst tutors and students within first-year teaching, and found this to be undermining of her confidence. However, survival of end-of-first-year exams had given her a greater sense of belonging by the beginning of the second year. But importantly, the extract shows Doreen's reliance on the currency of academic measurements *and* the extent to which this feels beyond her control.

A number of similar accounts go together to build up a general picture of the immense significance of assignment grades and feedback comments on assessed work for the self-perceptions of these students. Most students suggested, directly or indirectly, that numerical grades had a significance which was larger than it should be, or out of proportion in some sense. How are we to understand this significance? Some academics might be tempted to brush the issue aside, putting it down to a tendency on the part of students to over-react. However, in the remainder of this chapter I want to suggest that such questions can be approached in a number of ways. Two sections consider a 'technical' and an 'humanistic' perspective, respectively. These are followed by a section looking at a symbolic interactionist approach. In the final section, I suggest ways in which this approach can be built upon to make clearer connections between the actions of individuals and the structural arrangements within which these take place.

Technical Perspectives

The vast majority of discussion about assessment in higher education is conducted with a focus on *what to do* and *how to do it properly*, so that fairness, transparency, efficiency and validity in relation to standards are maximized. These are necessary concerns, especially as the political agenda moves ever more in the direction of increased control in the name of reassuring stake-holders. A technical approach may have an emphasis on important conceptual distinctions (such as that between assessment *methods* and *purposes*, which are often conflated in practice) or on issues such as comparing the reliability of different methods. Discussion may be at the level of the course, programme, teacher, institution or system.

One very useful example, aimed at teachers in higher education, is a short but comprehensive booklet published by the Higher Education Research and Development Society of Australasia (Crooks 1988). This booklet details eight 'important guiding principles' for tutors when they decide how to conduct assessment. Of particular relevance for the present discussion are principles such as 'Try to ensure that assessment procedures promote and reward desired learning activities and outcomes' (1988: 10); 'Communicate assessment requirements clearly to students' (1988: 14); and 'Strive for effective feedback to students' (1988: 14). These three (of the eight) principles proposed by the author are then given some elaboration, with practical suggestions. For example, with the first area tutors are advised to draw on Bloom's taxonomy to divide the intellectual skills they are trying to develop and measure into three broad types (recall and recognition; comprehension and application; critical thinking and problem solving) and to map their proposed assessment items against these in a schedule. Other practical suggestions include the use of marking sheets which list assessment criteria and a number of categories within each, though Crooks emphasizes that this is 'no substitute...for more detailed, line-by-line comments on the student's work' (1988: 26).

A second example of this approach can be found in a discussion document published by the Universities and Colleges Staff Development Agency. Having given a comprehensive account of a variety of ways in which assessment processes can fall short of even a modicum of reliability and validity, the report ends with a warning to those running courses and marking students' work in higher education:

assessment procedures in higher education are likely to become increasingly open to scrutiny, to candidates, and to candidates' appeals. The need for commonly-agreed marking procedures and techniques is obvious. If collective responsibility for candidates' results is to be maintained, full openness between colleagues and demonstrable internal consistency of courses and related assessment procedures are of vital importance.

(Partington 1995: 15)

It is highly probable that the recommendations in these texts, if allowed to shape changes to the practices reported by students such as those at RU, would result in an improvement in student experience. However, there are important limitations to the approach that this example represents, even in its own terms of leading to improved practice. Firstly, there seems to be an assumption that – at least collectively – tutors have complete control over all facets of the assessment process: yet in many courses, assessment practices reflect the traditions, regulations, wishes and even creativity of institutions, professional bodies, employers and other interests as well. One recent survey suggests an increasing involvement of new 'audiences' in assessment (see Hounsell 1997; Hounsell et al. 1996). Secondly, there is a problem in the way the approach overgeneralizes 'good' assessment practice. As with teachers themselves, different subject disciplines carry different pedagogic assumptions. Changes seen as improvements in one area may be seen as a step backwards in another. Tensions such as these are very familiar to people in staff and educational development in higher education. Their work, which necessarily rests on the notion of improving pedagogic quality through rational means, meets with more resistance in some subject disciplines than in others where there is less of a clash of cultures.

A technical perspective on assessment represents a necessary engagement with important issues. However, while it may promote practices which are in the interests of students as well as staff, it does not set out to give a socially located understanding of such practices.

Humanistic Perspectives

In a paper which focuses on assessment in higher education as a political issue to do with the exercise of power, Heron points out that there is a contradiction between (on the one hand) the level of rationality we assume students can bring to bear on their learning, and (on the other hand) that which we give them credit for in assessment and other processes:

How is it, then, that he [*sic*] [the student] is not entitled by the prevailing system to acquire and actively exercise a fully rational grasp of his own learning objectives, of the programme that is relevant to achieve them, of criteria of assessment and the actual process of assessment in his own work? He is seen as rationally competent to grasp the discipline taught by his academic superiors and to respond appropriately to their assessment. Yet, paradoxically, he is not seen as rationally competent to *participate* in

determining his own academic destiny, nor in assessing his own competence.

(Heron 1988: 78, emphasis in original)

Heron goes on to discuss the arguments which are advanced to justify this
state of affairs, which in his view amount to an 'initiation model' that is both
'hierarchical and authoritarian' (1988: 78). Academic staff are characterized as
being responsible for the bodies of knowledge which are central to the culture,
and must oversee an apprenticeship of the next generation of culture-carriers.
Heron then offers a critique of this model, again pointing to inherent contradictions:

> Unilateral control and assessment of students by staff mean that the
> process of education is at odds with the objective of that process. I believe
> the objective of the process is the emergence of an educated person: that is,
> a person who is self-determining – who can set his own learning objectives,
> devise a rational programme to attain them, set criteria of excellence by
> which to assess the work he produces, and assess his own work in the light
> of those criteria – indeed all that we *attribute* to and *hope* for from the
> ideal academic himself. But the traditional educational process does not
> prepare the student to acquire any of these self-determining competencies.
> In each respect, the staff do it for or to the students. An educational
> process that is so determined cannot have as its outcome a person who is
> truly self-determining.

(1988: 79–80)

Having explained the origins of all this in terms of historical hierarchical
concepts of the person, Heron offers an alternative model of the person and
traces some of the implications of this for educational (especially assessment)
processes. Self-assessment and peer assessment are discussed for what they can
contribute to meaningful assessment (in other words, that which supports
learning). Collaborative assessment is proposed as a transitional arrangement
between the current 'authoritarian' system and the preferable alternative. Here
the tutor can act straight away to begin to ameliorate the way assessment is
usually conducted. Collaborative assessment, says Heron, is the 'next step
forward, first with respect to students' course work, then with respect to final
essays and examinations' (1988: 90).

Heron's analysis has some affinity with the claim that a meaningful distinction may be drawn between pedagogy and andragogy (for example, Knowles
1990; see also Tennant 1988). Conceived as *adult learners*, most students in
higher education do not seem to experience assessment events that contribute
to the goals of self-determination. It is worth noting that Heron's initial argument
refers to the rational capacity of 19-year-old students, and could be presented
with considerably more force in respect of students in UK higher education,
over half of whom have been 'mature students' (over 21 years old on entry)
since 1990 (Department for Education 1992): we might reasonably expect such

students to have had even more opportunities than their school-leaver counterparts to develop their rational capacities.

A similar analysis to Heron's comes from the work of Boud, though here a 'learning' emphasis replaces the 'person' one at the centre of the account. Boud illustrates an 'inconsistency' between the high value placed by academics on critical analysis in their own work, and their uncritical acceptance of many traditional assessment practices. He goes on to draw on a wide sweep of assessment-related research that, collectively, gives a very 'bleak' picture:

> Despite the good intentions of staff, assessment tasks are set which encourage a narrow, instrumental approach to learning that emphasises the reproduction of what is presented, at the expense of critical thinking, deep understanding and independent activity. These findings indicate effects which are quite contrary to those which are sought...All this research has taken place in the context of assessment in which staff decide on the aims and objectives, the assessment tasks, the criteria for judgement and the final outcomes of the process.
>
> (Boud 1990: 104)

Like Heron, Boud compares this state of affairs with the ways in which academics *themselves* develop their work and are assessed, which is often characterized by 'self-assessment, feedback from others and much reworking' (1990: 107). He then suggests some alternative developments in the assessment of students in higher education. These include careful monitoring of assessment practices to see how valid they are in the eyes of students; challenging existing assessment on the grounds that it does not prepare the reflective practitioners needed in the world of work; the introduction of problem-based learning and assessment; and the use of more self and collaborative assessment. All these themes are taken further in Boud's subsequent work (such as Boud 1995).

Analyses like these provide an attractive set of ideas with which to examine both established and innovative assessment practices, because they are underpinned by a model of appropriate conditions and goals for adult learning. The experiences of the students cited earlier in this chapter *may* be understood in relation to the gap they seem to indicate between actual practices and such an ideal. In addition, humanistic reasoning about assessment (and other aspects of teaching and learning) can provide the motivation for an apparently 'technical' approach. A good example of this is a study demonstrating a high level of reliability when tutor, student, self and peer assessments in a biological sciences assignment were compared (Stefani 1994). At the level of the system, the former UK Employment Department published a report commissioned from the University of Newcastle-upon-Tyne which straddles both 'technical' and 'human-istic' approaches. While the main focus of the report was on the implications of competence-based National Vocational Qualifications for assessment in higher education, it also emphasized a number of general disparities between purposes and practices. For example, it stated that none of the 'four main purposes of higher education' (a general educational experience of intrinsic value;

preparation for knowledge creation, dissemination and application; specific vocational preparation; preparation for general employment) was 'particularly well served by current assessment policies and methods' (Atkins et al. 1993: 35, 63).

If the main concern of a 'technical' perspective is with the efficiency and effectiveness of current assessment practices, the humanistic perspective goes on to combine this concern with a philosophical view of the education of persons, deriving both a rationale and an agenda for change.

An Interactionist Perspective

A symbolic interactionist perspective might begin by trying to identify the meanings held – perhaps 'definitions of the situation' – by the various different 'actors' in the social situation, and the extent to which meanings held anticipate the actions of others and are redefined in interaction between, say, tutors and students or students and students. This was the approach taken by Becker et al. (1968) in their classic study of life in a North American university, entitled *Making the Grade*. Becker et al. described in considerable detail the different perspectives that were held by staff and students about the grading system, then not untypical of practices across large parts of North American higher education. They provided a rich description of the students' instrumental approach to learning and assessment, and highlighted the contrast between this 'Grade Point Average' perspective and the declared purposes of the institution. Contrary to common perceptions, the receipt and interpretation of grades was shown to be a fundamentally *collective* process for students. Underneath this was a contrast in the way that faculty and students saw the relation between academic achievement and individual ability. Becker and colleagues explained this as follows:

> Students and faculty view the relation between academic achievement and the *individual ability* of the student differently. The student, from a common faculty point of view, does as well in his [*sic*] academic work as his abilities and motivation allow him to do; if he does poorly, it is because he cannot or will not do better...Students do not share this view. They think that the student controls his own academic fate by the amount of effort he puts forth...They thus attribute variations in student performance to an unwillingness to give sufficient time and effort to academic work or to a deliberate decision to put one's major effort elsewhere.
>
> (Becker et al. 1968: 39, emphasis in original)

This type of analysis suggests that whilst they are a more or less public outcome of the most fundamental academic measurement, grades might mean one thing to students but something else to tutors. Comments associated with those grades might also reflect cross-purposes, if tutors see themselves as supplying justifications for numerical or alphabetical labels whilst students expect developmental information. In Becker's study, staff complained about the emphasis students gave to grades at the expense of scholarship. However, the study also demonstrated the rationality of the *student's* viewpoint, stating that 'a student can choose learning over grades, but only if he is willing to suffer the consequences' (1968: 58–9, 61).

Differences like these in staff and student perspectives are overlaid with a difference in power, the practical consequences of which are taken further in this approach than in the humanist perspective outlined earlier. Student experience is taken to encompass a number of 'areas' beyond learning (such as the organizational, political and the personal, in Becker's terms), an important point given the much narrower 'learner' focus of most writing about student experience in the UK (see Haselgrove 1994). In the area of academic work, the relationship between students and the university was one of *subjection* (Becker et al. 1968: 7, 133). This subjection arises from the fact that

> ...the power to define the terms of the contract lies largely in the instructor's hands. Students may argue over them or, in extreme cases, complain to a departmental head or dean. But they understand that, although they may make the instructor uncomfortable, they have no formal means of influencing the standards he sets for their performance. It is in such ways that the abstract idea of subjection occurs as a concrete reality in the student's daily life.
>
> (1968: 65)

This reality meant that in relation to academic work, 'students...[were] almost completely powerless' (1968: 7), subject to an array of regulations which maintained the staff in a superior position.

This rare study makes use of some of the major analytical ideas within symbolic interactionism (such as situational adjustment, commitment, adult socialization) to develop a rich and insightful account of situated actions and meanings. That is, it leads to a *sociological* understanding of student experience of assessment. However, there are two principal reasons for wanting to look beyond what it provides. The first is about empirical generalization, in that the study reflects a particular time and place. There are major differences between the circumstances of Becker's fieldwork and those of mature students in the UK of the 1990s: for the young students at the University of Kansas, grades were connected in fundamental (and often explicit) ways to so many other areas of student life, including membership of valued fraternity/sorority organizations, notions of 'maturity' and a whole range of obligations and social relations from the security of continued financial sponsorship, to 'dating' other students. For the mature students in RU in the UK, grades have an impact and a significance which is just as great but which seems to operate without the explicit organizational connections illustrated by Becker et al.

The second reason is theoretical, and arises from a recognition of the type of study that symbolic interactionism makes possible. As a form of interpretative sociology, symbolic interactionism is primarily concerned with actions and their subjective meanings. In Becker's own interpretation of the approach, social structures are conceptualized in terms of institutions or organizations seeking to socialize individuals, the effects of which are mediated individually and collectively (see Becker 1995). This is a useful conceptualization as far as it goes, but there are grounds for examining other facets of social structure, such as the sources of the subjection, the basis of the 'currency' of grades, or the historical features of the individuals and the organizations that come together in interaction. The effects of all of these 'structural' aspects are clearly visible in *Making the Grade*, but their origins and maintenance are largely unexplored.[3]

The cultural and political interests which act to maintain the grading system Becker et al. studied are not themselves studied. To an extent, such interests enter into the discussion at the point where the authors leave symbolic interactionism behind, in their conclusion. Furthermore, while the idea that past actions become part of the context for new actions – as 'regularized expectations' or 'the generalized other' – is fundamental to the approach, there is no vocabulary in the Chicago-style of symbolic interactionism to take such a (structural) discussion forward. Indeed, this was a principal reason for the emergence of the 'Iowa School' of symbolic interactionists whose adherents aim to ascertain trans-situational features of action.

Clearly, data like that introduced earlier in this chapter can be interpreted within a symbolic interactionist perspective, but this carries the risk that we focus on agency and end up asserting the distinctive rationality of the different viewpoints involved. Finally, then, is it possible to understand student experience of assessment events in a way that gives simultaneous consideration to this 'agency' *and* 'structural' features?

A Bourdieuian Perspective

Much of the work of Pierre Bourdieu is concerned with the mutual interdependence of structure and agency. A Bourdieuian perspective would suggest a focus on the social practices involved in assessment. What would this mean for an interpretation of the student's widely-shared view of the inadequacy of feedback on marked assignments at RU? Becker's work in Kansas led to the suggestion that there was a 'built-in irremediable conflict' in the system, whereby students engaged in information-seeking because of the importance of grades while tutors made ambiguous statements in response: if tutors were to give the level of detail desired by students, 'the function of examinations and assignments as measures of student ability would be destroyed' (Becker et al. 1968: 86–7). This seems like a useful analysis, but we should recall that all the RU students interviewed had recent experience of formal study in other settings, and that their complaints were made with reference to comparisons with these other experiences. Indeed, three of them were themselves qualified teachers of adults.[4] The feedback they received on assessed work violated their sense of what to expect from a pedagogic arrangement. Importantly, they *brought these expectations with them to the situation*, as part of a cluster of experiences from what seemed like comparable situations (as professionals, as students, as teachers and so on) and which therefore seemed to provide the tools for action. Bourdieu's concept of *habitus* is likely to be useful here, since it refers to socially derived but mutable dispositions that go to make up a sense of reality and a sense of limits for each individual. It offers the possibility of an explanation that is *situated* in an historical sense as well as in a current social reality (see Grenfell and James 1998: 14–18).

The acquired dispositions of the *habitus* allow (effectively infinite) possibilities for strategy. Students producing written work for assessment described their activities strategically, in terms which highlight the real (effectively limitless) scope they have for making choices to do with the process of production as well as the actual content. The burden of many of their complaints was that tutors did not give sufficient information for them to make these choices more intelligently, or in other words to modify their strategies. At the same time, the systematic arrangements for assessing written work (in large numbers, alongside staff's other priorities and so on) made such information hard to come by. Arguably, the students were in a situation organized to provide an initiation into an academic discipline rather than one designed to nurture them as learners (see James 1998). This in turn led them to overestimate the scope for the development of their capacities as learners.

Becker et al. showed how students have to make choices between competing activities with different kinds of reward attached. A Bourdieuian perspective would also lead us to look at 'rewards', but see these as forms of capital pertaining to a series of overlapping fields. The notion of 'field' may alert us to other, equally important questions. What are the rewards to academic staff for spending lots of time writing comments on items of assessed work which are sufficiently detailed to become grist to the mill of student development? How do these rewards measure in importance against other rewards for other activities, such as publication and research? What level of increase in student (and assignment) numbers would these rewards sustain? Other data in the study suggested that the rewards of operating some kind of rational pedagogy were far outweighed by the individual and collective rewards of producing high-quality publications and attracting high-prestige externally funded research contracts. Ironically, the results of these activities also seemed to maintain buoyant student demand. The *habitus* of academic staff can only be understood in relation to the fields in which they are enmeshed and which they themselves continually 'mesh'. The inter-institutional and international nature of some fields means that the academic is playing in several different 'games' at once, and that relations with students may only feature in some, or one, of these 'games'.

What of the impact of grades on students' self-perception, particularly self-confidence? Once again, the interactionist approach has much to tell us. Grades get much of their meaning and significance in interaction, and are socially 'produced' as well as 'consumed'. However, there are fundamental differences between the situations of the students at RU and those at Kansas in the way that grades connect with other areas of life. These differences draw our attention to the complete absence, in the RU data, of anything like the instrumental 'GPA perspective'. Instead, staff and students seemed to share a particular view of assessed work: their joint conception is a technical one, which emphasizes the rationality of judgements of worth of academic products against shared, explicable criteria. Indeed, students often insisted that such criteria (the expectations of tutors) should be better articulated, so that they might maximize their chances of success, and some tutors made conscious efforts to meet this need. Yet assessment was experienced and practised in ways which suggest that this technical conception is only one part of the story. Assignment grades seem to have a strong 'totalizing' tendency, so that the specificity of the conditions and parameters of each judgement are lost: that is to say the visibility of the conditions and judgements decreases as the grades in question are reinterpreted as a prime constituent of personal worth. This 'misrecognition' on the part of students may have parallels in the actions of tutors, where for example a rigid distinction is maintained between a student's grades (considered to be the result of a rational academic process), and a student's feelings about grades, or perhaps 'pastoral' issues such as the student's personal circumstances (which, note, in some exceptional cases, are allowed to influence grades awarded). A Bourdieuian approach asks whether students and tutors share a fiction or misconception of assessed work akin to that Bourdieu describes in relation to language and teaching (see for example Bourdieu et al. 1994).

The argument here is that assessment has to be understood relationally, in that the practices of both tutors and students do more than what we would expect from the interactionist analysis of opposing 'perspectives'. Together, they play a vital role in processes which elevate grades to the point where they appear as naturalized personal knowledge. Such processes have sometimes been assumed to have operated at the level of ideology and to be out of reach for the mere participant. Here I am suggesting that the maintenance of the legitimacy of grades and, of course, degree classification is a joint, active enterprise in which the *habitus* of staff and students operate within distinct but closely-related fields. These fields are increasingly harmonized as students progress through the course and become socialized into the ways of the academic discipline (James 1998). Staff and student practices maintain a situation in which a very specific set of differences between students are expressed in academic currency and are misrecognized as naturalized personal knowledge, much in the sense that Bourdieu suggests happens across whole education systems (for example, Bourdieu 1984: 397). As we saw earlier, mature students like Theresa, Myra and Doreen are wrestling with the inherent difficulty in interpreting grades which seemingly have a will of their own, refusing to keep their place as partial and technical judgements about specific academic performances. Instead, these judgements expand to fill out much of the perception of self, contesting even the most secure of other successes and achievements. This could be understood as a dynamic readjustment of subjective expectations in line with new ('objective') information about academic progress, as the *habitus* and field reconfigure.

Conclusions

At the time of writing, the dominant discourse with regard to assessment in

UK higher education is one of 'benchmarking' and 'threshold standards' as the national Quality Assurance Agency develops models which it is hoped will restore confidence amongst the various 'stakeholders'. To many, this seems to herald some sort of national curriculum for higher education. A 'learning society' rhetoric also continues, in some tension with the assessment discourse (see Broadfoot 1998). On the ground, there is little in the way of routine analysis of assessment practices amongst academics (Ecclestone and Swann 1999), although there are pockets of considerable interest in 'what might be described as an international movement towards "alternative assessment" which is also variously called innovative assessment, performance assessment and authentic assessment' (McDowell 1998). There is also evidence of increasing diversity in assessment practices across at least some higher education systems, and the recognition that this reflects fundamental changes in the nature of higher education (for example, Hounsell et al. 1996).

In this context, given the centrality of assessment events in student experience, it matters a great deal that different perspectives like those outlined in this chapter give us such different understandings. It is clear that the perspectives vary in terms of their scope and implications. The 'technical' one will offer relatively straightforward diagnoses and remedies, but may miss important social processes that jeopardise or prevent the success of its solutions. By contrast, a Bourdieuian perspective may provide an intricate and sophisticated purchase on social practices, but in itself offer few pointers to reform. While it is not the main purpose of this chapter to argue about the superiority or otherwise of a particular perspective, it is clear from the discussion that not all share the same limitations. I have argued elsewhere that a Bourdieuian approach to higher education does offer a better account of social practices in relation to teaching, learning and student experience (see James 1998), and it seems to me that this is also the case with assessment and its effects. However, the main purpose of this chapter has been the more modest one of mapping out some of the territory and illustrating ways in which different perspectives give us different questions and quite different answers.

Notes

1   In the UK, General Certificate in Education Advanced Level qualifications (usually referred to as 'A levels') represent a high-status and highly specialized academic curriculum pathway to higher education, where they function as the most visible of entry qualifications. Though they are aimed primarily at young people who stay on at the upper end of secondary schooling, A levels are also taken as part-time (occasionally full-time) courses by mature students aiming for a university place. As qualifications, they are often criticized for their cost, their narrowness in comparison to academic qualifications in other countries, and for the negative impact they have on the status of other routes in post-compulsory education.

2   From their beginnings in a small number of experimental courses in the late 1970s, Access courses expanded rapidly during the 1980s. By the late 1990s they numbered some 13,000 across the UK. They are usually one-year full-time or two-year part-time courses aimed at adults whose backgrounds have not given them rich educational opportunities in the past. The courses offer a route to higher education

which bypasses the traditional 'A levels', and in contrast to 'A levels', Access courses generally place as much emphasis on the skills required for successful study in higher education as they do on the content of subject disciplines.

3 However, I do not wish to suggest that symbolic interactionism does not allow for any analysis of such things as stratification and differences in economic and political power. Layder goes too far in suggesting that

> The weakness of SI [symbolic interactionism] is that it does not postulate *any* connection between...localised, face-to-face issues and wider structural features...It is the inability of SI to properly come to terms with this structural domain that limits its contribution to the macro-micro issue.
>
> (Layder 1994: 74, emphasis added)

The point here is that symbolic interactionism *does* postulate such a connection, but one which lives in and through interaction and the meanings generated and brought to bear on interaction. As Denzin has shown in his minutely detailed history of the approach, it is also possible to cite many recent examples of symbolic interactionist work which deals explicitly with structural issues. He concludes: 'The problem of the astructual bias in symbolic interactionism is a dead issue' (Denzin 1992: 63).

4 According to the staff list in the Prospectus at RU, none of the staff held such a qualification at the time of the study.

References

Atkins, M.J., Beattie, J. and Dockrell, W.B. (1993) *Assessment Issues in Higher Education*, Sheffield: Employment Department Group.

Becker, H.S. (1995) 'Personal Change in Adult Life', in R.G. Burgess (ed.), *Howard Becker on Education*, Buckingham: Open University Press (first published 1964 in *Sociometry* 27: 40–53).

Becker, H.S., Geer, B. and Hughes, E.C. (1968) *Making the Grade: The Academic Side of College Life*, New York: John Wiley and Sons.

Boud, D. (1990) 'Assessment and the Promotion of Academic Values', *Studies in Higher Education* 15(5): 101–11.

—— (1995) *Enhancing Learning Through Self-Assessment*, London: Kogan Page.

Bourdieu, P. (1984) *Distinction: A Social Critique of Judgement of Taste*, Cambridge, MA: Harvard University Press.

Bourdieu, P., Passeron, J.C. and Saint Martin, M. de (1994) *Academic Discourse: Linguistic Misunderstanding and Professorial Power*, trans. R. Teese, Cambridge: Polity Press.

Broadfoot, P. (1998) 'Records of Achievement and The Learning Society: A Tale of Two Discourses', *Assessment in Education* 5(3): 447–77.

Brown, S. and Knight, P. (1994) *Assessing Learners in Higher Education*, London: Kogan Page.

Crooks, T. (1988) *Assessing Student Performance*, Kensington, NSW: Higher Education Research and Development Society.

Denzin, N. (1992) *Symbolic Interactionism and Cultural Studies: The Politics of Interpretation*, Oxford: Blackwell.

Department for Education (1992) *Statistical Bulletin 18/92: Mature Students in Higher Education-Great Britain 1980–1990*, Darlington: DFE.

Ecclestone, K. and Swann, J. (1999) 'Litigation and Learning: Tensions in Improving University Lecturers' Assessment Practice', *Assessment in Education: Principles, Policy and Practice* 6(3).

Grenfell, M. and James, D. (eds) (1998) *Bourdieu and Education: Acts of Practical Theory*, London: Falmer Press.

Haselgrove, S. (ed.) (1994) *The Student Experience*, Buckingham: SRHE/Open University Press.

Heron, J. (1988) 'Assessment Revisited', in D. Boud (ed.), *Developing Student Autonomy in Learning*, London: Kogan Page.

Heywood, J. (1989) *Assessment in Higher Education*, Chichester: John Wiley and Sons.

Hounsell, D. (1997) 'Assessment, Learning and Teaching in Higher Education: Changing Practices and Their Implications', British Education Research Association Annual Conference, University of York.

Hounsell, D., McCulloch, M. and Scott, M. (1996) *The ASSHE Inventory: Changing Assessment Practices in Scottish Higher Education*, Edinburgh: University of Edinburgh, Napier University and Universities and Colleges Staff Development Agency.

James, D. (1995) 'Mature Studentship in Higher Education: Beyond a "Species" Approach', *British Journal of Sociology of Education* 16(4): 451–66.

—— (1996) 'Mature Studentship in Higher Education', PhD thesis, University of the West of England.

—— (1998) 'Higher Education *Field* Work: The Interdependence of Teaching, Research and Student Experience', in M. Grenfell and D. James (eds), *Bourdieu and Education: Acts of Practical Theory*, London: Falmer Press.

Knowles, M.S. (1990) *The Adult Learner: A Neglected Species*, 4th edn, Houston: Gulf Publishing.

Layder, D. (1994) *Understanding Social Theory*, London: Sage Publications.

McDowell, L. (1998) 'Editorial', *Assessment and Evaluation in Higher Education* 23(4): 335–8.

Partington, J. (1995) *Assessment Processes and Personal Judgement in Higher Education – A Discussion Paper*, Sheffield: Universities and Colleges Staff Development Agency.

Ramsden, P. (1992) *Learning to Teach in Higher Education*, London: Routledge.

Stefani, L.A.J. (1994) 'Peer, Self and Tutor Assessment: Relative Reliabilities', *Studies in Higher Education* 19(1): 69–75.

—— (1998) 'Assessment in Partnership with Learners', *Assessment and Evaluation in Higher Education* 23(4): 339–50.

Tennant, M. (1988) *Psychology and Adult Learning*, London: Routledge.

Thomson, K. and Falchikov, N. (1998) 'Full on Until the Sun Comes Out: The Effects of Assessment on Student Approaches to Studying', *Assessment and Evaluation in Higher Education* 23(4): 379–90.

Part V

Postmodern Perspectives and Implications for Assessment Practice

Editor's Introduction

Ann Filer

Postmodern Perspectives on Power, Culture and Educational Testing

The final pair of chapters in the book set out the challenges of postmodernism to the intellectual and cultural foundations of educational assessment and explore some implications for the way forward. In the opening chapter to this book, Patricia Broadfoot and Andrew Pollard began by talking of 'the complexities arising from the postmodern challenge to the established thinking and practices of late modernity'. They continue:

> This challenge, and reactivity to challenge has given rise to new priorities, new forms of contestation and regulation and new forms of discourse across post industrial nations worldwide…
>
> (Chapter 1)

The challenge to the philosophies and practices of modernity lies in the perception that they have failed to deliver on their promise of economic progress and emancipation through the accumulation of scientific and technical knowledge. Within postmodernist thinking, such 'grand narratives' have lost credibility. Throughout industrial and post-industrial societies, science and technology have contributed to rather than solved problems, and scientific knowledge is neither cumulatively coherent nor value-free. Claims for what constitutes knowledge emanate from the experiences, biases and power relations of particular cultural groups, and fail to incorporate culturally and socially diverse experience and perspectives. Thus postmodernism asserts that not only have the grand narratives of social and economic progress failed, but the knowledge that underpins them is delegitimized (Lyotard 1984: 37).

In the following chapter, Harry Torrance explores the nature of postmodern challenges to the theory and practice of educational assessment. As I described in the introduction to Part I, a prime function of assessment relates to the promotion and evaluation of the knowledge and skills deemed necessary for

economic progress, cultural continuity and the cultivation of individual potential. However, as Torrance describes more fully through his chapter, if the
credibility of the project (progress and emancipation) and the means (scientific
claims for 'truths' and 'reality') are under threat, then the ultimate justification
and legitimation of technologies of assessment are also under threat.

There is, of course, no unified 'postmodern' perspective and there is certainly
no agreement on its potential as an alternative emancipatory discourse within
education. As described above, and perhaps for most postmodern theorists, all
emancipatory narratives have lost credibility. For some, however, the analytic
power of large-scale historical and cultural narratives is still necessary for
constructing an adequate critique of social injustice in education (see suggestions for further reading, below). Indeed, it has been argued that some of the
most important aspects of postmodern critique have been prefigured in the
tradition of critical pedagogy that is traceable back to the 1960s (Morrow and
Torres (1995) cite Giroux and McLaren (1989) and Aronowitz and Giroux
(1991)). Probably a minority of authors in this book would describe their analyses as 'postmodern'. Nevertheless, as a body, the chapters in this book do that
which Torrance suggests postmodern studies of assessment should do. That is,
they challenge those who would claim to be able to 'stand outside the
discourse' to set standards and act with disinterested judgement. In making
'difference' itself a point of view, they also reflect that which, for Lovlie (1992:
120), is a key position of postmodernism.

However, notwithstanding new forms of discourse and contestation arising
from postmodernism, national systems of assessment continue to operate
within the 'sorting and ranking mind set' (LaCelle-Peterson, see Chapter 2 of
this book) of modernity. Allan Hanson opens his chapter in this book (Chapter
4) by graphically depicting American contemporary society as 'awash with
tests'. While testing may not yet be as pervasive in the UK as in the USA,
pupils in England and Wales, their teachers and schools are now subject to
more frequent, high-stakes testing than at any time in history. As Harold
Berlak points out in Chapter 10, the scientific assessment paradigm is at the
height of its influence over national educational policy in North America and
Britain at the same time as its claim to being a science is at its lowest. Berlak
also asserts that this increased political effort to gain control over the
curriculum comes about at a time when white, male Anglo-European political
and cultural dominance is increasingly being challenged. In the USA, for
instance, cultural minorities have challenged the hegemony of politicized,
centralized forms of knowledge assessment. These forms leave no space for the
voices of cultural minorities to articulate and legitimate their own diverse
cultural and historical meanings (Berlak 1995: 148–9). Similarly, feminisms
challenge the androcentrism of traditional Western thought and knowledge
production in which male is constructed as universal-rational-cultural; female
as partial-biological-emotional (Flax 1990; Nicholson 1990). In his chapter,
Harold Berlak discusses ways in which, in response to such challenges, assessment has now been used *explicitly* by dominant political and cultural groups to
promote ideas of national unity. He describes how, in opposition to claims for

culturally diverse representations, performance standards in US and UK schools are now being *overtly* constructed and articulated to reassert and promote (supposedly) underlying shared values and traditional knowledge. The hitherto implicit use of assessment for social and cultural control (see Introductions to Parts I and II) is becoming explicit.

Implications of the Postmodern Critique and Suggestions for Ways Forward

Through the previous chapters in the book, authors have set out implications and suggestions for ways forward in relation to their own fields of analysis. For instance, in various ways they assert the need for assessment practices to focus around the needs of individual learners and on descriptions of desired *learning* outcomes as opposed to graded and hierarchical outcomes. They also asserted the need for a greater awareness of issues surrounding assessment policy and practices among educational professionals and in society generally. This awareness would encompass functions of assessment concerned with social control and social reproduction, issues of differential power and knowledge relations and the production of inequitable outcomes, and of the interpretative, contextualized and value-laden nature of assessment practice.

The two final chapters in this book present further implications for the way forward that help to reframe these key issues in the light of the contemporary postmodern challenge. For Harry Torrance, the way forward includes the necessity for assessment practices to accommodate divergent experience, pupil intentions, wider dialogue and curriculum knowledge that can be local, provisional and 'what works'. In the final chapter, Harold Berlak sets out the case for democratically controlled assessment practices that would devolve power to a broad constituency of individuals and groups with legitimate interests in outcomes, and with a commitment to social justice at its centre.

In my introduction to this book, I stated the need for a clearer articulation of a 'sociological' discourse of assessment as distinct from the 'technical' discourse that prevails. The collection is intended, therefore, to give a more distinct profile to the range of empirical and theoretical enquiry being undertaken within this discourse. My hope is that this clearer articulation and profile will encourage more research in this field, as well as a more coherent development of that which exists. Assessment has become a highly significant area of interest in educational policy development worldwide. As the writers in this book have shown, this new interest in assessment means that it has become a highly contested area as the focus of complex political, economic and cultural expectations for change. The changing and often conflicting priorities for education, and hence for assessment, together with the public and policy debate that they generate, need the perspectives offered by researchers and writers in this field. In justifying this need, I can do no better that to quote from Mark LaCelle Peterson's chapter, 'Choosing Not to Know' (Chapter 2). In arguing the need for change in the 'sorting and ranking mind set (that) is deeply rooted in the history of testing' he states:

Assessment can and must be part of any meaningful transformation of schools and (dare we hope?) of society. Continued study of the ways in which assessment shapes educational outcomes and, more importantly, shapes our thinking about people and possibilities, will play a crucial role in any such development.

In essence then, the way forward has to be through a better understanding of what is inherently social about the practices and products of educational assessment.

Further Reading

In *Social Theory and Education* (1995), Morrow and Torres extensively critique theories of social reproduction and transformation through education and the challenge to them from postmodern theorizing. The authors construct an agenda for research based on the concept of 'critical modernism'.

In 'Social Criticism without Philosophy: An Encounter between Feminism and Postmodernism' (1997), Fraser and Nicholson illuminate the sometimes uneasy relationship between two of the most important political–cultural currents of recent years. This chapter appears in the wide-ranging volume *Feminist Social Thought: A Reader*.

In *Postmodernism and Education* (1994), Usher and Edwards provide a broad analysis of postmodernism, its impact on the theory and practice of education and an introduction to some key writers in the field.

References

Aronowitz, S. and Giroux, H. (1991) *Postmodern Education: Politics, Culture and Social Criticism*, Minneapolis, MN: University of Minnesota Press.

Berlak, H. (1995) 'Culture, Imperialism and Goals 2000', in R. Miller (ed.), *Educational Freedom for a Democratic Society: A Critique of National Goals, Standards and Curriculum*, Brandon, VT: Resource Centre for Redesigning Education.

Flax, J. (1990) *Thinking Fragments: Psychoanalysis, Feminism and Postmodernism in the Contemporary West*, Oxford: University of California Press.

Fraser, N. and Nicholson, L.J. (1997) 'Social Criticism without Philosophy: An Encounter between Feminism and Postmodernism', in M.D. Tietjens (ed.), *Feminist Social Thought: A Reader*, New York and London: Routledge.

Giroux, H. and McLaren P. (eds) (1989) *Critical Pedagogy, The State and Cultural Struggle*, Albany, NY: State University of New York Press.

Lovlie, L. (1992) 'Postmodernism and Subjectivity', in S. Kvale (ed.), *Psychology and Postmodernism*, London: Sage Publications.

Lyotard, J.F. (1984) *The Postmodern Condition: A Report on Knowledge*, Manchester: Manchester University Press.

Morrow, R.A. and Torres, C.A. (1995) *Social Theory and Education: A Critique of Theories of Social and Cultural Reproduction*, Albany, NY: State University of New York Press.

Nicholson, L.J. (1990) *Feminism/Postmodernism*, London: Routledge.

Usher, R. and Edwards, R. (1994) *Postmodernism and Education*, London and New York: Routledge.

9 Postmodernism and Educational Assessment

Harry Torrance

Introduction

Most introductions to or reviews of 'postmodernism' start with various disclaimers about how difficult a concept it is to define and describe. This chapter is no exception. Thus it is not my intention to offer an exact definition of postmodernism but rather to identify some of the parameters of the debates which surround the expression and identify some key issues, linked to key authors, which have implications for the theory and practice of educational assessment. The development of assessment procedures and practices during the twentieth century can be seen as the epitome of a 'scientific' approach to education and of the modernist project in education. The imperative has been (1) to control the measurement process in order to 'isolate the variable' of pupil performance, and thereby (2) to contribute to the Enlightenment project of social and economic development by the appropriate education of the populace. Clearly, challenges to the legitimacy of the modernist project must also entail a challenge to particular manifestations of it, including educational assessment, and it is some of these challenges which I want to try to identify and address in this chapter.

The fulcrum around which debates about postmodernism revolve seems to be a lack of faith in what has been termed the 'modernist' project of rational scientific progress and human emancipation. Thus the key legitimatory assumptions about how to determine truth and worth in the arts and sciences are under threat. However, while postmodernism has become an easily identifiable term, it remains a nebulous concept, or set of interlocking concepts, relating both to changing socioeconomic conditions on the one hand (postmodernity), and changing views of the status and legitimacy of scientific knowledge and the idea of progress (postmodernism) on the other. These basic parameters are played out in different ways in different subject areas. In the arts, the debate is about whether and how to borrow and merge styles from the past in a pastiche which, for example, celebrates the chaotic and profane development of a Los Angeles or a Las Vegas over and above the orderly lines of a Mies van der Rohe skyscraper or a Le Corbusier housing project. Fragmentation, playfulness and popular appeal is taken to be an equal achievement, if not indeed a more significant one, to that of the 'modernist project' of avant-garde elitism allied to social engineering (Connor 1989). In passing, we can note that the implication of rendering mass culture as equally valuable to elite culture could clearly be very worrying to those who have taken it upon themselves to defend 'traditional' values by incorporating them into the school curriculum.

In sociology and economics, and in related fields such as geography, the focus has been on the development of 'post-industrial society' and new forms of global capitalism, whereby a combination of technological change (particularly the introduction of computers, both to control production and facilitate instant electronic communication) and increasing global competition has resulted in major changes in industrial organization. Heavy primary production and manufacturing (coal, steel, etc.) is in decline; the remaining factories, and indeed other businesses, constantly strive to produce more output with fewer workers, and growth industries are those based on knowledge creation and cultural production (design, advertising and so on). Thus it is argued that the production of 'signs', of indicators of lifestyle choices and values, is rapidly replacing the production of 'things': we no longer just buy the car, or the coffee, we buy the idea that sells us the car or the coffee (see for example Kumar (1997) and Smart (1992), among many others). In turn, government tries to respond by focussing on education and developing the rhetoric of a 'high skill, high wage' economy: we cannot compete in primary production and basic manufacturing so we must compete in the knowledge creation and utilization business. Whether knowledge creation and utilization in the twenty-first century can be sustained and fostered by a rigid national curriculum and testing system is of course another matter.

This brings us on to the third subject area which it is important to acknowledge, that of social theory and philosophy, and the overall loss of faith in the idea of progress and the hitherto self-evident supremacy of western scientific knowledge and elite culture. As noted above, many observers and theorists have identified an increasing lack of faith in the ability of science and technology to 'solve' our social and economic problems, and indeed an absolute lack of evidence that they can do so. A century of unprecedented scientific advance has also seen a century of unprecedented human misery in two world wars and continuing conflict around the globe. Most recently in the UK, with the debates over BSE and genetically modified crops, our scientists have been unable to agree among themselves whether or not our food is safe to eat, far less convince us that it is. We are living in the 'risk society' (Beck 1992). In turn, the very idea of human 'progress', the core legitimatory idea underpinning the development of scientific and technological activity, is called into question. Things may change, but that does not necessarily mean that they are getting better, or that 'we' in the 'West', or 'North', are in an unarguably more developed state than those in the 'East' or 'South'.[1]

Thus postmodernist philosophy is calling into question the nature of knowledge, knowing, and the representation of what it is that we claim to know. Scientists, it is argued, are simply another cultural group, albeit currently an elite group, pursuing their own self-interests. They have no 'disinterested' ground on which to stand and 'observe' the social practice and progressive utility of their endeavours. As Carr (1995) has recently put it, since the Enlightenment, 'to engage in rational enlightened thought was to think in accordance with universal principles of rational justification that are independent of particular historical or cultural circumstances...' (1995: 76). Yet it is exactly this disinterested universalism which is now coming under sustained attack:

> whatever else it means, 'postmodernism' is intended to announce that...the 'age of reason' to which the Enlightenment gave birth – has now given way to a 'postmodern condition'...in which...Enlightenment ideas of emancipation, empowerment and rational autonomy are deemed to lack both analytic credibility and political legitimacy...a realisation that the values, assumptions and explanations that derive from the Enlightenment are no longer adequate...
>
> (Carr 1995: 78)

> In the debates about postmodernism the Enlightenment and its legacy have become a polarising axis, defended by those, such as Habermas, intent upon completing what they see as an unfinished, emancipatory project, and attacked by Lyotard and others as the ultimate source of the totalitarian and ecological nightmares that have bedevilled the twentieth century
>
> (Boyne and Rattansi 1990: 3)

In turn, the tendency of mainstream, 'modernist' social science, including educational research, has been to:

> cling to the belief that in principle the deep structure of reality is knowable, that it is intellectually and culturally penetrable...[and]...modernity...may... be defined in terms of an aspiration to reveal the essential truths of the world...
>
> (Boyne and Rattansi 1990: 7–8)

Postmodernism has, rather, made calls 'to abandon (the myths of) representational clarity and total accessibility to the subject' (Stronach and MacLure 1997: 4).

What then are the implications for educational assessment of such volatile movement in the tectonic plates of social science? Postmodernism may be hard to define, but its tendencies and implications cannot be ignored. If the legitimacy of mainstream science and social science is called into question, and with it the related practices and procedures of educational research, so too must be the theory and practice of educational assessment. Postmodernism is not a discrete entity, a 'thing' to which assessment must respond, but it is a constellation of ideas which represent a significant challenge, a *zeitgeist* which cannot and should not be dismissed. I propose therefore to review some of the key ideas of three of the field's most cited writers – Foucault, Lyotard and Baudrillard – whose work has very clear implications for education and educational assessment.

I will then try to conclude by suggesting ways in which assessment practices might change to accommodate at least some of the issues raised.

Examinations and the Creation of Self Discipline

While Foucault is not often regarded in the literature as a mainstream 'post-modernist', his ideas are of central significance to any treatment of the issues raised in this chapter since he wrote explicitly about the role of the 'examination', in both its generic and educational sense, in relation to the institutional creation and sustenance of authority structures and disciplinary procedures (Foucault 1977). Foucault's work is a key exemplar of how mechanisms of social control move from the explicit to the implicit, as societies move from feudal to modern forms of social organization, and in particular how the words that we speak and the thoughts that we think are situated within, and generated through, certain discursive practices. In turn, the fact that we 'create' what it is we speak of, within particular historical and social conditions, is hidden within the taken-for-granted parameters of particular discursive communities. Thus we simultaneously accede to and create the power of authority figures such as doctors, police and prison officers, teachers, social workers and others when we allow them to observe and examine us, while also endorsing the legitimacy of the very act of observation/examination and the role of such professionals in our society. Thus discourses are 'practices that systematically form the objects of which they speak...and in the practice of doing so conceal their own invention' (Foucault 1974: 49), while 'the exercise of discipline presupposes a mechanism that coerces by means of observation' (Foucault 1977: 170).

The meanings which arise from particular institutional practices, then, derive from both the form and the content of those practices, and effectively define what can and cannot be said. In particular, 'educational sites [are] generators of an historically specific...discourse...sites in which certain...validations of and exclusions from the "right to speak" are generated' (Ball 1990: 3). Foucault documents the move from the direct, explicit, feudal exercise of power through physical coercion, to the modern social practices of self-control and professional management whereby discourses of care, training, rehabilitation and treatment construe and construct – 'discipline' – individual behaviour in relation to normative expectations; with 'the examination' being *the* exemplary manifestation of normative disciplinary power. Foucault's argument is that the power relations inherent in examinations imply and depend upon a hierarchy of observational roles and the comparison of individual cases (results) with an established or assumed norm: 'The success of disciplinary power derives...from the use of hierarchical observation, normalizing judgement and their combination in a procedure that is specific to it, the examination' (Foucault 1977: 170). Measurement and comparison are crucial to the effectiveness of the practice:

> the art of punishing, in the regime of disciplinary power, is aimed neither at expiation, nor even precisely at repression...it refers individuals to a

whole that is at once a field of comparison, a space of differentiation...the constraint of a conformity that must be achieved.

(Foucault 1977: 182–3)

With respect to education, this is made all the more effective by the purpose and practice of school tests and examinations being to select and distribute, both within the education system, and subsequently beyond it:

the school became a sort of apparatus of uninterrupted examination... It became increasingly a perpetual comparison of each and all [pupils] that made it possible both to measure and to judge...a constantly repeated ritual of power...it is the examination which, by combining hierarchical surveillance and normalising judgement, assumes the great disciplinary functions of distribution and classification...

(Foucault 1977: 186, 192)

Thus examinations classify and standardize knowledge, defining both the 'subject' (history, geography, etc.) and the 'knowing subject' (the certificated individual). Examinations organize and legitimate knowledge in testable form, while at one and the same time creating/endorsing the fact that knowledge can be organized and tested, and, furthermore, that it is perfectly appropriate for people performing certain roles to organize and test knowledge (see also Hoskin 1990).

However, examinations are not simply 'imposed'. People (teachers and examiners) create them and other people (pupils/candidates) voluntarily submit to them. Here another of Foucault's key insights comes into play, namely that power is a process produced through discursive practices:

power...is not possessed as a thing, or transferred as a property; it functions like a piece of machinery...it is the apparatus as a whole that produces 'power' and distributes individuals in this permanent and continuous field...this network 'holds' the whole together and traverses it in its entirety with effects of power that derive from one another: supervisors perpetually supervised.

(Foucault 1977: 176–7)

Thus we are all implicated/co-opted – we all, from different positions within the hierarchy, have an 'interest' in examinations continuing to exist in one form or another – teachers for purposes of pupil motivation and classroom control; pupils and parents for purposes of credentialism and economic opportunity; and governments to measure performance and do unto teachers what they do unto pupils (with similarly parallel coincidental interests in the process and outcomes, of course).

The argument here, then, is not so much that examinations are a social construct rather than a neutral technological instrument (though of course they are, and this has been noted many times before, for example by Bernstein

(1971) and Broadfoot (1996)); but rather that the use of *any* such instrument underwrites the legitimacy of the process of measurement and comparison. Thus form is as important, if not more so, as content. The very fact that we allow ourselves to be subjected to examinations, or subject others to them, validates and endorses the construction of identity through discourses of 'passing and failing', 'knowing and not knowing', defining who becomes one sort of person and who another. Of course, it might yet be argued that 'it was ever thus': societies must reproduce social stability somehow, and the examination has evolved to distribute social and economic goods in a more meritocratic fashion than hitherto. However, the key insight from Foucault is that in doing this, examinations contribute to the accomplishment of many other aspects of social control, particularly with respect to our understanding and acknowledgment of authority and our internalization of self-discipline. Educational assessment can no longer claim to be naive about such matters or uninterested in them. Future theory and practice must be more self-conscious about these implications of the process; in particular, research and development in assessment must take more seriously the ethical issues of what counts as acting in the 'best interests' of the candidate, and take more trouble to ascertain candidates' views of the process and its outcomes.

The Meta-narrative of Meritocracy and the Performativity of Passmarks

Lyotard's concepts of 'meta-narrative' and 'performativity' are two of the best known and most often cited in discussions of postmodernism (Connor 1989; Sim 1996), and both present potent challenges to educational assessment. They take the debate about how society decides who has the right to speak, and about what, into even more provocative territory. Lyotard questions not only scientific procedure but what makes scientific procedure legitimate in the first place: in what sense can 'scientists' (including, for our purposes, assessment researchers and developers) stand outside of the discourse and practice that they are observing? Science claims to be distanced from everyday narratives and 'common sense' beliefs by developing observational methods and procedures, but ultimately, Lyotard claims, these procedures in themselves are only legitimated by taken-for-granted assumptions about 'higher' or 'grander' purposes: the 'meta-narrative' of technological progress and human development:

> I will use the term modern to designate any science that legitimates itself with reference to a metadiscourse...making an explicit appeal to some grand narrative, such as...the emancipation of the rational...I define postmodern as incredulity towards metanarratives...
>
> (Lyotard 1984: xxiii–xxiv)

Here then is the core of the attack on universal rationality: the claim that it is a 'meta-narrative' that privileges post-Enlightenment empirical science over and above all other ways of knowing and representing knowledge: 'What I say is true because I prove that it is – but what proof is there that my proof is true?' (Lyotard 1984: 24).

Of course, Lyotard is not without his critics (Benjamin 1992; Connor 1989; Haber 1994), with an obvious rejoinder being that his argument can slide into self-defeating relativism. My point here, however, is not to engage directly with Lyotard but to address the issue of what renders educational assessment legitimate; and clearly the ultimate justification is indeed a 'meta-narrative' of social and economic progress giving rise to a method for identifying individuals worthy of accreditation and selection within a meritocratic system. But (and especially in an increasingly multicultural society with global forms of communication) who is to say that one selection of knowledge is more appropriate than another; that one form of assessment renders a 'truer score' than another; indeed that a 'true score' can ever be produced for and adhere to an individual? Knowledge selections must be locally contingent, and assessment results must be a function of the interplay of task, context, individual response and assessor judgement. Thus provisional descriptions of multi-faceted achievements would appear to be the appropriate goal for a system of educational assessment that took such a challenge seriously.

However, while such a prescription would seem to accord with some of Lyotard's apparent preferred value positions *vis-à-vis* the postmodern (privileging the contingent and the local), it nevertheless runs counter to other trends that he identifies, particularly with respect to his other key concept, performativity. Thus while an affinity to the local and the conditional might imply a (nostalgic?) attachment to some sort of authenticity (local rather than universal 'truths'), 'performativity' implies that the very definition of what counts as truth, even under local conditions, has changed:

> No money, no proof – and that means no verification of statements and no truth. The games of scientific language become the games of the rich, in which whoever is the wealthiest has the best chance of being right…The question…now asked…is no longer 'Is it true?' but 'What use is it?' In the context of the mercantilization of knowledge, more often than not this question is equivalent to: 'Is it saleable?'…
>
> (Lyotard 1984: 45, 51)

Thus the goal of scientific activity is 'no longer truth but performativity' (1984: 46), whereby what 'works' *in situ* is taken to have more value than any pursuit of an absolute truth. Increasingly then, as means come to dominate ends, knowledge fragments into many competing 'micronarratives' (sometimes, quite literally, competing in the marketplace) while the focus of scientific activity becomes the improvement of the performance and operational output of the system.

In this, we have the core of a devastating critique of the whole standards, testing and accountability debate. It matters not that test results, or OFSTED inspection reports, or Research Assessment Exercises are 'true' (i.e., reflect with some degree of accuracy a real state of affairs); it matters only that one gets good results, or a good report. In turn, therefore, one's efforts are inevitably directed at practising for whatever items are likely to come up on the test, or manipulating whatever performance indicators are included in the inspection. Thus it does not matter whether test scores identify 'real' educational achievement, just so long as scores are going up; it does not matter whether schools are 'really' providing a high-quality educational experience, just as long as their paperwork is in order for an inspection. In saying this, of course, I am implying that this state of affairs is not, or ought not to be, acceptable, and that in some way there is indeed such a thing as 'real' educational achievement, which ought to be identified, described and encouraged by assessment practices which can indeed provide a more valid account of such achievement than narrow paper-and-pencil tests. I will return to this implicit claim in more detail below.

For the moment, however, I also want to acknowledge that, once again, there is an argument that might insist 'it was ever thus'. Teachers and pupils have always practised for tests, and indeed much has recently been written about turning this potentially negative dynamic into a more positive one by developing more challenging tests, practising for which will 'drive up standards' (for reviews, see Torrance 1995, 1997). Furthermore, examination results, it might be argued, have never pretended to be anything other than crude approximations to the truth of an educational performance; teachers and pupils alike have always 'crammed' for them, with it mattering not a jot whether candidates forget everything they have ever learned the minute they put their pens down, just as long as they pass. Yet this was also always regarded as a very undesirable consequence of an overemphasis on examinations, with test developers seeing such cramming as corrupting of the examination result. Moreover, within the UK this was in any case the orientation of a minority within a minority (essentially those who passed the 11-plus and went on to sit O and A levels), and their intuitive and voluntaristic accommodation to the system (see Foucault) seems to have been forgotten in the monolithic discourse of National Curriculum Test scores and standards. Thus while *some* teachers and pupils may always have regarded examinations as a 'game', results are now overwhelmingly important for *all*. Results brook no argument, or even critical engagement, and the government really does seem to believe that they mean something absolute about (universal) educational standards. Certainly pupils and teachers are having to deal with the arid consequences of that belief.

The Simulacra of Standards

This in turn brings us on to what one might term the ultimate expression of postmodern philosophy, Baudrillard's notion of simulacra (copies that have no originals) and the concomitant argument that our social and economic existence is now driven by the production and consumption of signs, indeed of hopes, fears, aspirations and fantasies, rather than the pursuit of the material, and in particular, material improvement in the quality of life.

Baudrillard, developing Marx's analysis of 'use value' and 'exchange value', argues that the driving force of social and economic organization is no longer production (factory organization, heavy primary industries and so on) but consumption (how goods are perceived and how they are designed to (apparently) satisfy needs and wants). In particular, he argues that the production and consumption of goods and services have gone through a four-stage transformation to create a 'political economy of the sign' (Baudrillard 1981, cited in Poster 1988: 57). Thus:

> needs and consumption are in fact an *organised extension of productive forces*...In the final analysis, the system of consumption is based on a code of signs and differences, and not on need and pleasure...The entire discourse on consumption aims to transform the consumer into the Universal Being...to make consumption the premise of 'human liberation', to be attained in lieu of, and despite the failures of, social and political liberation...
>
> (Poster 1988: 43, 47, 53, original emphasis)

Moreover:

> Whereas representation tries to absorb simulation by interpreting it as false representation, simulation envelops the whole edifice of representation as itself a simulacrum.
>   These would be the successive phases of the image:
> 1. It is the reflection of a basic reality.
> 2. It masks and perverts a basic reality.
> 3. It masks the *absence* of a basic reality.
> 4. It bears no relation to any reality whatever: it is its own pure simulacrum.
>
> (Poster 1988: 170, original emphasis)

Thus we have moved from the production and consumption of real things (goods and services) to the production and consumption of fantasies (lifestyles and political aspirations); a movement from use-value (utility) to exchange value (price) to ephemeral exchange value (the price of an idea) to complete sign value (whereby signs only have meaning and value in relation to other signs). Norris (1990) summarizes this as a position whereby:

> It is no longer possible to maintain the old economy of truth and representation in a world where 'reality' is entirely constructed through forms of mass media feedback, where values are determined by consumer demand (itself brought about by the endless circulation of meanings, images and advertising codes), and where nothing could serve as a means of distinguishing true, from merely true-seeming...habits of belief.
>
> (1990: 121)

Once again, Baudrillard has his critics (including Norris (1990), quoted above). Yet his insight is provocative and persuasive: think of the new shopping malls that we have become so used to of late, created out of concrete and cabling, yet able to convince us that we have just had tortilla and cerveza for lunch in 'The Old Cantina', and that later in the afternoon we should take tea and scones in 'Ye Olde English Tea Shoppe' (complete with thatch on the roof and wait-resses in starched uniforms). No Mexican border town ever had such a Cantina, no village green ever had such a Tea Shop, yet their memories are evoked to persuade us that all is well with the world. So it is with the National Curriculum: the perfect simulacrum of a high culture grammar-school-curriculum-for-all that never was. So it is with the debate over 'standards', which attempts to sell us not just the idea of educational improvement but the fantasy of economic redemption. Indeed so committed to image, rather than reality, has the Depart-ment for Education and Employment (DfEE) become, to be *seen* to be doing something, rather than *actually* doing something, that it engages advertising agencies to recruit teachers (see for example the *Independent* Education Section, 18 March 1999) and produces its own in-house magazine of the sort normally received from banks and building societies (*Teachers*, Issue 1, January 1999, published by DfEE). All of which is not to say that educational improve-ment and/or economic success are impossible to achieve, but rather that, insofar as they represent real goals that might be achieved, they depend on considerably more than simply being seduced into believing that they can be.

Thus to return to the concept of the simulacrum, there never was a time when 'standards' were universally 'high' and economic success derived from such a state of affairs. During the previous 'high water mark' of testing, selec-tion and streaming, in the 1950s and 1960s, no more than 20 per cent of the school population went to grammar schools, let alone took O levels and went on to A levels and higher education. Indeed, the school leaving age remained 15 until 1974, and most children did indeed leave at the earliest opportunity. Thus while universally high(er) standards for *all* might be considered a laudable aspi-ration, and indeed a significant development not hitherto achieved, it is unlikely to be accomplished by a return to the supposedly 'tried and tested' curriculum and teaching methods of the past – since they did not exist, at least not in the form now being invoked. And of course, economic success derived from the terms of international trade (still relatively favourable to the UK until the early 1960s), not educational standards. (For a more substantive review of the 'standards' debate, see Torrance (1997).)

Perhaps more interestingly for our purposes here, however, Baudrillard also notes widespread concerns about the disappearance of 'the real' – which has not happened without our noticing and thus provoking a sense of loss – and he alerts us to the parallel development of a struggle to preserve it. Thus alongside the production of simulacra:

> as though in response to the awareness of the fading out of the real, is a com-pensatory attempt to manufacture it, in 'an escalation of the true, of the lived experience'…the cult of immediate experience, of raw, intense reality…
>
> (Connor 1989: 56)

Now, while the raw, intense realities of 'bungee jumping' or 'sky surfing' have not yet made their appearance in debates about contemporary forms of assessment, the whole notion of 'authenticity', and the issue of practical competence, most certainly has. The argument is made in terms of standards, validity and fitness for purpose. If we want schools to develop challenging programmes for pupils, assessment tasks must encapsulate and test challenging goals. Thus assessment must be 'authentic'; it must present pupils with 'real' tasks and 'real' challenges, calling forth the skills and capabilities of enquiry, design, analysis and report writing through extended tasks, rather than just the recall of knowledge through paper-and-pencil tests.

Such arguments are currently being made in the context of debates about how best to use assessment to raise standards, though they are being given relatively little attention by policy makers. In the face of an apparently irresistible political will to simplify and narrow assessment to its lowest common denominator of externally written and marked tests, such arguments are seen as at best too complex, and at worst evidence of further self-interested lobbying by 'the educational establishment'. However, the key point for the purposes of this paper is that while such a position is seen as radical with respect to current political debate, and indeed might also be seen as radical with respect to the different forms of (potentially irreconcilable?) knowledge about a candidate that it might produce, at present, authentic assessment must still be seen as a scientifically modernist proposition. That is, it is premised on the ability of the assessment method to access an underlying reality; to identify 'authentically' the 'essential truth' of what a candidate can 'really' do. I will return to this point in the conclusion, but for the present we might simply note Baudrillard's contention that 'it is always a false problem to want to restore the truth beneath the simulacrum' (Poster 1988: 182). The implication is that there is little point in trying to render examinations more 'real', especially in present circumstances, for they will always be unreal, with the performance being context-bound and candidates always trying to discover and provide what it is they think the examiner wants to hear.

Implications for Educational Assessment

Others have noted the importance of postmodernism for educational research. Some, while recognizing the strength of the challenge, are resistant (Carr 1995; Kemmis 1992); others 'embrace' it (Stronach and MacLure 1997); still others distance themselves from its most radical implications while using its concepts and methods in their work (Ball 1994; Hargreaves 1994). Indeed, Hargreaves has previously dismissed 'imposed testing and curriculum requirements' as an attempt to 'restore and reinforce the crumbling edifice of modernity' (1994: 33). My conclusions will probably reflect this latter position; sufficiently convinced of the potential reality of a high(er) quality educational experience for pupils as to take the search for definition (and valid assessment) seriously, while rejecting the narrow definitions currently in mainstream political circulation and the concomitant 'meta-narrative' of universal standards deriving from and being driven by central intervention.

Clearly, present government policy on education and the use of educational assessment is inadequate to the challenge of postmodernity – to the complexity and fragmentation of contemporary social and economic life – even if it can be analysed in postmodernist terms and seems at times to be making use of post-modern strategies (performativity and the simulacrum of standards). A rigid, monocultural, centrally determined curriculum, policed by a narrow testing system, is unlikely to provide the circumstances in which innovative approaches to teaching, learning and assessment will flourish. More importantly for the discussion here, however, is to reflect on what alternatives have been posited by assessment researchers over recent years and what further developments may be necessary and desirable. As noted in the introduction, assessment in educa-tion can be treated as a special case of research in education – a form of enquiry into what pupils know, understand and can do – and as such can be seen as the enduring manifestation of modernism, indeed of positivism, in educational research. The presupposition is that for any task and in any circumstance, there is a 'true score' which can be ascertained and reported for an individual test taker. Of course test developers have always acknowledged threats to the reliability of their instruments, but they have not admitted that this fundamentally threatens the legitimacy of the exercise (Torrance 1986). Indeed, following Foucault and Lyotard, we can see that the development of instrumentation contributes to the maintenance of legitimacy within the confines of the 'discipline'. There have also been challenges to test taking *per se*, particularly with respect to the need to gather a wider range of evidence (coursework, practical work and so on) in order to come to a properly informed (valid and reliable) judgement. But this does not challenge the basic assumption that a valid and reliable result can be produced (see Murphy and Torrance (1988) for a fuller review). Similarly, Wood (1987) and Gipps (1994) have argued that there has already been a paradigm shift in assessment from an essentially psychometric model (measuring individual differences) to a more educational one (involving description and feedback to aid learning). Yet here too, as with the notion of authentic assessment mentioned above, it might be argued that there is still an assumption that the descriptions on which feedback is based derive from legitimate methods employed by teachers working in parallel with test developers. Thus all such developments can perhaps be seen to parallel the qualitative/quantitative debate in the mainstream of educational (and social) research: such developments challenge the positivist orthodoxy, but still legitimate the idea that teachers (researchers) can and should exercise power over their pupils (research subjects) to reach conclusions, while also contributing to maintaining the discourse of states of knowing, not knowing and who has the right to decide.

Perhaps more intriguingly, the Record of Achievement (portfolio) move-ment, which has ebbed and flowed over the past twenty years or so, has at times sought to elevate the voice of the pupil over and above simply providing employers and other third parties with a more comprehensive (teacher-written) report on pupils' achievements (see Broadfoot et al. 1988). The movement has also given significance to achievements outside the mainstream academic curriculum and indeed, on occasions, to achievements outside school. In this we can certainly see evidence of attempts to accentuate the importance of the local and allow the voice of the pupil to be heard. However, the emphasis in many schemes on dialogue and even negotiation between pupil and teacher might be interpreted as an attempt to keep faith with the notion of a true score, even perhaps to accomplish the ultimate modernist version of the truth through the creation of Habermasian 'ideal speech situations' in schools. Also, unfortunately, though perhaps predictably, such attempts seemed to fall foul of the unbalanced power relations between teachers and pupils very quickly (James 1989). In addition, Records of Achievement have been criticized for potentially exposing pupils to even more scrutiny (in the Foucauldian sense) than traditional examinations (Hargreaves 1989), since every aspect of a pupil's life, in and out of school, would be potential material for inclusion. Nevertheless, one has to start somewhere and I am minded to suggest that the rehabilitation of some of the more ambitious aspirations of the Record of Achievement movement is long overdue, as long as due attention is paid to identifying a wide range of accomplishments, as witnessed by a wide range of adults in and out of school, and is accompanied by a much more self-conscious commitment to privileging the pupil voice.

Certainly when one thinks about looking not just one or two, but ten, twenty or thirty years ahead in the theory and practice of educational assessment, accommodating difference would seem to be the most significant challenge. The bleakest postmodernist analysis would suggest that performativity and the production of simulacra have such a hold on social life that whatever is done in particular circumstances will have little consequence: it matters not that any 'real' educational experience is sought or encapsulated in 'authentic' assessment systems, just as long as the populace can pursue their chimerical desires within a virtual reality. Computer-generated and scored multiple choice tests, taken when wanted or needed for particular purposes via the internet, will suffice for the purpose. Nostalgia freaks can likewise take simulated 'authentic' tests in a virtual 'educational' environment.

Now it may be that some of this technology does indeed come to be used in ways similar to this, but the context must be one in which difference is protected, rather than punished, and dialogue and interaction between learner and teacher are paramount. Thinking more positively about performativity, a key implication is that 'knowledge' now resides in 'what works', what makes sense and solves problems at local level. This pragmatism seems to me to be a very important corrective to the grandiose claims of a uniform approach to educational assessment, especially when manifested in a 'national' system of curriculum and assessment. A key substantive issue for schools and attendant assessment systems to address is how to provide a meaningful educational experience for pupils with diverse needs and from diverse backgrounds in a world where trying to provide universally correct answers is inadequate to the educational task. So many 'answers' now revolve around the phrase, 'it depends on the circumstances', and it is precisely these circumstances that pupils ought to be encouraged to investigate and debate. A single 'correct' answer is no longer credible, but encouraging children to investigate what might count as a reasonable answer, and by what criteria and under what circumstances, would seem to be a core aspiration for both a curriculum and an approach to assessment in the twenty-first century.

One of the goals that Lyotard sets for postmodern science is precisely the identification of local knowledge(s) and surprises – 'paralogy' – or 'the search for dissent' (Lyotard 1984: 66), and it is accessing dissent that should now be explored in both research into and development of assessment. Postmodernist *study* of assessment would ask what social relations and assumptions about knowledge are inscribed in the assessment process, and would enquire into its origins and development, explore its embedded assumptions and resist abstraction and reification of key concepts such as ability and achievement – as do many of the chapters in this book. Postmodernist *development* of assessment would attempt to respond to the fragmented, individualistic, multicultural and post-colonial culture which we now inhabit, particularly trying to provide spaces for pupil response and dialogue to be heard. Theory and practice must respond to the challenge of divergent experience and address questions about who has the right to 'speak for others' by setting standards, who can claim to 'stand outside the discourse' and act as a disinterested judge of current achievement and future potential. Interestingly enough, Cooper and Dunne's research strategy reported in this book (see Chapter 5) might also provide a potential starting point for what such a response might involve, offering pupils the opportunity to reflect, to think again, and to change their 'answer' if they so wish. An approach to assessment which attempted to develop this more systematically would also resist legitimating the process of universal judgement – accepting that some pupils may be in a state between knowing and not knowing – learning, in fact, and being able to continue to learn.[2] Thus assessment should focus on identifying *what* pupils think is a reasonable answer in a particular context, but also *why* they think this – what are their criteria for response, and what do they think of the teacher/examiner's assumptions? Assessment should also be concerned to find out *what else* it is that pupils know, and *want* to know, since this will form the core of a genuine dialogue about the purposes, processes and desirable outcomes of schooling; the core, in fact, of a high(er) quality educational experience, leading to higher educational standards.

An immediate critical response might be that this is utopian stuff; aspects of it have already been tried and found wanting in the development of Records of Achievement, and the rest will simply never come to pass. My response in turn is that educational assessment is in need of some radical rethinking; the issues of complexity and difference cannot be ignored. If not this, then what? Perhaps this chapter will at least, in further turn, provoke others to respond to the question.

Notes

1 Similar issues are also being raised in anthropology with respect to who has the right to enquire into and speak for 'the other'; see Boyne and Rattansi (1990: 34–6).

2   Stronach and MacLure (1997) also report research strategies involving 'respondents' in continuing dialogues about method and substance which could be similarly developed.

References

Ball, S. (ed.) (1990) *Foucault and Education*, London: Routledge.

—— (1994) *Educational Reform: A Critical and Poststructural Approach*, Buckingham: Open University Press.

Beck, U. (1992) *Risk Society: Towards a New Modernity*, London: Sage.

Benjamin, A. (ed.) (1992) *Judging Lyotard*, London: Routledge.

Bernstein, B. (1971) 'Classification and Framing', in M.F.D. Young (ed.), *Knowledge and Control*, London: Collier-Macmillan.

Boyne, R. and Rattansi, A. (eds) (1990) *Postmodernism and Society*, Basingstoke: Macmillan.

Broadfoot, P. (1996) *Education, Assessment and Society*, Buckingham: Open University Press.

Broadfoot, P. et al. (1988) *Records of Achievement: Report of the National Evaluation of Pilot Schemes*, London: HMSO.

Carr, W. (1995) 'Education and Democracy: Confronting the Postmodernist Challenge', *Journal of Philosophy of Education* 21(1): 75–91.

Connor, S. (1989) *Postmodernist Culture*, Oxford: Blackwell.

Foucault, M. (1974) *The Archeology of Knowledge*, London: Tavistock.

—— (1977) *Discipline and Punish*, London: Allen Lane.

Gipps, C. (1994) *Beyond Testing: Towards a Theory of Educational Assessment*, London: Falmer.

Haber, H. (1994) *Beyond Postmodern Politics*, London: Routledge.

Hargreaves, A. (1989) *Curriculum and Assessment Reform*, Buckingham: Open University Press.

—— (1994) *Changing Teachers, Changing Times*, London: Cassell.

Hoskin, K. (1990) 'Foucault Under Examination: The Crypto-Educationalist Unmasked', in S. Ball (ed.), *Foucault and Education*, London: Routledge.

James, M. (1989) 'Negotiation and Dialogue in Student Assessment and Teacher Appraisal', in H. Simons and J. Elliott (eds), *Rethinking Appraisal and Assessment*, Buckingham: Open University Press.

Kemmis, S. (1992) 'Postmodernism and Educational Research', paper presented to ESRC invitational seminar, University of Liverpool.

Kumar, K. (1997) 'The Post-Modern Condition', in A.H. Halsey et al. (eds), *Education: Culture, Economy, Society*, Oxford: Oxford University Press.

Lyotard, J. (1984) *The Postmodern Condition: A Report on Knowledge*, Manchester: Manchester University Press.

Murphy, R. and Torrance, H. (1988) *The Changing Face of Educational Assessment*, Buckingham: Open University Press.

Norris, C. (1990) 'Lost in the Funhouse: Baudrillard and the Politics of Postmodernism', in R. Boyne and A. Rattansi (eds), *Postmodernism and Society*, Basingstoke: Macmillan.

Poster, M. (ed.) (1988) *Jean Baudrillard: Selected Writings*, Cambridge: Polity Press.

Sim, S. (1996) *Jean-Francois Lyotard*, Hemel Hempstead: Prentice Hall/Harvester Wheatsheaf.

Smart, B. (1992) *Modern Conditions, Postmodern Controversies*, London: Routledge.

Stronach, I. and MacLure, M. (1997) *Educational Research Undone: The Postmodern Embrace*, Buckingham: Open University Press.

Torrance, H. (1986) 'What Can Examinations Contribute to School Evaluation?' *Educational Review* 38(1): 31–43.

—— (ed.) (1995) *Evaluating Authentic Assessment: Problems and Possibilities in New Approaches to Assessment*, Buckingham: Open University Press.

—— (1997) 'Assessment, Accountability and Standards: Using Assessment to Control the Reform of Schooling', in A.H. Halsey et al. (eds), *Education: Culture, Economy, Society*, Oxford: Oxford University Press.

Wood, R. (1987) *Measurement and Assessment in Education and Psychology*, London: Falmer.

10 Cultural Politics, the Science of Assessment and Democratic Renewal of Public Education

Harold Berlak

Tests as Instruments of Science

In the USA and Britain today, educational policies are on similar trajectories. Dominating virtually all news and discussions of education policies are so-called 'league tables' in Britain, and their counterpart in the USA, rankings by standardized test scores. Although there is an increasing body of sceptical and critical professional and public opinion, there are no signs that the rush of governments to impose more testing and rankings of students, educational institutions and teachers is diminishing. Indeed, the inclination of elected officials is toward more public accountability, which in the USA and UK translates into greater use of mass-administered, high-stakes testing and rankings. In both nations, at all levels and in all sectors of the educational system, ratings and test scores play a determinate role in where and how individuals are educated and ultimately gain or fail to gain access to particular schools, jobs and professions. Based largely on students' performance on tests, entire schools are disestablished and 'reconstituted'. Increasingly hinging on test results are school budgets, the professional reputations and job longevity of educational officials, superintendents and principals, and whether teachers are credentialed, receive tenure and given salary increments.

While standardized testing and rankings by test score have long been a part of the educational landscape, particularly in the USA, reliance on testing and national, state and local rankings is on a scale that is unprecedented. The new policy thrust of attempting to raise national educational standards by tying them to nationwide measurements of results was developed and first imposed by right-wing free market conservative governments in the USA and the UK. In Britain Thatcher's 1988 Education Act, and in the USA the submission to President Bush and Congress of the 1992 report *Raising Standards for American Education* marked the beginnings of this new effort to shift the balance of power away from local authorities, schools and teachers toward centralized, bureaucratic state control. Now more than ever, the major issues of what and how to teach are being decided by politicians, government agencies such as the Office for Standards in Education (OFSTED), the National Goals Panel, state legislatures, state boards of education, and a raft of appointed committees, panels and commissions. These policies of centralizing power in matters of curriculum and pedagogy have not only been continued but are now championed by both the Clinton administration and the Blair government.

The justification for mandating measurement of results employing rankings and tests is that, while imperfect, they are the best if not the only basis for guaranteeing neutrality and for making fair and objective statements about the comparative worth and educational productivity of students, teachers and educational institutions. The logic for the policies appears unassailable, almost self-evident. Education is a labor-intensive and expensive enterprise, cost containment requires public oversight, and at present there is no feasible alternative to creating league tables and comparative rankings of educational performance without standardized measurement of educational outcomes.

The claim of objectivity and neutrality of tests and rating schemes that is essential to this system of national or state accountability rests on the scientific credibility of the twentieth-century science of mental measurement and evaluation, with its technology of specification and quantification of 'variables' and 'outcomes' and use of the 'normal curve' for constructing tests and for making comparisons within and among 'populations'. Test technology represents what Harry Torrance in Chapter 9 calls 'the epitome of the scientific approach to education and of the modernist project in education'. It is an exaggeration to say that the science of educational measurement, its ways of thinking and techniques, created the current obsession with using tests as the measure of educational productivity, but without the technology, current policies are simply unimaginable. This technology makes it possible to convert educational achievement or 'productivity' into an entity, a commodity which can be measured and compared quantitatively.

The advantage of giving scientific sanction to the commodity of educational productivity is enormous. It provides those who govern in with a technology to create 'standards' to measure the commodity of educational productivity and make presumably objective and unbiased quantitative statements about how little or much an individual, school, state or local educational authority possesses of this commodity compared to others. With a scientific basis for determining the educational productivity of individuals, schools and local districts, politicians and policy makers have the tools for making rational, cost-effective decisions. One can determine presumably, whether X amount of input placed here or there will lead to a net increase in productivity. It becomes possible to instil more discipline into the 'delivery system'. Authorities can identify the teachers, schools and local districts that fail to produce, and institute marketplace remedies, privatization, vouchers, charter schools and other policies that encourage schools to compete for students and resources. National curriculum goals coupled to standardized testing are seen as essential for maintaining control and disciplining the 'providers' of the commodity, local educational authorities, schools and teachers. Twentieth-century educational science, together with the field of applied educational statistics over the last seventy or so years, has constructed this conception of educational productivity and this way of thinking about the educational and the schooling process which today passes as common sense.

My first summary point is that this science for measuring educational productivity and its technology of testing is currently at the height of its power and influence in shaping government policy and the everyday process of schooling, at the very same time that its claim to scientific legitimacy is at its lowest. The case undermining the scientific standing of the science of educational and psychological testing has been developing for almost as long as such tests were created in the early years of this century. Charges by critics of the banality of the tests, and of cultural, gender and racial bias, have been and remain a constant. However, as writers in this volume have shown, the flaws in the scientific logic on which the credibility of the technology depend run very deep to its core. The difficulties are not of the variety that can be overcome by chasing down ambiguity and apparent cultural, racial and gender bias within particular test items and then reworking them. I will not attempt here to recapitulate the range of arguments made by other writers in this volume and elsewhere (see Kamin 1974; Gould 1981; Gardner 1983; Cherryholmes 1989; Berlak 1992; Raven 1992; Neil and Medina 1990; Hilliard 1991; Darling-Hammond 1995). I will, however, drawing freely from others, summarize what I see as a fundamental and fatal flaw, the question of test validity.

I begin with a position more fully argued by Allan Hanson in Chapter 4: that mental tests are not measures of pre-existing realities or qualities of mind, but rather, tests create that which they purport to measure. Thus, 'intelligence' as measured by a test is not a characteristic of a person's mind but an artefact of the technology of 'intelligence' testing. This is not to say there are no real differences among individuals in intellectual capacity, just as there are differences in visual or auditory acuity. A score on an IQ test is 'real,' but owes its 'existence' to items on an 'intelligence' test which has been composed by a panel of experts in accordance with their notions of what knowledge and abilities should be considered marks of intelligence, and the canons of measurement science. Whether there is any relationship between an IQ score and those qualities of mind and behaviour that we in this or any given society might refer to as 'intelligence' is quite another matter.[1] In the same way that numerical calculation of intelligence (or IQ) has no reality other than as a score on a test, so too there is no reality to 'academic achievement' as measured by a standardized test. One's 'achievement' in math, science, reading and so on as measured by a test is an artefact of the items on an achievement test. Again, it is not a question of whether genuine differences in human capacities and achievements in mathematics and other domains exist which may to some degree be measured and compared. Rather, the question is whether a test, for example, a reading test, measures what it claims to be measuring, a person's ability to read. A top rank or score in the 99th percentile on a particular test of reading ability tells us only how an individual or group score compares with others taking the same test, but says nothing whatsoever about whether persons who score well on a test have the capacity to read with meaning and understanding in the everyday world.

The science of measurement does offer a solution to the apparent circularity that psychological and educational tests merely measure whatever it is they measure. The purported solution was devised in the early decades of the twentieth century and refined over the ensuing eighty years. The credibility and usefulness of tests, according to the canons of the field, are said to depend on the reliability and validity of the 'instrument'. The term 'instrument', which is commonplace in social and behavioural sciences, is noteworthy. Instruments are things, objects that stand outside and apart from the phenomena being measured. In this sense, instruments are 'dispassionate' or neutral. The science of psychological educational testing adopted the metaphor of *instrument* along with the companion metaphors of *reliability* and *validity*. Test scores are from this perspective comparable to tic marks on a thermometer or meter stick. Whether scores, or percentiles that are calculated based on individuals responses to the items on achievement test or any standardized measure, say anything useful, meaningful or true about a person's actual educational performance or achievements depends upon whether the instrument possesses 'reliability' and 'validity'.

The leading theoreticians in the field of scientific measurement have been attempting to untangle the distortions and confusions produced by the uncritical use of these metaphors since my days as a graduate student almost forty years go. In those pre-postmodernist days, the metaphor of 'instrument' was taken quite literally, and the search was for technical solutions which yielded statistical indices of test reliability and validity. Since the 1950s, the American Psychological Association, the American Educational Research Association and the National Council for Measurements in Education have published technical standards and recommendations for establishing and reporting test validity and reliability. Both metaphors are problematic, but I focus on the concept of test validity because it represents the effort of the science of mental measurement to address the veracity or truthfulness of a measure.

In the last two decades, naïve behaviorism and simplistic operationalism have been in retreat in the academy. As criticisms of positive behavioural social science grew and qualitative research and theorizing gained more legitimacy, earlier notions about test validity shifted. The naïve empiricism of the early years has given way to a more nuanced and sensible conception of 'consequential' validity. The validity or worth of a test is now said to depend in part upon the actual consequences or effects of using an educational or psychological measure (Messick 1989). The invention of 'consequential validity' is an advance in that it is a tacit admission of the limits of operationalism and that context cannot be ignored. But the argument that the validity of an instrument depends upon the consequences of its use also means that the case that tests are technical neutral objects somehow detached from the ebb and flow of life is patently false.

The evaluation of consequences in human affairs is never a neutral or an unbiased act. The instrument metaphor in educational science has led us astray, sending us on a phantom search for 'objectivity'. There is no escape from 'qualitative' judgements made by fallible, biased human beings who are decidedly not objective or detached, and who have a point of view about which consequences are and are not desirable. If the validity of an educational measure cannot be determined without the intervention of human moral, educational and/or political judgements which the experts now admit, no scientific or technical process can exist for establishing the validity of a test on which its claims of fairness and objectivity rest.

Social Context: Measurement as Process

The fact that there is no basis for the view that standardized tests and rankings are scientific instruments, devices that stand outside of history, leads us to the rather unremarkable conclusion that educational tests are not things at all but a set of processes, social interactions between test creators, test givers and test takers. In the case of government-mandated tests, they are a set of carefully delineated administrative procedures for measuring 'educational productivity' and creating a quantitative public record of a target population's responses to these procedures, the records or tracings of these procedures being in the form of tables of scores, rankings or percentiles.

When the mystification of tests as scientific instruments is stripped away, along with it goes any claim that test scores transcend context. Put differently, it means that things such as standardized measures of educational performance are a mirage; they do not exist. Standardization requires that, for example, a given score on a reading test received by a student in school situation type A, a public or private school serving solidly white middle-class or upper middle-class families, is more or less equivalent in terms of educational productivity to the same score earned by a student in situation B, an urban public school that serves black and brown children who reside in the poorest, economically distressed areas. This proposition is clearly untenable, as the writers in this volume show. Context matters. Differences in numbers are not without meaning, but they can only be understood and interpreted in the context of the school situation, which includes the existing power relations in the school and in the larger society.

There is an overwhelming body of research conducted over the last two decades documenting that, beyond a shadow of a doubt, that the school context, the particularities of its history, the immediate and wider socioeconomic context, the language, race and social class of its students and their families, and the culture of the school itself have an enormous bearing on students' interest in and performance on all school tasks, including taking standardized tests and examinations. This volume is testimony to the range and depth of careful scholarship that has been carried out on the everyday process of schooling, on the epistemology of tests, and on the consequences of government policies that mandate the use of standardized measurement and ranking procedures as the means for raising educational standards. George Madaus in Chapter 3 shows how closely the technical and educational questions intersect with the broader issues of equity and social justice. Tests do not introduce more equality and fairness into the system, but less, with more streaming and stratification by family income, wealth and race (Hilliard 1991; Pullin 1994; Madaus 1994; Darling-Hammond 1994; Miller 1995).

The work of PACE (Chapters 1, 5, 7 and 8) (see Pollard et al. 1994; Croll 1996; Pollard and Broadfoot 1997) is noteworthy here. PACE was unique in that it was an externally funded, independent effort to map out in a systematic and meticulous way the consequences of the unprecedented changes that were taking place in British primary schools since the Reform Act of 1988 and the subsequent 1992 Education Act. The former introduced for the first time in the history of England and Wales a National Curriculum, and centralized control of what was taught. The latter shifted many of the powers over curriculum and pedagogy formerly vested in Local Educational Authorities and school-level professionals to London. This centralizing process included the abolition of the independent HMI (Her Majesties Inspectorate), which was considered to be too liberal in outlook and sympathetic to teachers. Inspection arrangements were put into the hands of a newly created entity, the Office for Standards in Education, or OFSTED.

PACE studies documented dramatic narrowing of the curriculum and learning opportunities, devaluation of teacher knowledge, declines in teacher and headteacher morale, and increases in pupil anxiety. PACE studies also document changes in school structure and governance. Headteachers once well insulated from the turmoil of national politics and bureaucratic regulations have become highly vulnerable to the vagaries of politics. (A recent issue of the *Times Education Supplement* ran an article on the difficulties of finding willing candidates for headships of schools in the lower ranks of the league tables, which serve the children of the urban poor.) PACE studies also reported various forms of resistance, efforts by teachers to hijack and undermine the prescribed curriculum and to circumvent top-down administrative procedures and rules.

What I find remarkable (or perhaps not so remarkable) is how little influence such research, analysis and critique has had on the direction of national educational policies in the USA and UK. What explains the political impotence of the research professions on teaching, learning and educational organizations? The fact that careful scholarship which fails to support current policies is routinely ignored by policy makers, politicians and the public raises profound and difficult questions, including questions about the future of educational research sciences. I return to this matter in the concluding paragraphs of this chapter.

Testing as Cultural Control

Mark LaCelle-Peterson in Chapter 2 speaks of the 'latent homogeneity' of standardized assessment practice. The term is apt because it captures the embeddedness and invisibility of the issues of language, culture, race, gender and class in current assessment practices, as well as the use of tests to define and construct a singular, standardized culture. That national and state-mandated curriculum and testing are an effort to centralize control of knowledge and culture is not a controversial claim. Tests mandated by government authorities are designed to visit on teachers and students a particular and singular view of the 'basics' of history, geography, literature, art and ways of looking and thinking about truth. Whatever else they may or may not do, tests and ranking schemes tell us all, students, teachers and parents, what counts and, perhaps more importantly, what does not count as public knowledge and cultural capital.

All school examinations and assessments, including those composed by classroom teachers, shape culture and distribute cultural capital. But standardization and centralization of curriculum and testing is an effort to put an end to the most valuable asset of a multicultural society, a vibrant cacophony of voices on what constitutes truth, knowledge and learning, and what the young ought and ought not to learn at school. It insists upon one set of answers, and only one.

The architects of these national policies know this. Most of the rhetoric in defence of testing focuses on raising educational standards as the key to national survival in the new global marketplace. However, it is clear that cultural control is the key collateral goal; the architects of these policies proclaim it. The 1992 report, *Raising Standards for American Education*, asserts that national education standards would 'bind together a wide variety of groups into one nation,' providing '*shared values and knowledge*' which will serve 'as a powerful force for national unity.' Lauren Resnick, a chief academic advocate for testing, a former president of the American Educational Research Association and a director of the New Standards Project, argued, 'Without performance standards, the meaning of content standards *is subject to interpretation*, which if allowed to vary would undermine efforts to set high standards for the majority of American students' (italics added). Nicholas Tate, current chief executive of the British government's Qualifications and Curriculum Authority, said in an interview, 'Today, we face the widespread belief that there are no underlying shared values in our society, that people are no longer willing to go along with what the school says. That is why we are beginning to make explicit, what has hitherto been implicit' (Tell 1998). It would be difficult for the Minister of Education in Orwell's *1984* to improve on such words.

National curriculum linked to so-called high-stakes testing is among the most powerful and pervasive forms of cultural control. Or to use the more apt language of Edward Said, the distinguished Palestinian-American scholar, it is a late twentieth century form of cultural imperialism. It is not coincidental that the concerted effort by central authorities to gain monopoly control over the curriculum arrives at the time that social movements have appeared and are challenging white, male, Anglo-European political and cultural dominance in the UK, the USA and other western colonizing nations. The formerly colonized, enslaved and oppressed clearly do not accept their ascribed cultural, racial and/or gender inferiority. They assert their rights to reclaim cultural power, and to create and forge their own cultural and social identities. Those who see these movements as cultural balkanization and as a threat to social stability and national unity view mandated testing as an antidote to cultural and moral disintegration, a way to manufacture consent and cohesion. For them, 'normalizing' and standardizing the curriculum protects the younger generation from the intellectual assaults of multiculturalists, anti-racists, feminists, child advocates and others who, in the name of social justice and cultural diversity, are threatening the fabric of the nation.

Movements for cultural, racial and gender equality and justice and the discontents that produced them may be temporarily contained and diverted, but they cannot be extinguished. The genie will not return to the bottle. These movements are destined to proliferate, strengthen and change. The root issues again are race, culture, gender and, of course, power.

Thus, centralized testing is deeply enmeshed in the so-called cultural war, or to give it a proper name, the multiculturalism question. Multiculturalism includes but is *not* mainly about *the content* of the canon: whose literature, history, ideas of art, music, cultural beliefs and ways of thinking are to be included and excluded in the curriculum and tests (important as this may be). Rather, it is about who in the end has the power to decide. Put another way, a mandated multicultural curriculum is an oxymoron, since the power to decide has not changed hands but remains largely in the hands of the culturally and politically dominant groups that run national and state governments.

From CLAS to STAR: A California Story

How these large cultural and political forces will play out in the longer term in the USA and Britain is not known, of course. But there are more than enough indications that governments' educational policies designed to control culture do not work as intended. There is no better illustration than the developments in California, my home state.

Despite chaotic, sometimes darkly comedic turns in California's electoral politics, what transpires in California is highly significant. First, California, with a tenth of the nation's school population, is by far the largest customer of the nation's multi-billion-dollar educational media and publishing industry. Thus what California chooses for its textbooks and curriculum frameworks shapes the textbooks and all educational products available throughout the USA.

Second, California is a case study of the pitfalls of even the most well-intentioned efforts to centralize standards and curriculum. For sixteen years, California has been a living laboratory trying to answer the question: is it possible to develop a single set of content standards that are not only challenging and of high quality, but sensitive to society's diversity and respectful of differences of opinion among various interests? To date, the answer is a resounding 'no'.

California's effort to mandate tests tied to curriculum began in 1983. California voters had just elected Bill Honig, an articulate and assertive State Superintendent of Instruction. Honig had campaigned on the platform that he would meet the challenge outlined in the national report, *A Nation at Risk*, that our schools are marked by a 'rising tide of mediocrity' threatening the country's very future.

California's Superintendent of Instruction is nominally a non-partisan office and Honig, a one-time elementary teacher and school administrator and a liberal Democrat, attempted to bridge party lines and forge a new bipartisan policy to promote educational excellence. His approach was simplicity itself: commission university scholars, and leading educators to write academically rigorous state curriculum 'frameworks' in all major school subjects, then align the frameworks to textbooks and to a system of state-wide testing.

Honig's response to the widely expressed fear that the tests would dumb-down the curriculum was to promise new forms of testing that would overcome the inherent limitations of commercially available standardized achievement tests. These new tests, he promised, would enhance academic learning, foster creativity and require 'higher order' thinking. Under Honig's plan, California would be the first in the nation to align tough new curriculum guidelines or 'frameworks' to mandated statewide testing.

California's new English and Language Arts Framework arrived in 1985 and was widely hailed as a breakthrough by the major newspapers and by mainstream and progressive educators alike. The only serious opposition came from the far right, which did not as yet have sufficient clout to block it. The new framework broadened the state's approach to early reading and language instruction, incorporating an assortment of practices for teaching reading and writing which had come to be known as 'whole language' or 'language experience'. The framework also broadened the literary canon, which became more inclusive and multicultural with the addition of more women, and of men and women of colour. In spite of charges by critics which were taken as true by the media, the framework, while it de-emphasized basal readers, did not forsake phonics practice or drill. It did, however, incorporate approaches to teaching writing that encouraged students to write from personal experience and feelings.

The first of California's new breed of test linked to the curriculum framework arrived in 1994 and was a language and reading test given the acronym CLAS (for California Learning Assessment System). The CLAS language test was given to California's students for the first and last time in the spring of that year, the same year Newt Gingrich proclaimed victory for the right-wing Republican 'revolution' and the first time in forty-two years that the Republicans gained control of the US House of Representatives. In California, it was a particularly bountiful year for nativism and xenophobia in electoral politics.

Governor Pete Wilson, a pro-corporate, pro-choice Republican and former mayor of San Diego, rode to re-election in the fall of 1994 on a wave of voter approval for two notorious ballot measures: Proposition 185, the 'three strikes and you're out' anti-crime measure that mandated twenty-five years to life in prison for three felony convictions, regardless of the seriousness of the crimes; and Proposition 187, which denied public services to non-citizens. Wilson embraced these propositions. Soon after the first results of the recently administered CLAS language test were announced, he seized upon CLAS and the curriculum framework as fresh targets for his attacks on liberals, who, he claimed, were not only soft on crime and immigrants, but staunch defenders of radical multiculturalism in the schools.

A number of objectionable test items were reprinted in local newspapers and cited by Wilson as clear evidence of political correctness and multiculturalism run amuck. One was a passage from Maxine Honig Kingston's *Women Warrior*, followed by the directions, 'Write an essay in which you interpret the moments of silence or inability to speak.'

With Wilson's re-election, the new language curriculum framework and the CLAS test were dead. Thus after an estimated 56 million dollars in public funds, and more than five years of development – and despite the efforts of the Educational Testing Service, the country's premier developer of tests and the prime contractor for the CLAS test – California could not deliver the promised new breed of achievement test that was to be academically rigorous, culturally sensitive and respectful of diverse opinions. The attempt was stillborn, consumed by California's ongoing cultural wars, destroyed by an electoral process heavily driven by right-wing corporate money, and by political campaigns that played upon fear of the other, often provoking class, race and cultural animosities.

For four years the state's language curriculum and testing programme lay in limbo, until 1998 when the state's newest new reading and language curriculum framework was approved. This time, basal readers and phonics are in. Out are whole language and language experience approaches – and just about anything else that might disturb the sensibilities of the religious and far right who remain in firm control of the state's Republican Party. It is not just the Republicans, however, who jumped on the right-wing bandwagon. Leading Democrats and the state's Superintendent of Instruction, Delaine Easton, generally seen as pro-teacher and a liberal, joined in the condemnation of the previous framework. She pronounced the new one as 'more balanced, and more focused on the basics'.

Along with the new framework, the state introduced a new assessment scheme called STAR (Standardized Testing and Reporting) as the replacement for CLAS. The STAR plan required all California districts to administer the Stanford 9 Achievement Test, an off-the-shelf standardized test published by Harcourt Brace. The test was not aligned to the new framework. And, it is important to note, it was certainly not one of the promised new breed of tests, but was one of the old-fashioned dumbed-down, fill-in-the-bubble variety that have been in use since the second decade of the twentieth century.

The controversy has not ended. In the Spring of 1998, superintendents from a number of the state's largest cities, including Los Angeles, San Francisco and Oakland, objected long, strenuously and publicly about the mandated use of the Stanford 9 test. They did not object to using standardized achievement tests, but to the requirement that all school districts use the same standardized test. They argued, correctly, that every school district in the state already administers a comparable off-the-shelf achievement test and that converting it to a single measure would be costly and add no new educationally relevant information. What the Stanford 9 and all similar tests produce is what many of its proponents want: a single yardstick for generating statistically comparable sets of scores, rank orders and/or 'norms' across all California school districts. The superintendents also protested that there was not an alignment between the test and the new framework. A spokesperson for the Department of Education acknowledged this, but promised this would be remedied next year. Not surprisingly, the remedy being chosen by many districts and teachers (and publicly acknowledged) is to adjust the curriculum and teaching to fit the Stanford 9.

A few weeks later, several city school superintendents protested again. This time, they were outraged that non- and limited English speaking students were being required by the State Board to take the Stanford 9. (Statewide, about 25 per cent of students fall into this category; 47 per cent in Los Angeles, and just over 30 per cent in San Francisco.) San Francisco Superintendent Waldemar Rojas openly defied the state directive and refused to administer the test to such students. He called the lack of exemptions 'flat out cruel, unnecessary, and meaningless'. The Los Angeles and San Francisco school districts subsequently, in separate actions, filed suit in federal court charging civil rights violations. Most school districts complied with the state's mandate, but a number refused to compile and/or release results and asked the court for relief. It is now a virtual certainty that over the next decade, many millions of public and private dollars will be consumed as a stream of litigation slowly makes its way through state and federal courts.

It is also important to add that the superintendents' protests took place amid two other developments: first, public protests over the reported effects of the state's anti-affirmative action measure on 'minority' enrolment in the University of California, and second, another xenophobic political campaign, this time for the ultimately successful Proposition 227, designed to eliminate bilingual education and install English-only policies in California's schools.

The language and reading framework and bilingual education are not the only issues caught in the crossfire of California cultural politics. Soon after, a front-page story in the *San Francisco Examiner* appeared with the headline, 'Math War Erupts as State Board Decides How It Should Be Taught'. Discounting concerns of school districts, mathematicians, mathematics educators, teachers, labor leaders and parent groups, the State Board of Education – once more aided and abetted by cultural conservatives – approved a new mathematics framework which, the report noted, 'emphasizes workbook drills, memorization and computation'. Several defenders of the new 'back to basics' framework, oblivious to the irony, argued that it was more important to boost test scores than increase conceptual understanding of mathematics. Several weeks later, the scenario was repeated in response to the state's new science framework. Not only is there no end in sight to the curriculum wars, but there is every reason to believe that they will become more fierce and poisonous as the state attempts to accomplish what it has not as yet succeeded in doing: aligning curriculum frameworks to high-stakes tests.

I have argued that the importance of California's experience goes far beyond its borders. It is not only the most populous state, but for sixteen years has been the living laboratory for the policies that were advocated in the 1992 national report, *Raising Standards for American Education*, and to this day remains as the blueprint for the policies that are now driving national and, with some exception, state educational policies. Indeed, the resemblance between Honig's

plan and the key recommendations in the aforementioned report is not acci-
dental. Honig served on the national 'Standards Task Force' that produced the
Report, in which California is used as the exemplary success story. From the
section of the report that argues for the feasibility of national standards and
testing:

> The fact that challenging and high quality content standards, even in sensi-
> tive and particularly complex areas as science and history/social studies,
> have been developed in a state like California, which has great diversity,
> indicates that the challenge of diverse opinion can be overcome by hard
> work and careful respect for differences of opinion among the various
> interests. California has developed sophisticated and complex curriculum
> frameworks in mathematics, social studies.
>
> (*Raising Standards for American Education*: E-17)

The facts as they unfolded support the opposite conclusion. There was a
rancorous grassroots rebellion in Oakland and several other school districts
against the purchase of textbooks which had been written to conform to the
state's newly mandated history–social studies framework. A main charge given
by the US Congress to the commission that produced the 1992 Report was to
study the 'feasibility of national standards and tests'. Yet every single instance
cited above and in the entire Report as exemplary proved unfeasible and ended
not 'with respect for difference' but the reverse, enmeshed in toxic racialized
electoral politics and as acknowledged failures. The 'challenge of diverse
opinion' was not 'overcome by hard work and careful respect for difference'.
Moreover, in this matter California is not unique. There have been numerous
high-profile failed efforts to write national standards, most notably in the areas
of history and of English language and literature, and if the past decade is any
indication, many more are on the way (Cornbleth and Waugh 1995; Nash and
Crabtree 1997).

The Future of Public Education and the Educational Research Sciences

In this chapter, I argue that the intellectual foundations of the entire edifice of
modernist educational research and evaluation are crumbling. The currently
used measurement technology cannot sustain its own claims about objectivity
and neutrality. It ignores or trivializes social context, including the critical
issues of culture, race, gender and power. I have also shown that raising educational standards in practice has come to mean standardization and centralization
of curriculum, and an effort by government to impose cultural uniformity. Finally,
I have shown how these policies in California have succeeded in creating new
arenas for racial and cultural warfare, enmeshing basic pedagogical, learning and
curriculum questions, how and what school children should be taught at school
in ideologically charged, demagogic electoral politics, and highly polarized
forms of cultural politics that invoke stereotypes, cultivate hatreds and fear of
the 'other'.

Even were we to accept as true the false proposition that test results are an adequate, if imperfect indicator of educational quality or productivity, there is no evidence to be found that after sixteen years, the effort by the state of California to centralize curriculum has yielded the promised results. California's place in the national rankings has not changed appreciably. The frequently repeated promise of enhancing educational quality and equality of opportunity made by advocates has not materialized. African-American and Latino students' achievement test scores are little changed. Drop-out rates are about the same and the inequalities between rich and poor schools have, if anything, widened. There are some changes and disagreements over progress, but these are quibbles about a few test score points, differences of no practical significance. It is also of note that it has been about a decade since the USA and UK have been on the same policy track, yet in international comparisons on academic achievement, both nations fare about as well or badly as they did in the mid 1980s.[2]

Why is it that, despite the absence of supporting evidence, and the failure to show any of the promised results, do the current national and state educational policies continue? This is a large question that I do not address here. However, one reason, is clear. From their beginnings in the 1980s, these policies have had the active political and financial support of the governing political elites. By governing elites, I refer to the nations' major political and corporate and financial leaders, major business lobbies, mainline corporate-endowed foundations and think tanks.

Though initiated by the right-of-center Bush administration and Major government, these policies are embraced by 'new' Democrat Bill Clinton and the 'new' Labour Prime Minister, Tony Blair, as well as by the mainstream of all political parties. Clinton was far more than a bystander. While Governor of Arkansas, Clinton, with Republican fellow governor of Tennessee, Lamar Anderson, later Bush's Secretary of Education, helped write a report of the National Governors' Association (*Time for Results* 1986) that was the immediate precursor to the seminal 1992 report. The leaders of both nations were elected to office as centrists who accept the world view of the corporate sector that the nation's ability to survive and prosper in the global marketplace depends upon an educated workforce and the cultivation of educational excellence, which in policy terms was translated to specification of so-called national 'content standards' monitored by standardized ratings and measures of academic achievement.

Given the enormous economic and political power of these groups and their ability to frame and set the terms of the policy debates in education, what are the prospects for challenge? In the USA, some efforts to centralize and standardize have been successfully resisted and defeated by organized political action, particularly when these policies impinge directly on the cultural sensibilities and interests of a politically active constituency. In 1997, Clinton's long-standing effort to install national tests in reading and mathematics was untracked by a coalition of Civil Rights groups, fair test advocates, progressive democrats and right-wing Christian cultural conservatives. Many right-wing

Christian cultural conservatives are fiercely anti-government, and distrustful equally of mainstream pro-corporate, Republicans and Democrats. The cultural right can be counted on to oppose at all levels efforts to centralize control of what bodies of knowledge, ways of thinking and civic values should be taught to their children – unless they are in control. Across the political spectrum in California and across the nation, there are living examples of anti-racist coalitions which have successfully demonstrated their power to obstruct, evade and circumvent state control. Bilingual education continues in the face of the anti-bilingual Proposition 227. In Oakland, a rainbow coalition composed of African-American, Asian Americans, Latino, Native and Euro-Americans managed to thwart the school district's effort to adopt the state-approved, presumably multicultural history and social studies textbook series which the coalition viewed as racist, demeaning and historically distorted.

I cannot speak to the possibilities for resistance and changing course in the UK. Clearly, there are major differences, in geography, history and the role of social and political movements. The British parliamentary system confers on the prime minister and the majority party virtually unlimited power to install and uninstall national educational policy.

Amelioration, resistance, circumvention, and legal obstructions to particularly noxious aspects of centralized control are vitally important. However, they do not represent a challenge to the current distribution of power; that is, moving power from the center and toward school-based professionals, teachers, communities and parents. Indeed, if the entire control apparatus erected in the USA and UK since the late 1980s were to be dismantled tomorrow, the nation's serious educational problems would not disappear, nor would it necessarily bring more democracy. The power of entrenched, hierarchical, bureaucratic school districts and the regimes of autocratic superintendents and educational administrators would remain intact, and use of standardized tests as instruments of top-down management of curriculum and pedagogy would continue much as before. Also, victories on single issues sometimes do not turn out as hoped. The Oakland coalition that managed to block the adoption of the state-approved social studies textbook series won an important victory, but could not produce the funds nor create an infrastructure for creating a promised replacement that involved teachers and the community. Teachers were left with (arguably) worse older texts, or with nothing at all. Clinton, though defeated in his bid for national tests in reading and mathematics, continues to press for his testing agenda. He now proposes a national system of high-school exit examinations and more standardized testing of teachers for purposes of certification and professional advancement.

Given the current situation, is a genuinely progressive devolution of power possible? Progressive devolution of schooling does not appear to have an obvious constituency, nor does there appear to be a plan of what a system of democratically governed schools would look like in practice, nor what short and longer political steps might be taken to reverse and replace current anti-democratic policies. For many, the ideal of democratic schools is an illusion. Grassroots school-site democracy and public accountability are seen as contradictions. Many millions of ordinary men and women, rich, poor and middle class of all races who do not share the interests and concerns of the Carnegie Forum or the Business Roundtable, have come to see tighter top-down centralized management through testing as the only feasible alternative if the nation's primary and secondary schools are to be reformed and improved.

However, history is not at a standstill; circumstances change. As it becomes increasingly apparent that more top-down management will not succeed, and that efforts to impose a unitary view of culture will almost certainly backfire and have unanticipated and potentially dangerous consequences, current national and state policies could lose some support of mainstream politicians and some within the corporate elite whose interests may not be well served by provoking more cultural, racial and gender warfare. A major shift away from public acceptance of economic globalization, and the unrestricted flow of capital (which is not unthinkable), would have far reaching consequences on the direction of all national domestic policy and politics, including education.

Whether such changes provide an opening for a renewed and vigorous movement for devolving power from the center to local school communities, teachers and parents depends on having a comprehensive, articulated agenda for decentralizing schooling and curriculum decisions that appeals to a broad constituency. The keystone to such policies is a convincing and workable assessment plan that is helpful to teachers, supports student learning and provides policy makers, educational officials and politicians at all levels with information they require for making informed decisions. The questions of cultural, racial, gender and social class equity are central, but the plan must also satisfy the legitimate practical economic concerns of the business sector, and of parents who want children to learn in school what they need in order to be eligible for decent paying jobs and/or entrance to favored colleges or universities. Such concerns are too often brushed aside by humanist and progressive school reformers.

Because it is the assessment system that in the end drives the educational priorities across the board – in classrooms and schools, and in the higher reaches of administration and government – an organized activist, progressive multicultural movement of citizens and educational professionals must take as first priority the design and advancement of a comprehensive agenda for democratic assessment. The challenge of organizing and sustaining such a coalition are intellectual and political. While there are often shared commitments to social justice, combating racism, sexism and cultural chauvinism, and to the renewal of public education, there are also profound differences in professional roles, outlook and experience. Those who would compose such a coalition, the great variety of practitioners, primary and secondary school teachers, counsellors, head teachers and principals, and academics, professors, and educational researchers from disparate intellectual and professional traditions, live in very different worlds and language communities. They often speak and write only for others of their own kind, and in prose that is often inaccessible to outsiders. There are also conflicting material interests and power differences, zones of mutual misunderstanding and mistrust. Many practitioners are deeply suspicious of researchers and experts whom they view as remote from the everyday lived problems of schools, and as having little regard for the practical knowledge and experience of teachers, principals, counsellors, paraprofessionals and others who work in schools with children and adolescents. All have a vital contribution to make, but they would need to overcome their language barriers, physical and professional isolation, and focus attention and energy on addressing the assessment question.

The most formidable barriers to building such a coalition are deeply rooted in culture which includes the omnipresent issues of race, gender, social class and ethnicity. Acknowledging mistrust and the living legacy of cultural imperialism, racism and sexism that pervade our social relations and the societal institutions that we ourselves inhabit is essential and, of course, extraordinarily difficult. Many in the academy, government and schools question the claims to legitimacy of these new cultural formations and movements and continue to misunderstand and underestimate the depth and power of the demographic forces that are transforming political, social and cultural life in the USA, the UK and nations across the globe (Gilroy 1993; Hall 1996; West 1993).

In spite of the difficulties and many problems, the intellectual and political resources for building a renewed and effective political movement for democratic devolution of schools exist. While modernist thinking and practice of social and educational research are no longer tenable, in the last ten to fifteen years there have been significant advances in the sophistication of ethnographic and participatory and survey methods and in the use of high-speed desktop computers (Richardson 1997; Denzin and Lincoln 1994; Clifford and Marcus 1986). There are lively intellectual and professional traditions that offer alternative ways of thinking about pedagogy, academic achievement, 'educational productivity', human growth and intelligence, moral development, the relationship of schooling, curriculum, and the relation of schooling to civic society, democracy and the economy. There have been major efforts to rethink the idea of 'accountability', and in the development of criteria for creating culturally and racially sensitive, qualitative and quantitative assessment approaches that promote student learning and educational justice.[3] Finally, there are in the USA and UK numerous outstanding examples of primary and secondary schools with teachers and staff who, in their daily practice, exemplify alternative conceptions about curriculum, pedagogy, learning, and the assessment process.[4]

Because in the end it is the assessment system that drives educational priorities in classrooms, schools, administration and government, an activist, progressive and multicultural movement of citizens and educational professionals, researchers and teachers must take as its first priority the design and advancement of a comprehensive agenda for democratic assessment. It is, admittedly, a difficult and complex task. But understanding the centrality of the assessment question is a step toward finding the right road.

Notes

1   There is a vast literature. For extensive bibliography and publications contact The

National Center for Fair and Open Testing (FairTest) www.fairest.org; email FairTest@aol.com.
2   See *Education Week*, 18 June 1997, 4 March 1998. For an extraordinary revealing examination of the inequalities that persist and are increasing in American schools, see Kozol (1992).
3   The National Forum on Assessment, is a coalition that includes FairTest, a national advocacy group headquartered in Cambridge MA, and several Washington, DC based civil rights organizations. The Forum (1995) produced a set of *Principles and Indicators for Student Assessment Systems* which are available online from FairTest (see note 1).
4   Networks and organizations include NCEA (National Coalition of Educational Activists); Rethinking Schools, in Milwaukee Wisconsin; and the North Dakota Study Group on Evaluation. Also see Wood (1992) for a description of a number of these schools in the USA.

References

Adams, E. and Burgess, T. (1992) 'Recognizing Achievement', in H. Berlak (ed.), *Toward a New Science of Educational Testing and Assessment*, Albany, NY: State University of New York Press.

Allen, D. (ed.) (1998) *Assessing Student Learning: From Grading to Understanding*, New York: Teachers College Press.

Ball, S.J. (1997) 'Good School/Bad School: Paradox and Fabrication', *British Journal of Sociology of Education* 18(3).

Berlak, H. (ed.) (1992) *Toward A New Science of Educational Testing and Assessment*, Albany, NY: State University of New York Press.

—— (1995) 'Culture, Imperialism and Goals 2000', in R. Miller (ed.), *Educational Freedom for a Democratic Society: A Critique of National Goals Standards, and Curriculum*, Brandon, VT: Resource Center for Redesigning Education.

Broadfoot, P. (1996) *Education Assessment and Society*, Buckingham: Open University Press.

Burgess, T. and Adams, E. (1985) *Records of Achievement at 16*, Windsor: NFER-Nelson.

Cherryholmes, C. (1988) *Power and Criticism: Poststructural Investigations in Education*, New York: Teachers College Press.

Clifford, J. and Marcus, G.E. (1986) *The Poetics and Politics of Ethnography*, Berkeley and Los Angeles: University of California Press.

Cornbleth, C. and Waugh, D. (1995) *The Great Speckled Bird*, New York: St Martins.

Croll, P. (ed.) (1996) *Teachers, Pupils and Primary Schooling*, London: Cassell.

Darling-Hammond, L. (1994) 'Performance-Based Assessment and Educational Equity', *Harvard Educational Review* 64(1): Spring.

—— (1995) *Authentic Assessment in Action*, New York: Teachers College Press.

Delpit, L. (1995) *Other People's Children: Cultural Conflict in the Classroom*, New York: The New Press.

Denzin, N.K. and Lincoln, Y.S. (eds) (1994) *The Handbook of Qualitative Research*, Thousand Oaks, CA: Sage.

—— (1998) *The Landscape of Qualitative Research; Theories and Issues*, Thousand Oaks: Sage.

English-Language Arts Framework (1987) Sacramento: California State Department of Education.

Gardner, H. (1983) *Frames of Mind*, New York: Basic Books.

Gerwitz, S. (1997) 'Can *All* Schools Be Successful? An Exploration of the Determinants of School "Success"', paper presented at the British Educational Association.

Gilroy, P. (1993) *The Black Atlantic: Modernity and Double Consciousness*, Cambridge, MA: Harvard University Press.

Gipps, C. (1990) 'The Social Implications of National Assessment', *Urban Review* 22(2): 145–60.

Gould, S.J. (1981) *The Mismeasure of Man*, New York: Norton.

Hall, S. (1996) 'Cultural Studies and its Theoretical Legacies', in D. Morley and K.-H. Chen (eds), *Stuart Hall: Critical Dialogues in Cultural Studies*, London and New York: Routledge.

Hilliard, A. (ed.) (1991) *Testing African American Students*, Atlanta, GA: Southern Educational Foundation.

hooks, b. (1984) *Feminist Theory from Margin to Center*, Boston: South End Press.

Kamin, L. (1974) *The Science and Politics of IQ*, New York: Halstead Press.

Kozol, J. (1992) *Savage Inequalities: Children in Americas Schools*, New York: Harper-Collins.

Madaus, G.F. (1994) 'A Technological and Historical Consideration of Equity Issues Associated with Proposals to Change the Nation's Testing Policy', *Harvard Educational Review* 64(1): Spring.

Medina, N. and Neill, M. (1990) *Fallout From the Testing Explosion: How 100 Million Standardized Exams Undermine Excellence and Equity in America's Public Schools*, Cambridge, MA: FairTest. www. fairtest.org

Messick, S. (1989) 'Meaning and Values in Test Validation: The Science and Ethics of Assessment', *Educational Researcher*, March.

Miller, R. (ed.) (1995) *Educational Freedom for a Democratic Society A Critique of National Goals Standards, and Curriculum*, Brandon, VT: Resource Center for Redesigning Education.

Nash, G. and Crabtree, C. (1997) *History on Trial: Culture Wars and the Teaching of the Past*, New York: Knopf.

Pollard, A. and Broadfoot, P. (1997) 'Symposium Paper for the Annual Conference of The British Educational Research Association', PACE (Primary Assessment Curriculum and Experience) Graduate School of Education, University of Bristol.

Pollard, A., Broadfoot, P., Croll, P., Osborn, M. and Abbott, D. (1994) *Changing English Primary Schools? The Impact of the Education Reform Act at Key Stage One*, London: Cassell.

Pullin, D.C. (1994) 'Learning to Work: The Impact of Curriculum and Assessment Standards on Educational Opportunity', *Harvard Educational Review* 64(1): Spring.

Raising Standards for American Education (1992) Washington, DC: US Government Printing Office.

Raven, J. (1992) 'A Model of Competence, Motivation, and Behavior, and a Paradigm for Assessment', in H. Berlak (ed.), *Toward a New Science of Educational Testing and Assessment*, Albany, NY: State University of New York Press.

Richardson, L. (1997) *Fields of Play: Constructing an Academic Life*, New Brunswick: Rutgers University Press.

Said, E. (1994) *Culture and Imperialism*, New York: Vintage.

Sarason, S. (1991) *The Predictable Failure of School Reform*, San Francisco: Jossey-Bass.

Simmons, W. and Resnick, L. (1993) 'Assessment as a Catalyst of Reform', *Educational Leadership* 50(5): 11–15.

Tell, C. (1998) 'Whose Curriculum? A Conversation with Nicholas Tate', *Educational Leadership* 56(2): 64–9.

West, C. (1993) *Prophetic Thought in Postmodern Times*, Monroe, MN: Common Courage Press.

Wiggins, G. (1998) *Educative Assessment: Designing Assessment to Inform and Improve Student Performance*, San Francisco: Jossey-Bass.

Wood, G.H. (1992) *Schools That Work*, New York: Dutton.

Contributors

Harold Berlak has had a career as a classroom teacher, teacher of teachers, educational researcher, administrator, curriculum writer, editor and educational activist. Currently he is an independent scholar and teacher living in Oakland, California. He is author-editor of *Toward A New Science of Testing and Educational Assessment* (State University of New York Press, 1992) as well as numerous articles dealing with the intersection of culture, politics, and schooling. He welcomes comments and discussion at hberla@infinex.com.

Patricia Broadfoot is Professor of Education in the Graduate School of Education and Dean of the Faculty of Social Sciences at the University of Bristol. She directed the School's Centre for Assessment Studies for ten years from 1987 to 1997. She is the author of a number of books and articles in the field of assessment and comparative education. She is the editor of two international journals: *Assessment in Education* and *Comparative Education*.

Barry Cooper is Professor of Education and Director of Research in the School of Education, University of Durham. His research interests include the sociological study of the school curriculum and assessment, maths education and Indian primary education. He has recently directed ESRC projects investigating national curriculum testing in maths. His publications include *Renegotiating Secondary School Mathematics* (Falmer Press, 1985) and *Assessing Children's Mathematical Knowledge* (with Máiréad Dunne, Open University Press, in press).

Máiréad Dunne is a lecturer in the University of Sussex Institute of Education and has international experience in Ireland, Kenya, Australia, Fiji and Pacific nations. Her recent work has been developing sociological accounts of school mathematics assessment through two major projects. These were the classroom-based ethnographic study of the micro-social processes of teacher assessment and an ESRC-funded study of pupil interpretation and performance on KS2 and 3 tests. Máiréad's research interests include relationships between culture, context and cognition, social justice, and education and development.

Ann Filer is a Research Fellow at the University of Bristol Graduate School of Education. Her research interests include the sociology of assessment, pedagogy and pupil and peer group perspectives. She is co-director (with Andrew Pollard) of the longitudinal Identity and Learning Programme, tracking the careers of pupils through their primary and secondary schools. She is co-author of *The Social World of Pupil Assessment* (2000).

F. Allan Hanson is Professor of Anthropology and Distinguished Lecturer in Humanities and Western Civilization at the University of Kansas. After many years specializing in the culture and art of Polynesia, he has recently turned his research attention to contemporary American society. His latest book is *Testing Testing: Social Consequences of the Examined Life* (University of California Press, 1993).

Cathy Horn is a doctoral student in Boston College's Educational Research, Measurement and Evaluation programme, and works as a graduate research assistant for the National Board on Educational Testing and Public Policy. Before attending Boston College, Cathy received a bachelor's degree from Rice University and taught at a public high school in Houston, Texas. Her research interests include equity issues surrounding test use, particularly as they relate to high-stakes assessments.

David James is Principal Lecturer in the Faculty of Education, University of the West of England, Bristol. Following a variety of manual and non-manual jobs, he gained a degree in social science and a teaching qualification as a mature student. He has taught in further and higher education since 1981. His research interests include student experience, learning and assessment in a range of post-compulsory settings. He completed a PhD in 1996 and is co-author (with Michael Grenfell) of *Bourdieu and Education – Acts of Practical Theory* (Falmer Press).

Mark LaCelle-Peterson is currently Associate Professor of Education at Roberts Wesleyan College in Rochester, New York. He served as co-founder and director of the Xerox Center for Multicultural Teacher Education at the State University of New York at Geneseo. While at the Evaluation Assistance Center East at The George Washington University, he provided technical assistance on student assessment and programme evaluation to bilingual education programmes across the northeastern USA.

George F. Madaus is the Boisi Professor of Education and Public Policy at Boston College. Dr Madaus is also a senior research fellow for the National Board on Educational Testing and Public Policy. He has been the Vice President for AERA Division D and a past President of NCME. He served on the 1974 and 1985 Joint AERA, APA and NCME Test Standards Committee as well as on the 1981 Joint Committee on Standards for Educational Evaluation. Dr Madaus was also the co-chair of the APA, AERA and NCME Joint Committee on Testing Practices and served on the subcommittee that drafted the Code of Fair Testing Practices in Education. His research interests include test use in public policy, the impact of testing on curriculum and instruction, test standards and programme evaluation.

Andrew Pollard is a Professor of Education within the Graduate School of Education, University of Bristol. His research interests range across teaching–learning processes, learner perspectives, reflective teacher practices and the impact of national and institutional policies. His present research includes the Identity and Learning Programme (ILP), a longitudinal ethnography that started in 1987 and is now in its fifth phase (co-directed with Ann Filer). He directed, with Patricia Broadfoot, the Primary, Assessment, Curriculum and Experience Project (PACE) that has tracked the impact of education legislation on practices and experiences of teachers and pupils in primary school classrooms during the 1980s.

John Pryor has been researching the micro-sociology of the classroom both as a practitioner researcher and more recently as Research Fellow and Lecturer in Education at the University of Sussex. He has published work on assessment, gender, groupwork, teacher research and education in Africa. His current ESRC project (with Harry Torrance) involves collaborating with teacher researchers to investigate formative assessment practices.

Harry Torrance is Director of the Graduate Research Centre in Education and Reader in Education at the University of Sussex. He has directed several research projects investigating various aspects of teacher involvement in classroom assessment and school-based examining. He has published extensively on assessment and evaluation and is the author (with John Pryor) of *Investigating Formative Assessment: Teaching, Learning and Assessment in the Classroom* (Open University Press, 1998).

Name Index

Subject Index